4.89.

SCIENCE PARKS AND THE GROWTH OF HIGH TECHNOLOGY FIRMS

SCIENCE PARKS and THE GROWTH of HIGH TECHNOLOGY FIRMS

C.S.P. MONCK, R.B. PORTER, P. QUINTAS,
D.J. STOREY with P. WYNARCZYK

CROOM HELM
London ● New York ● Sydney

Published in association with Peat Marwick McLintock

Croom Helm Australia, 44–50 Waterloo Road,
North Ryde, 2113, New South Wales

Published in the USA by
Croom Helm
in association with Methuen, Inc.
29 West 35th Street,
New York, NY 10001

British Library Cataloguing in Publication Data

Science park and the growth of high
    technology firms.
    1. Great Britain. High technology industries
    Growth. Role of science parks
    I. Monck, C.S.P.
    338.4′76′0941

ISBN 0-7099-5441-7

Library of Congress Cataloging-in-Publication Data
ISBN 0-7099-5441-7

Photoset by Mayhew Typesetting, Bristol
Printed and bound in Great Britain by Mackays of Chatham Ltd, Kent

Contents

Tables

Figures

Acknowledgements

In 1984 a number of Science Park Managers, who were engaged in stimulating the formation and growth of high technology firms, believed that what they were doing was relevant nationally, and so decided to establish the UK Science Park Association (UKSPA). From information that the Association had collected on firms it was apparent that Science Parks were significant centres of growth and that a more detailed examination of the firms was needed to look at their characteristics and performance. Thus in 1986 the Association, together with Peat Marwick McLintock, commissioned a major survey of 284 high technology firms on and off science parks. The survey was devised by a team consisting of David Storey and Pooran Wynarczyk, then at Newcastle University, David Wield and Paul Quintas then at the Technology Policy Group (TPG) at the Open University, Charles Monck, Business Support Manager at English Estates, and Dick Porter, an associate with Peat Marwick McLintock. The survey, which was piloted by Paul Quintas and David Wield, was undertaken by staff from the regional offices of Peat Marwick McLintock and co-ordinated by Rory Landman. Preliminary results were presented at the UKSPA conference in December 1986, and interest was such that the authors were encouraged to undertake further analysis and write-up the material more fully.

The authors are particularly grateful for the support and encouragement received from David Rowe and the Executive of UKSPA; from Bruce Bower, the partner responsible for high technology activities in Peat Marwick McLintock; from the Research Technology Policy Division of the Department of Trade and Industry who, with Peat Marwick McLintock, provided resources for the survey and the subsequent preparation of the book; and from English Estates for releasing Charles Monck. Our thanks also go to the Economic and Social Research Council, which through their 'Open Door' scheme first enabled the bridge between the academics and Peat Marwick McLintock to be built. Finally, special thanks are due to Pooran Wynarczyk for undertaking all the computations and to Rory Landman, now of Advent Technology, for organising the survey and contributing to Chapter 10 on finance, and to the managers of Science Parks and the firms who participated in the survey.

We wish to emphasise that the comments and opinions expressed are those of the authors and in no way reflect the views of the organisations who have supported this work.

Abbreviations

ACARD   Advisory Council for Applied Research and Development
BES   Business Expansion Scheme
DEC   Digital Equipment (Boston, Mass.)
DSIR   Department of Scientific and Industrial Research
HEI   Higher educational institution
IT   Information technology
MOD   Ministry of Defence
NRDC   National Research and Development Council
NSF   National Science Foundation (USA)
NTBF   New technology-based firm
OSG   Occupations Study Group
OTA   Office of Technology Assessment (USA)
QSEs   Qualified scientists and engineers
R & D   Research and development
SERC   Science and Engineering Research Council
SPRU   Science Policy Research Unit (University of Sussex)
TPG   Technology Policy Group (Open University)
UGC   University Grants Committee
UKSPA   United Kingdom Science Park Association

Part I

Science, Technology and Economic Progress

1

Introduction

This book examines the growth and development of Science Parks in the United Kingdom and is divided into three parts. Part I examines the contribution of science and technology to economic progress, and notes that it is probably only in the last century or so that science has played a key role. That role, whilst it may have been relatively modest even 30 years ago, is now of paramount importance and has been elevated to a central position in economic development, particularly in the USA and more recently in Japan. In Part I it is shown that the last 20 years have seen two key developments occurring simultaneously. The first is the growth of new technologies, many of which are applicable in a commercial form and on a much smaller scale than previously. Second is the importance of 'leading-edge' research, much of which is initiated in universities and other institutions of higher education.

It was in North America that these two developments merged soon after the war. The foresight of individuals such as Professor Terman at Stanford was such that he realised industry needed access to high quality research in order to be competitive in international markets. He, and others, also appreciated that academics might wish to commercialise the results of their research, and so the concept of a Science Park was born.

It was not until the late 1960s that these ideas crossed the Atlantic and Cambridge University pioneered this development in Britain. Whilst it was quickly followed by Heriot-Watt, no other British university developed a Science Park until 1981. Over the next six years there was, however, a fundamental change so that, at the time of writing, only six universities have not established a park and have no plan for doing so.

Clearly, there has been a massive 'bandwagon' effect, and it is

3

therefore appropriate to take stock of these developments. The purpose of this study is to provide that opportunity for reflection. In many respects the evidence presented is open to several interpretations, but that perhaps is inevitable since an assessment is being made of a development which is only just becoming fully established. Nevertheless, there is a need to conduct such an appraisal, albeit an imperfect one, at this stage, because many universities are now reviewing their developments in the area of external relations. Government is also continuously looking for ways of improving the return from the resources which it provides to the research community in general and for universities in particular.

Part II begins this assessment by presenting the results of a survey of firms located on UK Science Parks at the end of 1986. In all, just over half of all firms currently located on a park were interviewed and these were 'matched' with firms in similar sectors but which were located off a Science Park. In this way, it was hoped to identify the added value which Science Parks provided. Comparisons were also made with the results of a study of small firms in the UK undertaken in 1985, in which similar questions were asked. To provide a specific illustration of many of the points raised, six cameos of respondent firms are also included.

Part III assesses the results and identifies important new directions for public policy. It is indicated that Science Parks are serving an important function. It suggests that most universities should have such a park which should be the focus of linkages with the commercial world. Even so, there is considerable scope for improvement, with greater efforts needing to be devoted to the management of the parks. There is evidence that, where the park is able to provide business and financial support services, this provides significant value to tenants.

The results of the survey also have implications for government. They demonstrate the importance of new technology-based firms (NTBF) in the direct creation of employment and make a strong case that this group should be a focus for policy. To assist this group it is necessary to ensure that budgets to the scientific community in general, and universities in particular, are increased in real terms. Science Parks demonstrate the willingness and ability of universities to work successfully with the commercial sector. Policies must not destroy the strengths of universities they wish to exploit by substituting short-term economic criteria for longer term and wider objectives. Government may, however, direct additional resources

4

towards institutions able to demonstrate a willingness and ability to work successfully with the commercial sector. A thriving Science Park is a key element in that demonstration.

A policy to promote NTBFs, of which Science Parks are one element, also requires government to review its public purchasing policies. There appears to be strong evidence that newly established firms in the high technology sector experience significant difficulties in tendering for government work. Many referred to difficulties in this area and felt they were the subject of unfair discrimination. It is also important to note that, despite the spectacular growth in venture capital in recent years, very few firms took an equity investment from financial institutions, either at start-up or in the following few years. If NTBFs are of such importance, it suggests there is a case for directing public resources into this area, perhaps through the judicious use of the Business Expansion Scheme. The survey also shows that from a property perspective, Science Parks, even outside the favoured south-east of England, can provide a worthwhile return to the private sector. It is therefore somewhat surprising that private sector investment has been conspicuously absent from the property institutions, and it is hoped that the material presented here will encourage institutions to reconsider their attitudes.

In short this book highlights the importance of small science-based firms. It shows that Science Parks are an important vehicle for promoting the development of this group, but that the parks themselves, government, universities and the private sector all have an opportunity to make that contribution even more effective.

2

Technology and Economic Development

2.1. INTRODUCTION

Throughout history there have been many examples of contemporary commentators regarding themselves as living through times of exceptionally rapid change. Clearly, during the industrial revolution of the eighteenth century the UK experienced major changes in work and leisure activities. Even at the start of the twentieth century, when rates of economic growth in Britain were below those experienced by many of its competitors, its own citizens must have been bewildered by the disappearance of steam, and its replacement by the internal combustion engine, the invention of the steam turbine, the development of electricity, the massive growth in the use of the bicycle, the appearance of 'new' metals such as aluminium. Nowhere is this illustrated more graphically than in the spectacular growth of the London bus industry. Clapham (1963) reports that in the 1903–7 period, when London was switching from horse-drawn buses to those powered by the internal combustion engine, there was a chronic shortage of bus drivers. The bus companies became so desperate that horse bus drivers became targeted for recruitment, because they did not fear the traffic! The only stipulation made of drivers by the bus companies, according to Clapham, was that they shaved off their whiskers to prevent them being covered in oil!

It is argued by Freeman (1986), amongst others, that similar, although perhaps less colourful, developments are occurring today. The concept of long waves of economic development and scientific change is currently very popular. Long wave theory argues that there do appear to have been periods of boom and prosperity in the 1850s and 1860s, and again in the 1950s and 1960s. Each period is

6

separated by one of recession and depression. The boom periods appear to be associated with the exploitation and development of a key technical advance or group of advances — notably, steam power in the 1850s, electricity prior to the First World War, and consumer durables, automobiles and chemicals in the post-1945 period. It is not unreasonable to suggest, as does Freeman, that the next period of prosperity, if and when it comes, will be based upon the full exploitation of the microelectronics and information revolution.

The effect of technological progress over the last century is there for all to see, in terms of reduced hours of work for most people, generally improved working conditions, higher standards of health and greater life expectancy. Even so, it has to be recognised that these benefits are, in the minds of some, more than offset by the irrevocable damage to the ecological system through inadequate policies on resources depletion and waste management, the risk of nuclear conflict and the problems of stress which this and other hazards impose upon those living in the late twentieth century.

Such fears have led to the formation and growth of Green Parties in most advanced countries, to act as a counterbalance to potentially damaging new technologies. The fact that the remainder of this book will examine only the contribution of technological change to economic progress, and in particular the contribution made by (primarily small) technologically based firms to such developments does not imply that we are unaware of the potentially damaging effects of technical change. Instead it is to be hoped that the benefits of technological progress can be harnessed, with the minimum of social and environmental disruption.

2.2. SCIENCE AND TECHNOLOGY

That science and technology are closely associated would seem today to be a statement of the blindingly obvious. Indeed, the concepts of science and technology have become so interlinked in public consciousness that they have appeared to be interchangeable. 'Scientific progress' and 'technological progress' are assumed to be equivalent concepts, one substituted for the other without any change in emphasis. However, does this merging of science and technology reflect actual or approximate equivalence, or does it indicate a confusing blurring of meaning? If the words are equivalent, how can such phases as 'science-based technology' make sense?

For centuries technology developed without notable scientific input. The technologies of the industrial revolution, from the textile machinery of eighteenth-century Lancashire, through iron, coal, coke and the development of steam power to the railways, owed little to scientific discoveries. Today, however, no one would deny the importance of science as a major factor in technological development. There is, for example, not much doubt that integrated circuits and other microelectronic devices could not have been conceived of without the understanding gained from scientific research. The relationship between science and technology has become an ever closer one over the past century or so. However, having been acknowledged, this is not to say that scientific and technological development are one and the same. The relationships and the phenomena themselves are complex, and can only be dealt with briefly here. It is however essential to look at science and technology and their interactions in order to place current Science Park development in context. Before looking more closely at the relationship between science and technology, it is useful to discuss briefly what we mean by these terms.

2.2.1. Science

The words 'science' and 'scientific' are used in three principal ways. Firstly, they refer to the body of knowledge amassed in books and papers by the practitioners of science; this is scientific knowledge. Secondly, they are used to describe the activity of this scientific community; they practise science. At the core of this practice is the scientific method — the procedures of systematic observation and recording, hypothesis formation and experimentation. Thirdly, the words 'science' and 'scientific' may be used to describe the individuals, groups and institutions known as the scientific community, who are the practitioners of science. There are therefore two aspects of scientific endeavour which are central:

(1) science aims at the discovery and understanding of natural phenomena.
(2) science proceeds by means of a methodology based on observation, experimentation, and reason.

It should be emphasised that science is not merely a set of operational techniques or laboratory procedures: these alone would render science no more than systematic empiricism. Scientific knowledge is distinguished from other knowledge by its theoretical base; empirical research is framed by theoretical understanding and hypothesis testing. Much activity which is practised by personnel educated in the sciences has a deficit of theoretical underpinning: for example, in civil engineering, theory still cannot predict for all contingencies and so models are used and tested. The pharmaceutical industry similarly remains a 'highly empirical business' (*The Economist*, 1 February 1987), in which the effects of new compounds cannot be accurately predicted, necessitating complex trial techniques (Pavitt, 1987).

Science involves a spectrum of activities, and a distinction is often made between 'pure' or 'basic' science, and 'applied' or 'mission-oriented' science. An example of basic science would be high energy or particle physics research, and an example of applied research might be the research into long-chain molecules or polymers in the 1930s, which led to the subsequent development of nylon and other plastics. Such distinctions are difficult to maintain, however, and boundaries are far from clearly defined. Basic research into nuclear physics — about which Rutherford said, in 1933, 'anyone who looks for a source of power in the transformation of atoms is talking moonshine' (Rose and Rose, 1969, p. 3) — had within a decade become research applied to the solution of just that problem. In the example of polymer research, the applied research was closely linked to basic scientific understanding of molecular structure.

Before moving on to discuss 'technology', it is interesting to note that public perception of science and the scientist has undergone significant changes, even over the last 50 years, and a notable shift is currently occurring. As Rose and Rose (ibid.) observed, before the First World War, scientists appeared in novels and films as 'rather endearing, absent minded figures, possibly mad, preferably possessed of pretty daughters, but on the whole fairly innocuous, inventors of machines that did easy things in a complex way but which often failed to work' (ibid., p. xiii). By the time of writing in 1969, Rose and Rose observed that the scientists had become either sinister figures of power or naïve tools in the clutches of despots, inventing death rays, atomisers, and human-devouring microbes. More seriously, science has become a major issue of concern for a public newly aware of the environmental damage caused by pollution and resource depletion, to add to the widespread anxiety over nuclear weapons. Politicians and public had become aware of the scale of consumption of financial and human resources in ill-fated military projects such as the Blue Streak rocket and the TSR-2 aircraft.

In the 1980s there has been quite a large shift in the public, and hence the politicians' view of the role of science and scientists. Science has become rehabilitated in many people's minds because of its apparently central role in technological advancement, and thus its importance for economic growth. This is the understanding at the heart of the Science Parks phenomenon, and a focus for much of the following discussion.

2.2.2. Technology

Given the above statements about science, the first point to be made about technology is that it is not simply 'applied science'. J.K. Galbraith provides a clear statement of this in his book *The new industrial state*: technology, he says, is 'the systematic application of scientific or other organised knowledge to practical tasks' (Galbraith, 1967). However, as will be shown below, the relationship between science and technology is not a fixed one, but varies over time and between sectors. Most significantly, the importance of scientific research to technological development has increased dramatically over the past century or so.

Technology is both a body of knowledge concerned with the solution of practical problems — what we might term 'know how' — and also the tools and artefacts which are used to achieve those solutions: it is both 'software' and 'hardware'. The word 'tools', as used here, covers everything from a knife to a manufacturing system or a communication satellite. In terms of the 'software' or 'know how', technology includes knowledge about the particular system which contains the problem being tackled, and knowledge of the techniques of how to manufacture and use the tools or technical aids necessary to achieve the solution. The technology required to build a water wheel in the fourteenth century would, for example, include knowledge of the river system which would provide the motive power, and also the needs of the users of the mill, in order to estimate the required size of the water wheel, and to make adequate provision for transportation access. Thus, technology must be seen as being part of a social process, and its 'hardware' seen in the context of the problem being tackled. The hardware without the software, both in terms of understanding the problem system and in terms of the set of techniques required for solution, is less than useless.

From the example of the water wheel used above, it is clear that technology has been successfully developed for centuries without any scientific input. Indeed, up until about 100 years ago science in Britain was regarded as a hobby, the private pastime of a small privileged minority of 'amateurs and gentlemen' (Rose and Rose, 1969). Only within the last century or so has science been regarded in the UK as an organised form of activity with professional status.

What other forms of knowledge apart from science might be identified as being inputs to technological development? The examples of the spectacular European cathedrals of the eleventh and twelfth centuries provide one example. Their builders lacked scientific knowledge about structure, Newtonian mechanics and the properties of materials. Their ability to build the high vaulted ceilings of stone was based on craft knowledge, gained from experience and the successes and failures of others, passed on through successive generations of master masons.

Craft knowledge is thus knowledge acquired by doing, by trial and error, and knowledge learned from the experience of others. A brief example taken from Flood (1986) will illustrate this. For around 100 years, the Pelton Wheel has been one of the most efficient and trouble-free ways of extracting power from flowing water. It consists of a wheel which has cup-shaped buckets around its circumference, the jet of water driving into the buckets and forcing the turbine round at high speed. The key feature invented by Lester Pelton in the USA in 1880 was to split the cup shape into two halves, the jet of water thus dividing and exiting from the turbine on both sides. Pelton was a carpenter who worked as millwright in the mining industry for 13 years before beginning intensive experimentation to develop a more efficient cup design. He learned from a standard textbook how to set up test equipment to measure efficiency, and tried between 30 and 40 designs of cups. A chance happening — a loose screw allowing a cup to swing round and the water jet to strike its edge, instantly increasing the wheel's speed — led Pelton towards the split-cup design. The importance of serendipitous happenings such as this are of course dependent on the 'prepared mind' of the observer. Thus, Pelton's invention resulted from his own expertise and acquired knowledge of the requirements of the industry, from his many predecessors and the accumulated knowledge gained from their successes and failures, and from his own 'trial and error' experimentation which accidentally hit upon

11

the solution. Of course, his device depended upon many developments by others — in particular, the spear valve which produced a controlled jet of water. In addition, there were other individuals who claimed to have invented the divided-cup design before Pelton (Flood, 1986).

Nevertheless this example illustrates that technological development, for most of industrialised history, has depended on craft knowledge, and each successive generation building on the experience of others. In many industries, the 'trial and error' became increasingly systematic, and indeed, systematic empiricism continues to have a major input into technological development. However, over the past century of so, science has played an ever-increasing role, and it is to the relationship between science and technology that we now turn.

2.2.3. Science and technology

As has been argued above, the relationship between science and technology is a dynamic one, changing over time, between industrial sectors, and between nations. In 1914 Britain found itself at war with a power which had in large part based its industrial growth on new 'science-based' industries. The German chemical industry supplied crucial synthetic substitutes for rubber, nitrates (for explosives and fertilisers), and motor fuel. Ironically, Germany was the source of supply for some of Britain's vital chemicals for the war, which has become known as 'the chemist's war'.

Germany, building on its chemicals, steel and machinery industries, had been the major beneficiary of Britain's industrial decline between 1870 and 1913, when the latter's share of world trade fell from over 40 per cent to 30 per cent. By 1913 Germany's share of European production in chemicals, steel and machinery was roughly twice that of Britain (Walker, 1980). The new chemicals, electrical and transport industries were closely linked to the increasing application of science to industry. Britain lagged behind Germany, France and the US in developing science-based industry, and in particular in scientific education: they 'entered the twentieth century and the age of modern science and technology as a spectacularly ill-educated people' (Hobsbawm, 1969, p. 182). Even with the outbreak of war in 1914, the crucial importance of scientific expertise was only slowly recognised in Britain. There was a fall in the already small output of scientists, and many scientists were enlisted and sent to their deaths as ordinary soldiers, the brilliant physicist Mosely being among them. Only in 1917 was the Department of Scientific and Industrial Research (DSIR) set up to link scientific effort to strategic goals.

In contrast, science had been harnessed in nineteenth-century France and Germany for both strategic and economic goals. In the 1830s French science was applied to hydrodynamics for water turbines, and in the 1850s Carnot and Clausius developed the science of thermodynamics, which both stemmed from, and fed back into, the further development of steam engines. In Germany the chemicals industry, which dominated world production for over 50 years, resulted from direct government encouragement to science (Bernal, 1939).

It is not suggested here that Britain's comparative failure to move into 'science-based' industry was the only cause of industrial decline: other factors such as the role of captive markets in the Empire, and simply the inevitable eroding of Britain's lead in industrialisation as more countries became competitors rather than customers, played their part. Nevertheless, the relative slowness with which Britain moved into the new industries of chemicals, electrical systems and products, and transportation was significant.

The increasing importance of science to technological development is manifest in the growth of corporate Research and Development (R & D) laboratories from the late nineteenth century: in the UK, Lever Brothers, 1889 and the United Alkali Company, 1892; in the USA, Edison, 1876, Arthur D. Little, 1886, Kodak, 1893, B.F. Goodrich, 1895, General Electric, 1900, Du Pont, 1902, and Bell Labs, 1907 — all are examples of early R & D laboratories. The massive profits generated from science-based technological innovations such as General Electric's electric lamp, and later Du Pont's nylon, both of which gave these corporations monopolistic control of the market, provided a clear demonstration of the potential benefits from industrial R & D. Through two world wars, science, even in Britain, has become ever increasingly applied to technological development.

How, then, are we to understand the current relationship between science and technology? Does science 'push' technological development by making scientific breakthroughs which have clear and irresistible application advantages? Or, at the other extreme, does science itself respond to the demands of technological development and, ultimately, the market place? It has been suggested, for example, that Isaac Newton's work on mechanics, dynamics and pendulums was indeed pushed by economic imperatives (Hessen, 1968). Clearly, the placement of government and corporate investment largely determines the direction of scientific enquiry: the work of scientists must be paid for, and areas of research which do not accord with either public or private sector imperatives will not receive funding (a current example of which in the UK is research into energy from waves).

Whether technology develops because of 'science push' or 'market pull', or indeed a mixture of the two, is a major focus of debate. 'Science push' or 'market pull' implies a monocausal, perhaps even linear process, a model of innovation which is found to be over-simplistic, as will be discussed later. In terms of the relationship between science and technology, it is however clear that there is much more likely to be a two-way interaction than the unidirectional model implies. Often, science follows rather than precedes technological development. The development of the steam engine promoted and preceded scientific understanding of the principles and laws of thermodynamics. This century, short-wave radio use led to important scientific discoveries about the ionosphere; and new alloys such as Duralumin preceded scientific understanding of 'age hardening', and prompted research into crystallography and atomic structure. There are, of course, many examples in which scientific knowledge has provided the basis of new technologies, and even new industries, as was the case with scientific knowledge of electricity and magnetism and electrical engineering.

Very often, developments in science are interlinked with the development of new experimental techniques and instruments: for example, the development of the electronic microscope and the ultra centrifuge (for separating molecules) were instrumental in promoting a paradigm shift in biology, to the new discipline of molecular biology, according to Yoxen (1983). Conversely, the electronic microscope itself followed scientific breakthroughs in a different branch of science – nuclear physics. The development of the electron microscope and the ultracentrifuge was financed by the Rockefeller Foundation as part of a programme to 'modernise' biology (Yoxen, 1983).

Several studies of the relationship between science and technology have aimed at establishing empirically the extent of linkages. Project Hindsight, funded by the US Department of Defence, found that technological progress in weapon systems resulted not from pure scientific research but from mission-oriented projects and engineering R & D (Office of the Director of Defence

Research and Engineering, 1969). The study has been criticised for being biased against basic science inputs, and in particular, for arbitrarily cutting off basic science inputs dating back more than 20 years (Mowery and Rosenberg, 1979). A study by the Batelle Research Institute (1973) found rather greater scientific input. A total of 533 significant 'events' in innovation processes were identified as being 'decisive events'. Basic scientific research accounted for 34 per cent of the significant events, applied research for 38 per cent, and development for 26 per cent. However, of the decisive events, only 15 per cent resulted from basic research, 45 per cent from applied research, and 39 per cent from development activity.

A study which has been interpreted as a counter to Hindsight was commissioned by the US National Science Foundation (NSF) in the late 1960s. TRACES found that 70 per cent of important 'events' in the innovation process resulted from non-mission research, 20 per cent from applied research, and 10 per cent from development. TRACES had no time limit cut-off, and found that 45 per cent of basic science inputs were from research completed more than 30 years before the innovation, and 80 per cent of basic research was more than 15 years old (Illinois Institute of Technology, 1968). This finding is particularly relevant to our present study, and suggests that the application of basic scientific research is a long-term process.

Recent work discussed by Pavitt (1987) suggests that in many sectors, technology builds on previous technology, with little interaction with science. However, in specific fields such as pharmaceuticals, chemicals, biotechnology and electronics, there is a much closer link with scientific research. Thus, the relationship between science and technology is a variable one both through time, and at the present time between different industrial sectors.

2.3. TECHNOLOGICAL INNOVATION

According to the OECD (1982), innovation can take many forms:

— a familiar product manufactured from new materials (such as clothing from new types of synthetic fibres);
— a fresh combination of existing products to give improved performance (for example, stronger materials from a mix of wood and plastics);
— adaptation of an existing product to meet new demands (for

15

example airships for the carriage of freight);
— a new product utilised to perform a new function (for example photo-electric cells to collect solar energy);
— a new process either to make a new or modified product or to lower production costs (for example, shoe-making equipment to exploit new adhesives that replace stitching).

Innovation can be regarded as the *total* process of the inception of an idea, into the production of a product, and finally to its ultimate sale. It therefore *includes* invention and the many stages of implementation such as research, development, production and marketing.

Somewhat confusingly, different authors have used the terms 'innovation' and 'invention' in rather different contexts. The OECD, for example, uses invention to describe the creation of a new product or object, whereas for Norris and Vaizey (1972), invention was the creation of new technological knowledge, with innovation being the embodiment of this knowledge in the production process. In this sense the latter authors have a narrower view of innovation, specifically excluding the commercial viability of the product. For our purposes the wider definition of innovation will be employed.

Freeman (1982) credits Schumpeter with the key distinction between invention and innovation: 'An invention is an idea, a sketch or model for a new or improved device, product, process or system.' (ibid., p. 7.) The majority of inventions do not lead to technological innovations. 'An innovation in the economic sense is accomplished only with the first commercial transaction involving the new product, process, system or device, although the word is used to describe the whole process.' (ibid.) These points should be emphasised: first, that technological innovation refers both to the first launch of a new artefact or system, and also to the *process* of innovation, from invention to launch; and secondly, that technological innovation includes discrete *products*, from a new type of nut and bolt to a machine tool; new *processes*, such as 'ribbon growth' production of solar cells; and whole new *systems* such as a monorail transit system.

In his work, which placed technological innovation at the centre of economic development, Schumpeter emphasised the discontinuous nature of technological progress. He focused on the role of technological innovation in explaining the high level of instability in capitalist economies (Schumpeter, 1939). To Schumpeter, waves of product innovations swept away old industries in a 'gale of creative destruction'. Graphically, he wrote that economic progress did not come from price-cutting by harness-makers, but from the innovative output of motor manufacturers which destroyed harness-making as an economically viable activity (Schumpeter, 1942).

Thus, Schumpeter's emphasis was on radical changes in technology which promoted discontinuous and irreversible change in production functions. Conversely, other writers including Marx, Usher (1929) and Gilfillan (1935) emphasised the evolutionary or 'incremental' nature of technical change. Fishlow (1966), for example, showed how massive productivity gains in nineteenth-century US railway construction stemmed from a succession of minor improvements.

Freeman (1986) distinguishes four types of innovation. *Incremental innovations* are the undramatic (and often unrecorded) steady changes which occur fairly continuously in most branches of industry and in services. They often result from suggestions by users and production workers rather than R & D effort, and are the principal examples of 'demand-led' innovation. This type of innovation represents the majority of patents. Incremental innovations are thus not individually dramatic but, when taken together over time, may represent significant advances in productivity or efficiency. However, as Freeman has said, no amount of incremental innovations to coal-fired power stations would have led to nuclear power.

Radical innovations are discontinuous events which occur unevenly across sectors and through time. Radical product innovations provide new market opportunities, and radical process innovations lead to significant advantages in terms of production costs and quality. Radical innovation may involve combinations of product and process innovations, often coupled with organisational innovation. Individual radical innovations may have significant economic impact, but only over a period of decades. There is much less evidence of market-led radical innovation than in the case of incremental innovation, since the market has to be educated about the radically new capabilities and opportunities. However, as Freeman points out, those technologists developing the innovation clearly have a perception of a market potential: 'As Carlota Perez puts it: the search is always to turn base metals into gold and not vice-versa'. (ibid., p. 16.)

Freeman's third category of innovation is *the technological system*. These are combinations of radical innovations, coupled with organisational innovations across many firms. Technological systems thus affect more than one branch of the economy, and may

17

themselves spawn new sectors. As an example of a new techno-logical system Freeman gives petro-chemical innovations, synthetic material and plastics innovations, injection moulding and extrusion machinery innovations, and the associated applications innovations introduced in the 1930s, 1940s and 1950s.

Freeman's final category is *technological revolution*, or change in techno-economic paradigm. Here Freeman develops Schumpeter's 'creative gales of destruction' concept — massive transformations associated with the diffusion of a new techno-economic paradigm, involving radical innovations and new techno-logical systems, which have economy-wide applications and effects. Such technological revolutions drive the upswing phase of the Long Wave (long-term variations in the world economy known as Long Waves or Kondratiev Cycles). The selection process from which a new techno-economic paradigm emerges may take ten or more years and, as the name suggests, involves an interplay of technological and economic factors.

These rarely occurring revolutions involve changes in product and process technologies, in business and production organisation, and in social and institutional systems. Freeman gives the examples of steam power and electric power technologies as being associated with such fundamental change, and argues that today the diffusion of microelectronics and computer technologies should be regarded as such a transformation, affecting every sector of the economy, as well as creating new sectors. By contract, nuclear power, for exam-ple, has no such economy-wide application, and cannot be considered a new techno-economic paradigm.

The major effects of a new paradigm are felt with its widespread diffusion. However, such diffusion will be a painful process since the new paradigm will require radical changes in the existing social and institutional structures. The new paradigm offers a plethora of new product opportunities, which may require market 'leading' or educating, and the opportunity of drastic cost reductions in all sectors, from manufacturing to personal services. The take-up of the new paradigm by 'leading-edge' sectors evolves into a best-practice set of procedures, methods and organisational factors which demonstrate the competitive advantage gained by adopting them.

In the economist Carlota Perez's view, economic depression (the downswing of the Long Wave) results from the old social and institutional spheres being out of phase with the 'best-practice' characteristics associated with the new techno-economic paradigm. Only when drastic changes are made in the old social structures and institutions can the opportunities offered by the new paradigm, in terms of both cost reductions and employment generation based on new investment and market opportunities, be realised. Technological and economic supremacy has shifted geographically with each Long Wave. Perez argues that specific historical circumstances in certain locations produce a social and institutional environment which is best able to exploit a new technological paradigm.

How, then, does technological innovation come about?: what are the processes involved, and are there generalisable patterns recognisable in different cases and across sectors? Is there a model of the innovation process which can inform policy and direct future developments? The foregoing discussion on science and technology identified a commonly held current perception — that technological innovation follows on after scientific discovery in a sequential fashion. This 'linear model' of innovation assumes a progression something like:

BASIC $\Longrightarrow$ APPLIED $\Longrightarrow$ TECHNOLOGICAL $\Longrightarrow$ MARKET
SCIENCE   SCIENCE   DEVELOPMENT   PLACE

This model, as well as assuming that the progression is linear and proceeds in discrete stages, also suggests that science pushes technological innovation. As the previous discussion about the relationship between science and technology suggested, such a view is not supported by historical evidence in any widely generalisable sense. The view of technological innovation presented here as a substitute for the simplistic linear model builds on the understanding, stated above, that innovation is a process: new products and processes result from a complex interaction which is not reducible to one simple universal model.

As Schmookler (1966) and Freeman (1982) have emphasised, technological innovation is a process requiring, on the one hand, technological knowledge (possibly but not exclusively containing scientific knowledge), and on the other, the awareness of a need in the economy or the community. The word 'need' is value-dependent, and economists generally prefer to talk of market demand; but for radical innovations (for which there is no pre-existing market), the terms potential market demand may be substituted. The process of innovation is crucially one which unites both technological opportunity with market demand (or potential demand). Schmookler likened this process to the operation of two blades of a pair of scissors, the one useless without the other

(Schmookler, 1966). We may add that 'the market' here includes elements such as public sector procurement (e.g. defence). The 'social economy', and innovation to meet social needs for which there is little 'demand' in strict economic terms, are often ignored in discussions of technological innovation, but consideration also needs to be given to those issues. Indeed, alternative models incorporating social need have been discussed recently by Mole and Elliott (1987).

Returning, then, to our main theme, the process of innovation, uniting technological opportunity with market demand, involves within it a range of activities, the relationship between which is neither constant over time, between sectors, or even within sectors. As well as the recognition of technological opportunity and potential market demand, the innovation process for a manufactured product might include (by no means necessarily in this order);

Customer liaison/market research   development
prototype manufacture   design
testing and re-design   production engineering
manufacturing system design   applied research

Note that 'applied research' does not come at the beginning of the innovation schema, nor 'market research' at the end. Applied research may be required to solve problems with production engineering after the prototype stage. Similarly, some perception of a market is implicit in that applied research which takes places prior to the emergence of clear technological opportunity. The need for close involvement of customers at an early stage in the innovation process has been emphasised by Von Hippel (1976), and by the SAPPHO project at the Science Policy Research Unit (SPRU) at the University of Sussex (summarised in Freeman, 1982). Thus, the innovation process must be seen as involving a complex interaction of factors, some of which are external to the innovating organisation, such as markets and possibly inputs of scientific and technological knowledge. An interactive non-linear model has been suggested by Rothwell (1983), and is shown in Figure 2.1. The innovation process may be iterative, with re-design and re-development following testing and evaluation. Recent authors have therefore suggested that an iterative spiral model is more appropriate than a linear one (Figure 2.2). Most importantly, discussion of innovation and attempts to develop generalisable models often may be attempting to impose, *post hoc*, a rationality upon a process

Figure 2.1: Interactive model of the innovation process

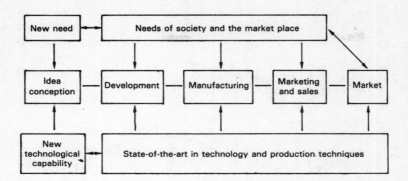

Source: Rothwell (1983)

which is inherently volatile and uncertain. Mowery and Rosenberg, in their critique of innovation studies, said

> the pervasiveness of uncertainty in the innovation process is ignored by most of the empirical studies . . . The attempt to decompose neatly the complex, stochastic and uncertain process which is that leading to innovation into a set of events that can simply be cumulated to yield an innovation, is as gross an oversimplification as is the 'black box' approach of the surveys of business firms. (Mowery and Rosenberg, 1979, p. 234)

How, then, does such a complex phenomenon ever succeed in taking place? One popular explanation might be termed the 'heroic' view of innovation, dependent on the individual technological entrepreneur. In his earlier work, Schumpeter emphasised strongly the key role of the entrepreneur in seizing both technological and market opportunities, and steering the innovation process. Very often, historically the entrepreneur was not the same person as the inventor of the new product or process (as Pelton was), but fulfilled the role of recognising the importance of the inventor's creation and its market potential, and set up the manufacturing capability to produce it. This is the role played, for example, by Boulton in his association with James Watt. The role of the Schumpeterian entrepreneur was and is a risky one in that they are anticipating

21

Figure 2.2: The innovation spiral

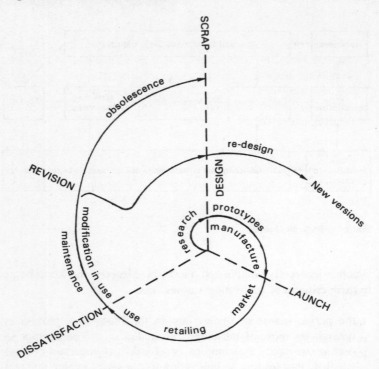

Sources: Roy (1983) and Walker (1986)

market demand rather than following it. For Schumpeter, the qualities possessed of the entrepreneur verge upon the superhuman: 'successful innovation is . . . a feat not of intellect but of will. It is a special case of the social phenomenon of leadership' (Schumpeter, 1928).

In his later work, however, Schumpeter acknowledged the increasing dominance of the large corporate R & D laboratories, and modified his view to take account of this institutionalisation of the innovation process. As the twentieth century has progressed, more and more fields of technological development have become the sole preserve of the large laboratory, both corporate and within universities, and the role of the individual inventor/innovator working alone has greatly diminished. This is graphically emphasised by

Braun and Macdonald in their account of the development of micro-electronics:

> Nobody other than a highly qualified scientist could have made any contribution in this field. There is no way in which semiconductor devices could be tinkered with at home; no way by which a skilled craftsman could improve their performance. . . . all old fashioned inventiveness proved of no avail. (Braun and Macdonald, 1978)

The shift to the large laboratory results both from the nature and scale of twentieth-century technologies such as pharmaceuticals, synthetic materials and aerospace; and the increasing role of scientific R & D in innovation. Nevertheless, many observers acknowledge the continuing role of small firms in innovation, in specific sectors and market niches. This is returned to in Chapter 3.

2.4. TECHNICAL PROGRESS AND ECONOMIC DEVELOPMENT

Intuitively, it is plausible to state that, setting aside the problems of measurement, the output of an economy is positively affected by technical progress. Demonstrating this by using a more formal definition of technical progress, however, presents major problems. It requires a recognition that in a modern society, output will increase because of an increase in the quantity of resources (primarily, capital and labour) and the quality of those resources (primarily through technological change). This is illustrated by assuming that over a period of time, output in an economy rises from X_1 to X_3, whereas if no improvement in the quality of resource input had occurred, then output would only have risen to X_2. Hence the contribution of improved quality of resources is $X_3 - X_2$.

The best known empirical studies which have estimated the contribution of technical progress to economic development were undertaken by Denison (1967, 1974) who found that during the period 1948–73, approximately one-third of the growth in output, and nearly one-half of output per head in the UK were due to advances in knowledge. The methods used to obtain these results have been the subject of considerable criticism, since technical progress is estimated as the residual element once the effect on output of increasing the quantity of resources has been identified.

This means that the residual includes not only technical change but also education and training (qualitative improvements to labour) together with the measurement errors in all factors. To some extent these criticisms appeared to be justified when subsequent research indicated that during the 1970s, the contribution of the residual (technical change) was negative (Denison, 1974).

Whilst there are reservations concerning methods of quantification, it is acknowledged that technical progress is a significant contributor to economic development in all developed countries; but even so, major uncertainties remain. If there is a clear relationship between the performance of an economy and its rate of technological change, then this should be statistically verifiable. Unfortunately, it is not possible to measure technical change directly and so the surrogate measure of expenditure on R & D tends to be used. However, the absence of an association between the growth of an economy and its R & D expenditure makes it clear that whilst technical change is an output R & D expenditure is an input. The factors which influence the productivity of this input are unclear.

We now propose to review these issues briefly, drawing heavily upon the work of CURDS (1987). This identifies seven dimensions of economic development and argues that R & D expenditure has been shown to be positively associated with each of these elements. Firstly, it argues that R & D expenditure is frequently a prerequisite for the provision of totally new goods and services and that it is these which provide the basis of economic growth in the longer term. Secondly, CURDS quotes the work of Nolan *et al.* (1980) on the UK pharmaceutical industry, indicating that expenditure by firms in that industry on R & D is positively correlated with sales growth. Thirdly, firms spending heavily on R & D expenditure are significantly more likely to be major exporters than firms spending more modest sums on R & D, with work on the UK mechanical engineering industry by Rothwell (1979) being cited. Fourthly, productivity growth has been shown by the OECD (1986) to be positively associated with R & D expenditure for individual sectors. Fifthly, it is argued that R & D expenditure will lead to reduced inflationary pressures in the economy since the introduction of new products and processes might be expected to lead, in part, to lower prices, most notably where the R & D leads to improvements in existing products. Sixthly, R & D expenditure and profitability at the sectoral or enterprise level are also significantly positively correlated. Here, however, it can be difficult to identify the direction of causation. Thus, it is difficult to be certain whether expenditure

on R & D leads to increased profitability tł
products, or whether high levels of industrial con(
high profits, which in turn lead to a greater willing
R & D in order to indulge in non-price competition
R & D is also shown to be positively correlated w
growth, with employment growing fastest in industr
most heavily on R & D. Finally, Thwaites (1982)
relationship between rates of product development a
change within UK manufacturing.

Despite assembling this impressive evidence it has to be admitted
that the relationship between expenditure on R & D and the performance of an economy is not clear-cut. It certainly appears that inputs
on R & D provide positive returns. What is less clear is whether,
at what point, and under what circumstances, these returns diminish
or possibly become negative. This is likely to depend on the nature
of the R & D undertaken and the ability of the firm/group of firms
to 'manage' that input effectively. Given this uncertainty it is not
surprising that, even before comparable international statistics
became available, doubts were being expressed over the presence of
a relationship between any individual country's science and
technology input and its performance in terms of growth. Jewkes *et
al.* (1969) point to changes within the UK attitudes in these matters.
In 1956 the British Advisory Council on Scientific Policy declared:

> The correlation between increases in industrial output and
> increases in the number of scientists in employment is more than
> fortuitous. Modern science, whether basic or engineering
> science, is the source of almost all the ideas on which the
> development of modern industry depends.

Yet in 1963 the same Council was forced to admit: 'We know no
way to determine precisely what proportion of any country's gross
national product should be devoted to the advancement and exploitation of science'. As in many other instances, excellent work by
OECD in collecting comparable statistics on R & D expenditure by
country has served primarily to indicate that if R & D expenditure
is related to economic performance, then the relationship is
complex. At the most simple level if R & D is so central to technical
progress, and if technical progress is so central to economic
development, then surely those countries spending most heavily on
research would be expected to exhibit the highest rates of growth.
There have always been counter-illustrations of this relationship

Figure 2.3: Trends in general expenditure on R & D (GERD) as a percentage of GDP in the 1960s and 1970s

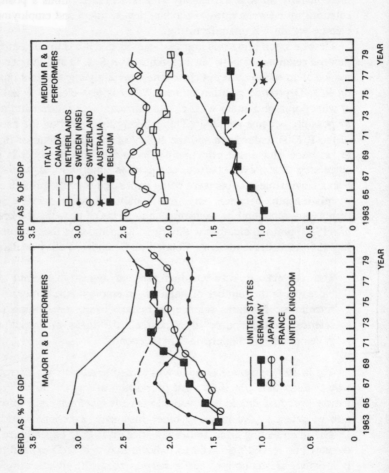

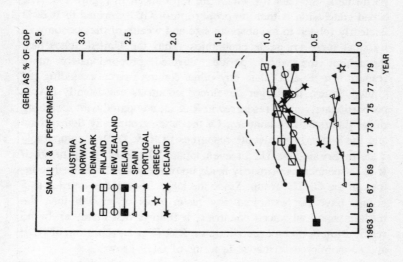

SMALL R & D PERFORMERS

GERD AS % OF GDP

AUSTRIA
NORWAY
DENMARK
FINLAND
NEW ZEALAND
IRELAND
SPAIN
PORTUGAL
GREECE
ICELAND

YEAR

1963 65 67 69 71 73 75 77 79

0 0.5 1.0 1.5 2.0 2.5 3.0 3.5

Source: OECD (1986)

throughout history, however, and it is likely that such exist today. In the nineteenth century, when the UK was the leading industrialised nation, it was France which was the champion of the European Scientific Community. In the 1950s and 1960s when Japan was experiencing rates of economic growth which were more than double the average of OECD countries, it devoted only very modest resources to R & D and to research in particular.

Recently, statistics on Total Domestic Expenditure on R & D as a percentage of GDP have become available for most OECD countries over the period since 1963. They show that countries can be sub-divided into three groups: Large, Medium and Small R & D performers, the data for which are reproduced in Figure 2.3. The broad conclusion is that the proportion of GDP devoted to R & D is clearly related to the absolute size and wealth of the economy — i.e. that there are scale economies. Thus the United States has, throughout the whole period, devoted proportionately more resources to R & D than any other country. Even excluding the United States, the larger developed countries consistently devote proportionately more resources to R & D, compared with the group of medium/smaller countries. Of the latter group only Switzerland and the Netherlands devote resources to R & D on a comparable scale to Britain, the US or even Japan. The third group of small R & D spenders is primarily made up of the lesser developed countries in the OECD group. Since the large advanced countries, as a group, have not exhibited any faster rates of growth than the medium/small advanced countries, it follows that there can be no relationship between expenditure on R & D as a proportion of GDP and economic performance in terms of GDP growth.

The absence of any apparent relationship may be due to several factors. Firstly, the measurement of R & D expenditure could be flawed. Thus, for example, the relatively high spending on R & D in the USA and the UK could merely reflect the relative importance of defence expenditure in the two countries which, in turn, might be expected to have a smaller impact upon the growth of an economy than a similar level of expenditure by industry. It could be argued, for example, that high expenditure on defence would lead to a 'crowding out' effect whereby qualified scientists and engineers are attracted away from the private sector by the prospects of employment in defence-related sectors. On the other hand, it could be argued that expenditure on defence leads to significant 'spin-off' for the private sector firms in that economy. On the grounds that the effect on the overall economy of research undertaken by the defence

Table 2.1: R & D expenditure by country and an index of competitiveness

	Total R & D expenditure as proportion of GDP (%) 1979	Defence R & D expenditure as proportion of GDP (%) 1979	Competitiveness indicator 1982
United Kingdom	2.3	0.68	94.3
United States	2.4	0.58	99.7
France	1.9	0.50	100.1
Sweden	1.9	0.22	117.2
West Germany	2.3	0.13	128.9
Japan	2.3	0.01	138.3

Source: Kaldor *et al.*, (1986), p. 32

sector is, *a priori*, uncertain, it might be better to *exclude* expenditure on defence from all international comparisons. The significance of this adjustment is shown in Table 2.1, taken from Kaldor *et al.* (1986).

Table 2.1 shows for six leading countries that four devote approximately 2.3 per cent of GDP to R & D expenditure, with France and Sweden somewhat lower at 1.9 per cent. It is also clear that this is not correlated with the index of competitiveness in the third column. However, once the defence component is identified, as in column 2, it is clear that there is a negative correlation between defence R & D and competitiveness. From this it appears that, for a given R & D Budget, the greater the proportion spent on defence, the lower the impact on industrial competitiveness.

Other problems associated with correctly measuring R & D expenditure in various countries may arise. It could be argued, for example, that it is relevant to distinguish between those resources devoted to R & D by the public sector and those devoted by the private sector, on the grounds that the former are less likely to be related to economic performance, at least in the short run. A further distinction might be made between expenditure on Research and expenditure upon Development: for example, until recently, Japan has been viewed as a country undertaking relatively little Research; instead, it has licensed technology from abroad and devoted resources to Development and subsequent commercial exploitation. Hence, for any given level of R & D expenditure, the higher the proportion devoted to development, the greater might be the expected effect on the performance of the economy.

29

Whilst it is possible to propose hypotheses of this type, the data for most countries is insufficiently robust to justify detailed analysis. Of more importance, perhaps, is the fact that the absence of a clear relationship between expenditure on R & D and the performance of a national economy reflect more fundamental issues. It should always be recalled that whilst a plausible case can be made that technological change is a factor influencing the performance of an economy, it is less clear to what extent expenditure on R & D affects the rate of technical change. Again, we emphasise that R & D may be viewed as an input, but its contribution depends on how that input is managed. Even if good ideas are developed through the research process, much depends upon the skill with which they are commercialised. Furthermore, it seems likely that different countries will show different aptitudes in developing research ideas. This appears to reflect the popular view (at least in the UK!) that the British are relatively good at invention and providing Nobel prize winners in science, but relatively poor at developing the full commercial benefits of these ideas. Some support for this view was provided, according to EIU (1985), by a recent report from the Japanese Ministry of Trade and Industry, which found that a staggering 55 per cent of significant post-war inventions were attributable to Great Britain.

Two countries with identical expenditure on R & D might then be expected to have very different rates of commercial development. This is illustrated in Foxall's (1984) review of both the successful and unsuccessful launches of new products. He shows that the successful new products combined both technical proficiency and marketing awareness. Interestingly, he reports on the results of a study by Cooper (1973), which investigated 114 new products which failed, and shows that it was 'a consequence of inadequate market awareness or marketing competence (specific or latent), rather than technical impediments'. Cooper comments that 'this result is quite provocative, particularly when one considers the relatively minor amounts spent on marketing research compared to the large sums spent on R & D'. A similar point is made by Freeman (1982) in examining successful and unsuccessful innovations in Britain. In his view the key element distinguishing the two was that, in the case of the successful innovations, the needs of the user were better understood. Whilst this may appear obvious, or even tautological, it is striking that Freeman found that companies which reached the market first with a new product were frequently unsuccessful. Rather, it was the company which provided the product 'with all the bugs ironed out' that was successful. Hence, the combining of technological skills and market understanding is critical.

In looking at the linkages between technical change and economic growth, there is a danger of underestimating the importance of the 'softer' factors associated with industrial innovation. Thus, for example, two of the major industrial innovations of the twentieth century which resulted in massive cost reductions and virtually unassailable competitive advantage to the innovating companies were largely innovations in work and production organisation. Ford's assembly line production systems using mass-production interchangeable components and low-skilled labour, though including some technical product and process innovations, were principally a radical change in work organisation. Similarly, the rise of the Japanese motor cycle and motor car industry in the 1950s and 1960s was based on organisational innovations in such areas as inventory control, elimination of waste, and quality control. Interestingly, the Japanese motor industry has moved into product innovations over the last decade or so, going against the classic model in which industries move over time from product to process innovation (as, indeed, the US motor industry has done) (Altshuler et al. 1984).

Clearly, then, the ability of the firm to convert ideas into new commercial products is fundamental to technical change and to economic progress, yet varies markedly from one firm to another. Several different approaches have been made to investigate the factors influencing the ability to convert ideas into products. The first approach reflects the concern of economists with the most appropriate form of market structure for maximising rates of technological change. In simple terms, does a competitive market provide a greater incentive for invention than a monopolistic one, or are monopolists more able to finance the necessary R & D than competitive firms? It was Arrow (1962) who formally showed that firms in a competitive industry have stronger incentives to supply a new invention than those in monopolistic industry and that society incurred a welfare loss by permitting a reduction in competition. Although the basis of this was subsequently challenged by Demsetz (1969), the debate was conducted within the conventional 'comparative static' context, which is of questionable relevance to a discussion of technological change. For this reason it is the ideas associated with Schumpeter (1942) which are more influential. In his later work he suggested that the benefits from research were so uncertain that only large firms would be prepared to undertake it.

31

Furthermore, only industries with high profits — presumably arising because of high levels of industrial concentration — could afford to devote resources to R & D. Finally, R & D activity is likely to be subject to scale economies, so giving a comparative advantage to larger firms. Conversely, however, firms in monopolistic positions may have less of an incentive to innovate, particularly if they perceive themselves as being protected from the threat of new firms entering the industry and so reducing the monopolist's profits.

It is therefore an essentially empirical question as to what types of market structure are most conducive to R & D, and it appears to be broadly true that research intensity increases directly with market concentration (For a review, see Clarke, 1985). Even so, the direction of causation is unclear in the sense that it is not possible to distinguish whether R & D intensity leads to high industrial concentrations or vice versa. Finally, it has to be emphasised that these studies only examine R & D expenditure, and not the effectiveness of that expenditure in generating products.

A second approach has been pioneered by Rothwell and others at SPRU, University of Sussex. They investigated the role played by different-sized firms in more than 4,000 significant UK innovations over the period since the war. Rothwell showed that small firms, with less than 200 employees, produced a smaller proportion of significant innovations than might be expected, given their share of total output and employment. He also shows that the share of small firms in these innovations has been rising over time and that, perhaps for the first time in the 1980s, smaller firms produced a higher proportion of significant innovations than would have been 'expected', given their contribution to output or employment. These matters are discussed more fully in Chapter 3, but for the moment it is important to recognise that the broad thrust of Rothwell's work is to show that there is a dynamic complementarity between larger and small firms. Taking the case of the US semi-conductor industry, Rothwell shows that whilst large firms played a crucial initiating role in invention and innovation, much of the dynamic growth and market diffusion came about as a result of the formation of and growth of NTBFs.

This illustrates a further important point, that technological advance does not take place in a single firm. The effective advance is one which is replicated, almost certainly with modifications, by many firms. This is the process of diffusion, and may be regarded as the process of spreading technological advance. The pattern of this spread is likely to vary, depending on factors such as the nature

Figure 2.4: A model of innovation diffusion

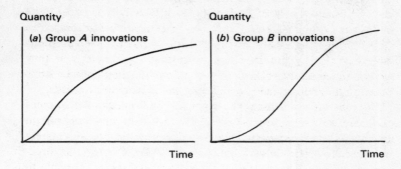

Source: Davies (1979)

of the technology, the nature of the product market, the form of patenting, etc. In his study of the diffusion of technology, Davies (1979) makes a distinction between Group *A* and Group *B* diffusions. The former he classifies as 'inexpensive, technically-simple and produced off-site', whereas Group *B* diffusions are 'elaborate, costly, and custom made'.

The predicted diffusion path, for these two groups are shown in Figure 2.4. Here, the technically simple innovation has a more marked *S* shape than the more sophisticated advances. Hence, at any point in time, Group *A* innovations are more diffused, although over time the Group *B* innovations narrow the differential.

Figure 2.5 then attempts to summarise the complex relationship between expenditure on R & D and the achievement of economic progress. As we noted earlier it cannot be inferred that in practice the relationship is of the simple 'linear' form, with the direction of flow being in a single direction. Nevertheless, even if this most simplistic assumption is made, it can be seen that expenditure upon R & D has to undergo four key transformations before — if ever — it results in identifiable economic benefits. These transformations are shown as arrows in the top row of the figure, but the extent to which the transformation is made depends upon the factors identified below the arrow. Thus, the first transformation is the extent to which expenditure upon R & D leads to new inventions. This is shown to depend upon several factors — notably, the quality of the scientists themselves, the extent to which R & D expenditure is focused upon

Figure 2.5: Diffusion of technological advances

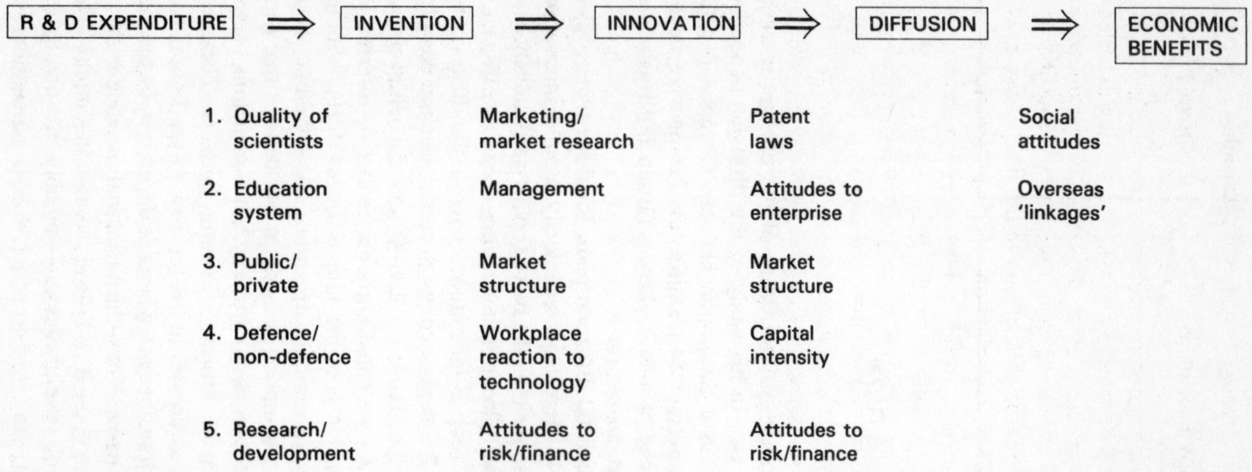

R & D EXPENDITURE	→	INVENTION	→	INNOVATION	→	DIFFUSION	→	ECONOMIC BENEFITS
1. Quality of scientists				Marketing/ market research		Patent laws		Social attitudes
2. Education system				Management		Attitudes to enterprise		Overseas 'linkages'
3. Public/ private				Market structure		Market structure		
4. Defence/ non-defence				Workplace reaction to technology		Capital intensity		
5. Research/ development				Attitudes to risk/finance		Attitudes to risk/finance		

basic research or upon defence/military applications, and the extent to which it is undertaken in the public or private sector.

Similarly, the extent to which inventions are transformed into innovations also depends upon several factors: for example we have noted that the vast majority of new products which fail do so because of inadequate marketing/market research. In other cases they fail simply because management does not recognise their potential, and it is only when a rival develops the product that the error is recognised. We have also discussed the role that market structure and the nature of competition in the market can play, although it is unclear which combination of characteristics or price/non-price competition, competitive/concentrated structure or large/small firms dominated is likely to be the most productive in leading to direct economic benefits. The extent to which new products, and particularly new processes, are accepted in the workplace can also be an important consideration. This is likely to be dependent upon some factors outside the control of the firm, such as the prevalent levels of unemployment, and partly upon factors which the firm can influence, such as levels of training and unionisation rates. Finally, the ability or willingness of the firm to finance such developments is also important. Where the innovation process is undertaken by a large firm, then financing decisions are 'internal' to that firm, but even here, particularly in the case of quoted companies undertaking high-profile research, the market value of the company is clearly related to possible new products. Given also that a company may wish, for short-term reasons, to raise the value of its share price (for example, to fight a take-over), there may be a temptation to use new inventions as a weapon in broader financial battles. Attitudes to risk of the wider financial community are probably even more crucial to success in the case of a new firm, without a track record and perhaps without even a fully tested prototype model. Clearly, the growth of venture capital in the United States and some European countries, some of it focused specifically upon technologically sophisticated ideas, indicates that it is possible to obtain finance for this type of project. Nevertheless, as we shall demonstrate later in the book, relatively few new firms, even in the high technology sector, seek external equity participation from a financial institution at an early stage in the life of the business, and of those, only a small proportion is able to persuade the institutions to participate.

Factors affecting the extent to which innovations are diffused and so lead to economic development are shown under the third arrow from the left in Figure 2.5. Diffusion depends upon some of the factors identified earlier, notably, market structures and attitudes to risk, etc. At this stage, however, new factors enter — most notably the willingness of individuals or firms to take up these innovations — and this we call attitudes to enterprise. This includes the willingness of both existing businesses to sell new products and process, and propensity of existing firms to incorporate new production technology and components, and the willingness of individuals to establish new businesses. As the Davies (1979) research noted, the extent to which these benefits are diffused also depends upon the nature of the technology, patent laws, etc.

The extent to which these processes lead to direct economic benefits, even after all these stages, also depends upon a final set of factors — most notably social attitudes and overseas 'linkages'. Nuclear power, for example, has had some clear economic benefits in terms of employment amongst UK suppliers as well as relatively low-priced electricity from the older generation of reactors. On the other hand, it has led to concern amongst many groups over the processing and disposal of nuclear waste and the risks of accidents at power stations. Conventional coal-fired power stations also impose costs upon the community in Britain, and more particularly overseas, through discharges of sulphur dioxide into the atmosphere. It is therefore important to recognise that although the criteria for assessing technology is referred to here as economic benefit, this is used in the widest sense of referring to the welfare of a community, thus including conventional or measurable economic benefits and associated 'social' gains and losses.

The extent to which any individual country benefits from R & D expenditure depends on whether it can ensure that it is able to harness the competitive advantage to be gained from product or process innovation and diffusion. As we noted earlier, the United Kingdom has been relatively effective in undertaking research and producing inventions but relatively poor in moving these inventions on to the innovation and diffusion stages. This has meant that the lion's share of economic benefits of UK inventions, notably manufacture and distribution, has been obtained by foreign nationals. However, many observers argue that, in many areas of new technology, most of the 'added value' is at the R & D end of the spectrum rather than in manufacturing and distribution. For these reasons, manufacturing has been transferred to developing countries paying relatively low wages — particularly in South-east Asia, with the advanced countries specialising in the provision of advanced services — notably the provision of software and the undertaking of 'frontier' R & D. The trend in manufacturing to seek cheap-labour locations abroad is, however, being reduced by the increased automation of production systems, the need for flexibility and for closeness to suppliers, and for quality.

Figure 2.5 has identified the variety of factors influencing the relationship between expenditure on R & D and economic development. Given the complexity of these relationships, it is not surprising that there should be an absence of any clear statistical relationship between the variables. Indeed, it would be surprising if one existed. The real value of Figure 2.5, however, is that it demonstrates that the transformation of R & D expenditure into economic development is dependent upon four key stages, and at each of these stages there is a wide variety of factors influencing the transformation. In some cases public policy can clearly be directed towards improving the transition through the provision of more scientists, improvements in the general quality of education, better patent laws, encouragement to enterprise, etc. Even so, two major problems remain. Firstly, it is unclear which of the factors influencing, for example, the transition from invention to innovation, are the most important or which are the most amenable to changes in public policy. Secondly, for some factors, such as market structure, even the ultimate objective of public policy is unclear — should it be more or less competitive markets?

Concern with the elements in Figure 2.5 has recently resurfaced again in Britain, most notably in the ACARD (1986) report on *Exploitable areas of Science*, which stated:

> With growing competition in the world's industrialised markets and increasing technological sophistication of the products of those markets, most industrialized countries require a strong science-based economy, decision-making procedures on national science policy must balance judgements on scientific and technical potentials against social and economic developments. (p. 41)

Implementation of such policies, however, is more difficult since it is unclear, in terms of Figure 2.5, either at what stage the UK is weak or what the appropriate policies for rectifying such weaknesses actually are. Nevertheless, within the UK there has been a clear shift of emphasis of government policy towards science as part of a change in the overall ethos of government economic policy. In particular there has been a redirection of resources away from the public and towards the private sector. Bowles (1985), for example, shows that whilst in 1972, 29 per cent of R & D employment was in the public sector, this had fallen to 24 per cent by 1983. There has also been an attempt to encourage those scientists working in the public sector either to place greater emphasis upon the commercial relevance of their work or, even better, to commercialise their own work by making it into a business in which they have an equity stake. These initiatives are key elements within the government's broader economic policy themes — notably, those of privatisation and the encouragement of entrepreneurship.

The remaining chapters will examine aspects of these initiatives by focusing upon the role played by universities and other higher education institutes — and particularly by smaller high technology firms. It is towards a review of the role of these groups that we now turn.

CONCLUSION

This chapter has painted a broad historical canvas to facilitate our understanding of the role of technical change and economic development, into which will be placed the relatively recent combination of small, hi-tech firms, universities and Science Parks. It has been emphasised that no single model exists which relates R & D, technical progress and economic development. Nevertheless, it is clear that in the long run, the adoption and diffusion of technical innovations is central to economic progress. What is less clear is the appropriate configuration of policies to promote these developments.

3

New Technology-based Firms and the Universities

3.1. INTRODUCTION

The previous chapter illustrated the links that exist between scientific knowledge and its application to economic progress. Key elements of that link are the universities and other institutions of higher education which train individuals with the appropriate technical and scientific skills and smaller technology-based firms which can provide the vehicle for invention to take place and for innovations to be diffused.

The universities and the smaller-firm sector have always played a part in economic progress, but it was perhaps only in the 1980s that, at least in Britain, the two were given a major role. Furthermore, it is only in very recent times that their roles were seen to overlap and complement one another, most notably in the establishment of Science Parks.

This chapter considers the role of new technology-based firms in the British economy. It also examines the changing role of universities, primarily conditioned by the reductions in central government funding. Only in this way is it then possible to examine the context of the growth of Science Parks in Chapter 4, which can be seen as the fusion of university and technology-based small-firm developments.

3.2. INNOVATION AND THE SMALL-FIRM SECTOR

Chapter 2 began a discussion of the role which different-sized firms played in technical innovation. It referred briefly to a long-standing debate on the most appropriate form of market structure for

Table 3.1: Innovations produced by sector in the UK since 1945

	Number of innovations used	Employment in 1976 (000)	Innovations per thousand employees	% of all innovations
Food, drink & tobacco	112	761.3	0.15	2.6
Chemicals & oils	421	438.9	0.96	9.6
Metal manufacture	186	470.1	0.40	4.2
Machinery	573	407.6	1.41	13.1
Mechanical engineering	558	1,031.4	0.54	12.7
Instruments	332	154.0	2.16	7.6
Electrical engineering	346	347.0	1.00	7.9
Electronics	428	359.3	1.19	9.8
Shipbuilding	67	178.2	0.38	1.5
Vehicles	212	560.8	0.38	4.8
Aerospace	85	206.9	0.41	1.9
Textiles, leather & clothing	144	966.6	0.15	3.3
Bricks, pottery, etc.	157	258.6	0.61	3.6
Paper	54	213.4	0.25	1.2
Printing	29	338.9	0.09	0.7
Other manufacturing	91	612.2	0.15	2.1
All other sectors	583	NK	NK	13.3
Total	4378			100.0

Note: NK — not known
Sources: Pavitt *et al.* (1987); *Business Monitor*, 1976

promoting innovation, and concluded that a competitive environment in which there were both large and small firms was appropriate. It nevertheless remains a key area of debate as to whether large or smaller firms are more 'innovative'. If, for example, small firms were shown to be more innovative, then there would be some case for considering policies to promote their development and vice versa.

In principle, it is possible to obtain an answer to this question by reference to a data base housed at the Science Policy Research Unit (SPRU) at the University of Sussex, which covers information on significant technical innovations introduced on a commercial basis in the UK since 1945. The sectoral composition of innovations is shown in Table 3.1 and it illustrates several important points — firstly, that there is a clear concentration of innovations in sectors such as machinery and in mechanical engineering which, between them, provide 25.8 per cent of all significant innovations. When account is taken of the size of the sector, and innovations normalised by number of employees in 1976, then instruments and electronics are seen to be the most innovative. Secondly significant innovations are almost absent in the service sector — other than in business services, even though services are now the major UK employer. Thirdly, it shows that significant innovations have taken place in 'unfashionable' sectors of manufacturing such as shipbuilding, metal manufacture, building materials and food — in fact, these industries in aggregate provide about 12 per cent of all significant innovations.

The SPRU data base is also very helpful in pointing to the fact that there are major differences in the size of innovating forms. Rothwell (1985) says,

In the scientific instruments industry, small firms have enjoyed an average of 58.5% of total sectoral innovations between 1945 and 1983 . . . In pharmaceuticals, in contrast, SME's share in innovations averaged only 14% over the 38 year period and it has been zero since 1974.

Rothwell attributes these sectoral differences to variations in entry costs. In the pharmaceutical sector, for example, development costs for a new drug are generally very high, in part because of the regulatory costs of specified testing procedures, whereas development costs in instrumentation are generally much more modest.

The innovating performance of different-sized firms is then likely to be strongly related to the sector in which it is operating. Even so, it would appear that, from the data presented in Table 3.2(a), there have been changes in the propensity of different-sized firms to introduce innovations. The table shows that the small-firm sector, i.e., enterprises employing less than 200 workers, increased its share of innovations from around 13–14 per cent in the 1950–64 period to around 26 per cent in the 1980–3 period. Equally interestingly, very large firms — with more than 100,000 workers — also appear to have increased their share of innovations from around 10 per cent in the 1945–55 period to 15 per cent in the 1980–3 period. From this it is clear that the middle-sized firms experienced a consistent drop in their share of innovations over time.

These data take no account of considerable shifts in the size structure of manufacturing enterprises over the period. To normalise for these differences, Table 3.2(b) provides data on both the proportion of total manufacturing employment in small (less than 200 workers)

Table 3.2(a): Innovation share by size of firm

	<200	200–999	Size of firm employees 1,000– 99,999	100,000+	Total number of innovations	%
1945–9	16.8	12.8	60.2	10.2	226	100
1950–4	14.2	14.0	62.6	9.2	359	100
1955–9	14.4	19.2	54.5	11.9	514	100
1960–4	13.6	15.2	58.5	12.7	684	100
1965–9	15.4	16.7	54.7	13.2	720	100
1970–4	17.5	15.3	53.2	14.0	656	100
1975–9	19.6	17.1	48.8	14.5	823	100
1980–3	26.3	16.4	42.1	15.2	396	100
					4378	

Table 3.2(b): Innovations per employee in small firms

Year	% of total manufacturing employment in enter- prises with less than 200 workers (a)	% of innovations in firms with less than 200 workers (b)	$\dfrac{b}{a}$
1958	24.0	14.4	0.60
1963	21.3	13.6	0.64
1968	20.8	15.4	0.74
1974	21.5	17.5	0.81
1980	24.3	19.6	0.81
1983	26.5	26.3	0.99

firms and the proportion of innovations undertaken in this sector. It shows that over the period 1958–83, there has been a continuous improvement in the 'productivity' of the small-firm sector in terms of innovation, rising from 0.60 to 0.99 over the 25-year period. Pavitt *et al.* (1987) in further analysis of the SPRU data base show that, in fact, the relative share of innovations provided by both large and small firms has increased over time, with medium-sized firms experiencing a decline.

A second effect which may explain the apparently substantial increase in the share of total innovations provided by small firms is a possible 'structural' or 'compositional' effect. It was noted earlier, for example, that small firms were traditionally a major source of new innovations in electronics and yet were relatively unimportant in pharmaceuticals. If there is an increase in the number of innovations in instrumentation and a decline in pharmaceuticals, then aggregate data of the type shown in Table 3.2 will identify the structural shift, rather than a 'pure' firm-size effect. In other words, is there a structural shift amongst innovating industries away from those in which medium-sized firms are found towards those in which small and large firms are found? On the other hand, a 'pure' size effect would be where there was, *in all industries*, evidence of small firms becoming responsible for an increasing proportion of innovations.

These issues are addressed empirically in Pavitt *et al.* (1987), who show that the generally increasing share of both large and small firms in innovation is far from uniformly found throughout all sectors. Instead, only in the chemicals and electronics sectors is there significant evidence of such a development, although in machinery, instruments, shipbuilding and vehicles the innovative performance of small firms appears to be increasing. On the other hand, large firms in metals, mechanical engineering, electrical engineering, aerospace, textiles and building materials, significantly increased their share of innovation. The increasingly clear U-shape of innovatory performance thus seems to reflect polarising sectoral differences rather than a general development across all sectors.

To Rothwell (1986), however, the question of whether it is large or small firms which are the major source of new innovations is irrelevant for two reasons: firstly, because both large and small firms have advantages and disadvantages in introducing new innovations and that these change from one time period to another and from one industry to another; and secondly, Rothwell argues that the most effective innovations are where the advantages which large and small firms possess are combined. Thus, whilst small firms have the ability to react quickly, are more willing to take risks, and have better internal communications than large firms, they generally lack the large firms' access to finance, lack its ability to market products through established dealer networks and lack the large firms' expertise in dealing with government bureaucracy which can be very important in the case of new products.

In practice, Rothwell believes that small firms have often played a crucial role in the diffusion of new technologies, particularly in the relatively early stages of the product's life. He quotes the example of the semi-conductor industry in the United States, in which diffusion of the new technology took place through several research scientists leaving Bell Laboratories to establish their firms. Rothwell describes it thus:

> What in fact occurred during the evolution of the US semiconductor industry was a classical example of the dynamic complementarities that can exist between large and small firms. Existing large firms provided much of the basic, state-of-the-art technology, venture capital and technically skilled personnel, which were essential to new technology-based firm start up, the new technology-based firms provided risk taking entrepreneurial drive and rapid market exploitation. It was a synergistic relationship.

To summarise, therefore, innovation has been concentrated in the manufacturing sector, rather than in services. Within UK manufacturing, significant innovations have occurred in most sectors, but they appear to be increasingly concentrated in the new or high technology sectors such as instruments and electronics. These sectors are still relatively youthful and here there is evidence that smaller firms, frequently in conjunction with larger firms, can play a key role in the diffusion of innovations. We now review some studies of these firms.

3.3. NEW TECHNOLOGY-BASED FIRMS

Whilst the subject of innovation within different sizes of firm is of importance, it is a subset of such firms — the new technology-based firms (NTBFs) which are of key interest. The interest which they generate stems from several factors:

— They are thought to embody the technologies of the future and hence provide secure employment opportunities for several generations.
— In the United States NTBFs have exhibited spectacular rates of employment growth.
— The areas in which NTBFs are important in the United States (Boston, Massachusetts; Palo Alto and Orange County in California) have also exhibited major job creation in the business and consumer service sectors locally.
— The quality of the jobs provided in NTBFs are significantly better than those in traditional manufacturing.

The first major comparative study of NTBFs was undertaken by Little (1979). They compared the growth of NTBFs in the USA with those in the UK and in Germany, and immediately encountered problems over definition. Eventually they settled on the following characteristics of an NTBF:

(1) It must not have been established for more than 25 years.
(2) It must be a business based on a potential invention or one having substantial technological risks over and above those of a normal business.
(3) It must have been established by a group of individuals — not as a subsidiary of an established company.
(4) It must have been established for the purpose of exploiting an invention or technological innovation.

The results of the Little study were spectacular. It was able to identify 41 firms in the USA satisfying the above conditions which in total employed 334,000 workers and had sales (in 1974) of virtually $10 billion world-wide. The clear implication of the Little study was that these were merely the 'First Division' firms, but that it would have been possible to have obtained many other qualifying firms experiencing rapid growth. After an exhaustive study, Little was able to identify 93 companies in the UK which satisfied the criteria. The British companies were, however, very much smaller than those in the US listing, and whilst it is not possible to make direct comparisons, it is clear that the total number of workers employed was approximately half that of Hewlett–Packard alone at the same time. In Germany there appeared to be even fewer NTBFs than in the United Kingdom.

Since the Little study there is little evidence that the gap between the USA and Europe has narrowed. Oakey (1984), for example, undertook comparisons between high technology firms located in the San Francisco Bay area of California, Scotland and south-east England. He defined high technology to be the sectors of instruments and electronics. In the decade prior to 1978 the Bay area employment in these sectors increased from 58,000 to 111,000 — an increase of 91 per cent. Over the same period, employment in these sectors rose from 46,800 in Scotland to 65,400 — an increase of 40 per cent, whereas in south-east England it actually fell by 12 per cent. Even so, there are areas of Britain which have experienced a rapid growth of high technology firms, notably the area around Cambridge which has been studied by Segal Quince (1985), Keeble

Table 3.3: Employment growth in Cambridge 1983–7

Size (employees)	Annual % rate of employment growth	
	High-tech	Conventional
< 26	+ 43.00	+ 12.25
26–50	+ 13.50	+ 17.00
51–75	+ 26.00	− 7.00
76–100	+ 7.50	− 1.50
101–200	+ 10.00	0.00
201–500	+ 7.50	− 2.25
501–1000	+ 0.25	+ 0.75
> 1000	+ 0.25	− 1.25
All businesses	+ 6.5	+ 1.2

Source: Cambridge City Council (1986)

and Kelly (1986) and Cambridge City Council (1986). The other major area in England experiencing a rapid growth in the number of high technology firms so called is the 'M4 Corridor', studied by Sayer and Morgan (1985), and by Breheny and McQuaid (1987).

In both these areas, the growth of high technology employment is very recent. Ellin and Gillespie (1983) and Gibbs *et al.* (1985), for example, using definitions of high technology based upon groups of Minimum List Headings (MLHs) could find no evidence of an 'M4' effect using employment data for the period 1971–8. Breheny and McQuaid (1987), however, report the results of their own work, together with employment surveys conducted by both Hampshire County Council and Berkshire County Council. Broadly, these show that employment growth in the high-tech sector is significantly faster than elsewhere. This is clearly illustrated in an examination of employment trends in Cambridge in the 1983–7 period. This survey, conducted by Cambridge City Council (1986), was of 420 manufacturing firms. Of these, almost 200 were classified as high tech and 220 were in conventional manufacturing. This is shown in Table 3.3, which projects that over the period 1983–7 high-tech manufacturing firms in the Cambridge area will grow by 6.5 per cent whereas those in the more conventional sectors will grow only by 1.2 per cent. The table also illustrates that the more rapid rates of growth will be experienced by the smaller firms in both the high-tech and the conventional sectors.

It is important, however, that these figures are interpreted cautiously, since their method of calculation consistently leads to an upward bias in the performance of small firms and a depressing of the performance of large firms. Furthermore, the figures include employment in firms which moved in to, or started up in, the area, and so employment growth is not solely the result of in-firm growth. Finally, the projected growth in employment of 1.2 per cent in manufacturing firms in conventional sectors also deserves comment since this is also an 'exceptional' performance. We have no national data with which to make comparisons, but there can be few areas of the UK in which manufacturing employment will rise during the 1983–7 period. It suggests that, if Cambridge is typical, then in areas in which high technology firms are concentrated, it is not just high-tech firms which perform well in terms of employment creation, but that even firms in the conventional sectors perform better than elsewhere.

This raises a more fundamental question about the overall employment creation performance of these areas. Is it, for example, the nature of the overall business environment which enables both high-tech and conventional-sector firms in these areas to perform better overall, or is it the purchasing power which fast-growing high-tech firms provide which stimulates growth in the more conventional sectors? In other words, does the growth in high-tech firms lead economic development or is it merely the most clear outward manifestation of the good business environment in which all firms prosper? To some extent, this is the same issue raised by Storey (1985a) in his comparisons of new firm formation in East Anglia and the Northern region. He speculated that if northern England, a traditionally depressed region dominated by old and declining industries, had created high-tech firms at the same rate at which they were being created in East Anglia, a thriving region generally regarded as the centre of high technology in Britain over the same period, then perhaps there would have been an extra 500 jobs in northern England. The effect of this upon unemployment in the North would have been minimal, suggesting that the direct contribution of high technology firms to employment creation and unemployment reduction was minimal.

At that time, however, it was not possible to make direct comparisons between the two regions because the northern England data ended in 1978, whereas the East Anglia data covered the period until 1981. It is now possible, however, to make rather more explicit comparisons since Northern data up to 1981 are now available. The comparison is made in Table 3.4 and shows that much depends upon the definitions used. Assuming that we take the original definitions used by Gould and Keeble (1984), i.e., including chemicals, then

Table 3.4: Employment in high-tech firms, East Anglia and northern England, 1971 and 1981

	Total employment in high-tech sectors in 1971		New firms in high-tech sectors in 1981			
	Including chemicals	Excluding chemicals	Including chemicals		Excluding chemicals	
			Number	Employ.	Number	Employ.
East Anglia (Norfolk, Suffolk and Cambridgeshire)	19,943	17,004	72	1,065	68	1,012
Average employment				14.8		14.9
Northern England (Durham, Cleveland and Tyne and Wear)	44,503	9,830	80	808	70	655
Average employment				10.1		9.4

Note: High technology is defined as MLHs: 271, 272, 354, 364, 365, 366, 367 and 383, according to the 1968 Standard Industrial Classification

new firms in East Anglia in 1981 provided a 5.3 per cent increase in employment over and above the 1971 employment in those sectors (1065 ÷ 19,943). New firms in the North, however, provided only 1.8 per cent (808 ÷ 44,503). If the North had experienced the same contribution as East Anglia, it could have expected 2,360 new jobs — an increase of just over 1,500. In both economies, however, the vast majority of new firms are in the electrical and scientific sectors and so it is probably more relevant to compare their performances. In these sectors new firms in East Anglia in 1981 added a net 5.9 per cent to the stock of 1971 employment, whereas in the North new firms added 7.0 per cent. In this sense, therefore, the North actually performed better than East Anglia over the decade.

The real differences between East Anglia and the North, however, are reflected in differences in the average size of new firms. In East Anglia the average employment size in surviving firms is 14.9 workers, whereas in the North it is only 9.4 workers. In short, this suggests that the direct impact on employment of new high-tech manufacturing firms in two very contrasting regions may only be of the order of only 1,500 jobs — and is probably very much lower — over a decade. It suggests that in no way does the direct contribution of new high technology firms explain the fundamentally different economic performance of these two contrasting regions.

In response to this situation, several points may be made. The first is that whilst the comparisons made have yielded only modest differences in the 1971–81 period, the major changes have occurred in the post-1981 period. Even so, it should be recognised that two-thirds of the companies included in the *Cambridge phenomenon* by Segal Quince (1985) were present in the city in 1981. In terms of employment, although the figure is not provided, it is safe to assume that about 90 per cent of 1984 employment in high-tech firms in Cambridge was in firms present in 1981, and that the 'phenomena' was well developed even at that time.

A second response is that whilst areas such as Boston, Massachusetts, have shown that the growth of high technology firms leads to a major expansion in both producer and business services, it is less easy to see why there should be a direct 'spin-off' to more conventional manufacturing. In the case of Boston it is clear that the growth of high-tech firms has led to the development, for example, of a sophisticated venture capital market and the growth of a major financial services sector. The wealth created by the growth of (initially small) high technology firms has created a booming sector for the provision of consumer and personal services. It is less clear,

49

however, why the growth of high-tech firms should lead directly to an improved performance on the part of the conventional manufacturing sector — primarily because the high-tech sector would be expected to purchase relatively little from this sector. Furthermore, high-tech firms are likely to pay relatively high wages, thereby bidding up local wage rates and placing the conventional sector at a comparative disadvantage because of their location. Of course, the growth of high-tech firms can lead to improved opportunities for other high-tech firms in the locality. Keeble and Kelly (1986), for example, cite the case of a leading new firm in Cambridgeshire, having a turnover in excess of £75m, which claims to have created indirect to direct employment in the ratio of more than 20:1 through its subcontract work. What is less clear, however, is whether this indirect employment occurs within Cambridge or the UK, or even overseas.

The fact that areas in which high technology firms are concentrated also experience an 'above-average' performance in their conventional sectors can be explained in two ways. The first, which we have discussed above, is that the high-tech sector 'leads' economic development and that the conventional sectors benefit from the additional purchasing power generated. If this explanation is valid, it suggests that those wishing to promote development can do so by focusing efforts upon the high-tech sector and that ultimately this will lead to an overall performance in the whole economy.

The second but contrasting explanation is that the type of 'environment' which induces the establishment and growth of high technology firms is also one likely to lead to growth amongst conventional businesses. There has been some discussion about the nature of this 'environment'. Keeble and Gould (1984), for example, in their discussion of the East Anglian region, appear to place emphasis upon new firm founders identifying 'a pleasant environment as a place to live' as a key consideration. In this they are presumably referring to amenity and cultural benefits. Whittington (1984) places emphasis upon the fact that the levels of education, managerial experience, etc. are higher in the existing prosperous areas of the UK and it is these which explain differential performance. Finally, many of the new areas such as Cambridge, the M4 corridor, etc. are not encumbered by traditional attitudes to work and trade union practices, and thus the greater flexibility required by the high technology firms may lead to an overall improvement in industrial relations and hence to better performance throughout the whole economy.

If these observations are correct it suggests that an environment likely to induce the establishment and growth of high technology firms is also one in which the rest of the manufacturing and services sector would prosper. It suggests that whilst high technology firms, even in these areas, perform better than 'conventional' sectors, the latter perform better than the national economy as a whole. It seems unlikely that it is possible to abstract these elements of the successful economic environment and apply them to localities in which there has been no spontaneous upsurge of growth amongst high-tech firms. It also suggests that policies which concentrate upon promoting the growth of high technology firms in areas where the economic environment is poor is likely to meet with very modest success. To deepen our understanding of these factors, a better appreciation of the characteristics of the high-tech entrepreneur are needed.

3.4. THE HIGH-TECH ENTREPRENEUR

The classic study of high technology entrepreneurs in Europe and the United States was undertaken by Little in 1979. It made several recommendations about how the number of NTBFs in Europe could be increased and how growth in this sector could be promoted. These included:

— Provision of financial assistance to such companies.
— Changing cultural attitudes to give greater encouragement to entrepreneurs to make money out of a business.
— Changing the behavioural constraints which inhibit the willingness of Europeans to start businesses.
— Changing patent laws giving individuals the right to exploit patents which their employers refuse or fail to exploit.

In the report Little places great emphasis upon the need for changes in the tax system, enabling individuals in business to retain a high proportion of the profits earned in their business, and since 1977 many of the barriers identified by Little have been reduced in both Britain and Germany. In Britain rates of personal income tax have been consistently reduced since 1979, and the government has placed considerable emphasis on the social acceptability of entrepreneurship. The period has also seen the growth of private venture capital, much of it directed towards high-tech projects, on a previously unheard-of scale. In Germany, since 1983, a scheme to promote comprehensively the growth of NTBFs has been in operation whereby different levels of public subsidy are available for the stages of concept-testing, development and marketing of an NTBF (Keil (1986), Kulicke (1987)).

Whilst the subject of entrepreneurship has received extensive study in the UK in recent years (see Curran, 1986 for a useful recent review), the high-tech entrepreneur has received less study than might have been expected. In particular, it is important to know whether the types of incentives which are clearly relevant to the growth of NTBFs in the USA are also relevant to the growth of NTBFs in Europe. In this context the study by Segal Quince (1985) on high technology firms in Cambridge is of importance. This demonstrates the difficulty of identifying a 'typical' NTBF and that, in some respects, the aspirations of their owner(s) and the problems which they face do not differ significantly from those of other firms of similar age. Even so, Segal Quince see the so-called 'soft–hard' model developed by Bullock (1983) as relevant. They note that many NTBFs are established as 'soft' companies, often by academics, providing services or writing software, in a consultancy capacity. Since there is little direct capital outlay, the 'soft' company is a low-risk business. However, once the market for the product/service is better assessed, and perhaps the product/service better developed, the academic may have to make a judgement about whether to turn the business into a full-time activity. Here, the 'risk' to the individual increases, but the product/service becomes 'harder' since the business is likely to be providing a more customised service. A third stage may involve the provision of a new product — perhaps only a prototype — sold on only a very limited scale, whilst a fourth stage would be full-scale production. At each of these stages the business becomes 'harder', and the 'risk' to both the entrepreneur and any possible outside financier also becomes greater.

According to Segal Quince, there were in Cambridge a number of classical 'soft' developments which became increasingly 'hard', although currently, many companies remain, and probably always will remain, at the soft end of the spectrum. This ability of NTBFs to start 'soft', and so have relatively modest capital requirements, and to become 'harder', with this being financed by retained profits, is one reason why Segal Quince claim that a shortage of capital is not a factor limiting the growth and start-up of firms in Cambridge.

Comparisons and contrasts with the US experience are

particularly relevant here. We noted earlier that the Little study recommended a change in social attitudes to enterprise in Europe. This has clearly occurred in Cambridge with the establishment of many NTBFs in recent years. It is clear that, following the US example, the establishment of many NTBFs is the direct result of 'spin-off' either from Departments of the University, or from existing firms in the area. There is also a core of high-tech business experience being built up in the area. As Segal Quince comment: 'There are already also a number of cases in which recently retired company directors of wide experience are working with young companies. The ''recycling'' of the technical entrepreneurs themselves, will make a significant contribution'.

Nevertheless, it has to be recognised that there is one key aspect in which the British developments fail to match the United States — and that is in the scale of the activities. Segal Quince note that many of the Cambridge companies seemed to be owned by individuals who did not see their objectives in terms of major growth, which might lead to diseconomies of scale through poorer internal communications, an inability to respond rapidly to market pressures, etc. In short there appeared to be no NTBFs in Cambridge which were likely to be growing into a major international company within 10–15 years of start-up. It is perhaps for this reason that the whole of the Cambridge Science Park could be placed in the car park of the Hewlett-Packard factory in Palo Alto, California!

It would also be unwise to infer that in the UK, NTBFs are formed only by those with direct and strong university or related links. A study by Kelly (1987) of new firms in the computer electronics industry, for example, shows that whilst the highest rates of firm formation are in Cambridgeshire and Oxfordshire (primarily rural counties with a premier university), there are also high rates of formation in counties of south-eastern England without a university — notably Hertfordshire. Kelly shows that out of the 78 firms founded in Cambridgeshire, 24 were set up by individuals with a primarily academic background. On the other hand, out of the 37 firms founded in Hertfordshire, 26 were initiated by individuals with a background in the computing industry and only two by individuals with primarily an academic background. It seems reasonable to believe that firms established by those with an academic background might be expected both to perform differently and respond to different incentives from those founded by personnel from the computer industry. To some extent we are able to test this question in our survey, the results of which are reported in Part II.

53

In many respects, similar developments have been taking place in Germany. Kulicke (1987) reports that over the period 1973–84, perhaps 2,000 NTBFs were registered, with the rate of formation increasing sharply in recent years. As with the UK, the firms tended to be located in the existing prosperous areas such as Munich and Stuttgart, and started by individuals already living in those areas. Of the firms studied, Kulicke was surprised to find that only 24 per cent were started by individuals with an academic background. However, the Germans are currently undertaking a detailed study of the performance of the NTBF sector with a view to assessing the effectiveness of the public financial assistance upon job creation.

The extent to which universities and other colleges of higher education contribute to the growth of NTBFs is, then, a matter of some debate. The development of Route 128 around Boston, Massachusetts has been related to direct academic spin-off from the concentration of academic institutions such as the Massachusetts Institute of Technology (MIT) in the Boston area (Roberts and Wainer, 1968). However, this much-quoted study included in its definition of 'spin-off' people who had left MIT up to ten years prior to setting up their firm (with an average time lag of 2.5 years). The early growth of Silicon Valley in California was more related to spin-off from the research laboratories of industry than to university spin-offs. In the UK the work of Kelly clearly shows that in some prosperous areas, NTBFs are formed by personnel with an academic background, whereas in other prosperous areas, previous experience of founders is industrial rather than academic. Overall, in Germany only about one in four NTBFs are founded by academics. Hence whilst the direct contribution of universities to the formation of NTBFs is a matter of some speculation, it is perhaps also true that in both countries, about one in four NTBF founders were former academics. Kelly, in his study of computer firms in Cambridgeshire, Hertfordshire and Scotland, obtains a figure of 21 per cent.

It is also clear that institutions of higher education play a major indirect role in the provision of education and the formal and informal areas of technology transfer. We know from the studies by Kelly that 34 per cent of computer-firm founders had a PhD and 79 per cent had a first degree (compared with 5 per cent of founders having a first degree in a survey of all UK small firms — Johnson and Storey, 1987). Clearly, therefore, the training which a university provides is vitally relevant in this case. It may also be relevant in a less formal context, even to those who are not either former staff or students. Links with local firms may be established through work experience for students, employment of staff as consultants, etc. It is for this reason that we now investigate the role which universities play.

3.5. UNIVERSITIES AND NEW TECHNOLOGY-BASED FIRMS

Since the mid-1960s at least, British universities have been under pressure from government and employers organisations to make their activities more relevant to the needs of the workplace, and hence contribute more to the economic development of the country. It was argued by the Finniston Committee in 1980, for example, that UK degree courses in engineering were inferior to those of many other countries because of weaker links between British universities and industry. The key problem was that the courses offered were too 'academic' and provided insufficient practical training to students.

The direct provision of students to satisfy the needs of industry is only one element of the role played by universities. According to Williams (1985a), there are, in fact, five main ways in which universities may contribute to the development of NTBFs and to economic development more generally:

(1) By providing opportunities for students to acquire skills and attitudes which could be used to create or promote the success of NTBFs.
(2) By promoting research in high technology which may create opportunities for innovation by small firms.
(3) By encouraging staff to provide advice and consultancy services in the field of high technology.
(4) By allowing staff to create or take part in the creation of firms to exploit high technology.
(5) By creating companies to exploit the research or design and development activities of staff in fields of high technology.

Whilst the skills and qualities of the graduate student from UK universities have been the subject of some criticism, we shall not dwell upon this issue, since it is with the concept of enterprise creation with which we are concerned. Before passing on, however, it should be mentioned that a further criticism of the higher education system in Britain is that not only is the graduate inadequately trained, but that the training tends to be directed towards the goal of achieving employment as an employee, and very often as an employee in a large firm. This is unfavourably contrasted with the United States where a much higher proportion of college students either establish their own business immediately upon graduation — or who aspire to business ownership at some point in the future. These matters have begun to change in the UK with the establishment of programmes such as 'Graduates into Enterprise' (Scott, 1987) — although here it has to be admitted that the typical graduate starting a business tends not to be in the high technology sectors.

Although there has been a shift by British universities towards greater involvement with industry — and particularly high technology firms — progress has been uneven for several reasons. These are articulated by ACARD (1983), which argues, firstly, that there has traditionally been an emphasis in British universities upon academic excellence, which was judged in terms of peer-group assessment, which in turn depended upon publications, very often in learned journals. Clearly, time devoted to commercial activities means that less is available for producing publications and so there was a clear choice facing the academic between career advancement and financial return. Secondly, at least until 1983, there was no incentive for British universities to earn additional income from non-exchequer sources, since this was simply deducted from their overall allocation of funds from the University Grants Committee (UGC). Since 1983, however, this rule has changed, and most universities have become significantly more active in obtaining supplementary sources of funding. Thirdly, there are logistic problems in encouraging academics to become involved in 'external' activities since teaching commitments had to take priority and this could present difficulties for commercial sponsors. Fourthly, there was a clear problem of encouraging academics to undertake work in which they were not interested. By their choice of profession, academics place a high premium on job satisfaction (they are not in it for the money!) and it can be difficult for commercial organisations to ensure that only the most intellectually satisfying tasks are undertaken by the academics. Finally, problems may arise over questions of confidentiality, whereby a commercial organisation wishes to keep secret even that research being undertaken, whereas the academic is concerned to disseminate the results of research.

The absence of strong links in the past between British industry and the academic world is not wholly attributable to the attitudes of the universities. ACARD (1983) points out that many British industrialists, especially those without high academic qualifications themselves, may feel intimidated by university academics. There is also a feeling amongst industrialists that only products which they have developed are of the necessary standard (The 'not invented here' syndrome).

In spite of all these problems, the period since 1980 has seen a major growth in links between universities and industry — and most notably with high technology firms. Five factors have been important in this context. Firstly, in 1981 the government-funded UGC announced a cut of 11 per cent over the following three years in the monies which it would provide for universities. Secondly, it also became clear that these 'cuts' were not to be uniformly distributed across all universities, but were to be concentrated amongst those which had traditionally specialised in applied sciences and had strong links with industry. Salford University, for example, experienced a 44 per cent cut, Bradford University a 33 per cent cut and Aston University a 31 per cent cut. Thirdly, as noted above, the UGC indicated that, when distributing income to the universities, it would no longer penalise those institutions which obtained external income. Indeed, by 1985, the UGC stated that it would look favourably upon institutions in which there was clear evidence of external linkages, such that it would give greater weighting in the distribution of its own funds to those universities for which external funding was of greatest importance. The wheel had indeed turned full circle in just over two years! Fourthly, the period also saw the salaries of university staff grow appreciably less rapidly than many in the public sector, and substantially behind those of 'comparable' individuals in the private sector. For those with computing/electronic skills, the salary differentials between the private sector and the universities widened enormously, and the only way in which universities could retain staff was to allow them to undertake consultancy. Fifthly, in 1984–5, changes took place in the statutory rights of individuals to exploit the results of government-funded research. Until 1984 the National Research and Development Council (NRDC) had the right to exploit all university-funded research. Similarly, the Council had the first rights to exploit work funded by them. However, at this time matters changed, with the NRDC losing its rights and the Research Councils transferring their rights to the university in receipt of the grant.

The form of these links with industry, which were established as a result of the aforementioned changes, varied considerably from one university to another. In most cases universities recognised that it was their ability to sell a high-value product or service in the market-place which would yield them additional income, since they were normally at the forefront of their particular research fields in the areas of high technology.

The form of responses adopted by universities has been grouped into four categories by EIU (1985):

(1) facilitating communications;
(2) providing professional and financial support;
(3) establishing enterprises and research centres; and
(4) collaboration with outside bodies.

We shall discuss each of these responses in turn, but it should be recognised that the nature of the response varied considerably from one university to another. Some adopted a positive, active yet centralised strategy whereby leadership was exercised by the university, examples of which are the developments at Salford and Warwick. Others appear to have concluded that their external relationships were satisfactory and that, whilst encouragement should be given to existing developments, no centralised initiatives were required. The principal university in this group was Cambridge. Finally, and probably the most numerous, were those universities which have moved towards establishing stronger industrial links, but with varying degrees of success.

Facilitating communications. Once it became an objective of policy for universities to improve their links with industry, it was quickly apparent that whilst individual businesses were aware of some of the activities within the university, most firms were almost totally unaware of the expertise within their local university. To overcome this lack of awareness a number of very different initiatives were developed. Thus, for example, senior members of Queens University, Belfast, set out to meet the Chief Executives of all large and medium-sized companies in the Province. Several universities and polytechnics have produced video presentations about the services which can be provided, whilst a UK research data base, controlled from the University of St Andrews, is designed to provide a comprehensive list of research activities in all British universities.

In order to establish links with local business several universities have provided the title of 'Visiting Professor' to appropriate individuals. The University of Salford has also developed industrial sponsorship for so called 'Integrated Chairs', whilst an increasing number of universities have financed chairs whereby the individual works part time in the university and part time in an appropriate local business.

Several British universities have followed the US model of establishing formal networks in which companies pay a fee in order to obtain access to information on research taking place in the institution. In the United States, probably the best-known network is that at MIT to which more than 250 firms, world-wide, subscribe. In Britain this scheme, albeit on a much more modest scale, is being implemented at the Universities of Salford and Surrey.

Providing professional and financial support. The key element in the effective transfer of technology from universities to industry is the provision of a support framework for the individual academic. During the 1980s, most universities either appointed an industrial liaison officer for the first time or expanded the scope and capacity of the existing officers. The function of such individuals varied according to whether the university took a centralised (Salford-type) or a decentralised (Cambridge-type) view of industrial links. Cambridge University, for example, pursued a policy of having a liaison officer who linked outsiders with the relevant university staff, but the general policy of the university is that it takes no responsibility for any contracts entered into by its staff with outside bodies. On the other hand, Heriot-Watt University requires staff to enter into negotiations with outsiders only through its own liaison service which, in turn, provides specialist advice on contracts and provides insurance for academic staff. Similarly, Salford requires all academic staff to register their outside activities, which are strictly monitored by the University.

Establishing enterprises and research centres. Several universities have established their own companies to market their services, with these holding companies themselves having a variety of subsidiaries. Probably the best known of these is VUMAN, which is a wholly owned subsidiary of Manchester University, established to under-take R & D with its own staff. VUMAN has four divisions: lasers, robotics, industrial controls and model analysis, and although only established in 1982, had a turnover in excess of £1m by 1985.

Other initiatives include the establishment of new research centres. The Leicester Biocentre, for example, has been established to undertake research on genetic manipulation, funded by both government (the Department of Trade and Industry, the Science and Engineering Research Council) and private sources (Whitbread,

Distillers, Dalgety), whilst Austin Rover has established a major advanced manufacturing technology centre at Warwick University. The centre will undertake research not only for Austin Rover but also for other commercial clients.

Collaboration with outside bodies. Given that one objective of these initiatives is the transfer of technology, some universities have collaborated with other outside organisations to establish technology transfer centres. The University of Newcastle upon Tyne, for example, has collaborated with Newcastle Polytechnic and Newcastle City Council to establish, with support funding from the EEC, a technology centre, the purpose of which is to commercialise the technology within the university and polytechnic.

In no way should this brief review be thought of as a comprehensive statement of the flowering of initiatives taking place in British universities to promote the transfer of technology and to improve industrial links: instead, it has attempted to identify by the use of examples some of the major trends. Segal Quince (1988), in their review of these developments, note that whilst there is no clear model of success, there are major differences between universities in the way in which they have responded to both a shortage of funding and a need to demonstrate greater 'relevance'. These differences between universities are thought to reflect the following factors:

— the urban and industrial context of the university;
— the 'culture' and traditions of the university;
— the fields and quality of the research conducted;
— the presence of talented, supportive and motivated individuals and institutions;
— the availability of resources for special institutions;
— time; and
— public expenditure.

Broadly, Segal Quince argue that universities in areas experiencing industrial decline are likely to have greater problems than those in more prosperous locations. Nevertheless, the fact that Aston and Salford appear to have prospered, while Newcastle has not developed to anything like the same extent, is attributed to the presence of dynamic leadership at key positions in the former institutions. Furthermore, it is helpful if the university has some exceptional research areas where there is a commercial demand.

Segal Quince emphasise, however, that whilst a great deal has been achieved in a few years by some universities, it is unwise to expect a major change in cultural attitudes. So much depends on the ability of key university officers — normally the Vice Chancellor — to exercise qualities of leadership.

3.6. CONCLUSION

This chapter has examined the role of small firms in the new technology sectors and the changing role of British universities. It has shown that during the late 1970s and early 1980s smaller firms were becoming a more important source of innovation than at any time since the war. It also appears that larger firms are becoming more important, with middle-sized firms experiencing significant decline. In part these changes reflect sectoral shifts in the economy, away from heavy industry and towards electrical engineering, computers and electronics which, being 'new' industries, have many new and small firms.

Those working and founding firms in these industries need high educational qualifications: for example, one-third of all founders of computer firms in the UK had a PhD. This means that institutions of higher education, most notably the universities, are central to the generation of both labour and entrepreneurs in these key industries. It is therefore particularly significant that, at this time, universities are experiencing pressures from two directions. The first is to ensure that the activities of the university are 'relevant' to the needs of industry and commerce, and the second is to make these adjustments at a time of reduced central government financing.

There can be little doubt that most universities have adjusted to these pressures, although some have been significantly more successful than others. Perhaps the clearest outward sign of this adjustment to the new realities is the creation of a Science Park, and it is to a review of progress in this area to which we now turn.

4

The Evolution of Science Parks

4.1. INTRODUCTION

This chapter provides an overall view of the growth and development of Science Parks in Britain. It is not possible to discuss these developments in isolation from experience derived from abroad — most notably from the United States. For this reason, after discussing the problems of defining a Science Park, the chapter then provides a brief description of developments in the United States.

Turning to the UK, there are two clear phases during which Science Parks developed. Phase I was in the late 1960s when Cambridge and Heriot-Watt were established. Whilst drawing to some extent upon the US experience, these were most strongly motivated by technological considerations. Phase II occurred in the 1980s and drew much more heavily upon US developments. Phase II Science Parks also differed significantly from the earlier parks since they were a product of the contemporary economic pressures and conditions in Britain, which are also discussed in this chapter.

Finally we conclude with a snapshot picture of Science Parks in Britain which provides the background for the survey of firms which is presented in Part II of this study.

4.2. DEFINITIONS

There is no uniformly accepted definition of a Science Park and, to make matters worse, there are several similar terms used to describe broadly similar developments — such as 'Research Park', 'Technology Park', 'Business Park', 'Innovation Centre', etc. Some writers such as MacDonald (1987) claim that each of these terms are used interchangeably to describe the following package: firstly, a property-based initiative close to a place of learning; and secondly, one which provides high quality units in a pleasant environment.

On the other hand, Currie (1985), and Eul (1985) have attempted to distinguish between Innovation Centres, Science Parks and Research Parks. For Currie, *Innovation Centres* are small developments which provide facilities which enable start-up and small businesses to develop ideas, but which do *not* provide accommodation either for such businesses once they have grown, or for existing medium-sized or larger businesses. On the other hand, *Science Parks* provide accommodation for both start-up and medium-sized establishments, generally in a 'green field' setting, where small-scale manufacturing can take place. Finally, Currie argues that Research Parks differ from Science Parks in the sense that they prohibit all manufacture, except for the production of prototypes.

Eul (1985), however, defines an Innovation Centre as a group of buildings, close to a centre of academic excellence, providing managed short occupancy term accommodation for the development of strategic research or prototype development. Eul's Science Park definition is similar to that of Currie, but his definition of a *Business Park* is a development which provides high quality accommodation in which a wider variety of activities such as manufacture, showrooms, distribution, etc. can take place. According to this definition, the Business Park does not necessarily have to be linked to an institution of higher education or have tenants which are exclusively in high technology industries.

Whilst it is possible to construct consistent definitions, many developments choose to call themselves Business Parks or Science Parks without conforming to these definitions. The Newcastle Technology Centre, for example, provides no accommodation for its clients, and relies instead upon facilitating technology transfer between the higher educational institutions in the city and local firms through networking. On the other hand, Aston Science Park, which is generally acknowledged to be amongst the most successful of British parks is, according to some definitions, not a Science Park at all because of its relatively poor 'environmental' setting. It is located in a formerly almost derelict area in the centre of the city of Birmingham. Even so, it does satisfy other criteria, having close links with the University of Aston, providing 'managed' services and, in its first phase, was concerned with small and start-up firms which undertook only very limited manufacturing.

These problems over definition mean that we have to employ a rather pragmatic approach to developments which we call Science Parks, and define them as members of the United Kingdom Science Park Association (UKSPA). Because of these problems, UKSPA evolved a definition which sought to distinguish between 'pure' real estate (high specification) developments primarily designed to accommodate high technology firms and schemes developed in partnership with a centre of technological excellence (university research institute or corporate laboratory) where a primary objective is the transfer of technology and management skills, etc. Implicit in the UKSPA definition is the concept of selectivity of tenants on grounds other than planning. According to UKSPA, a Science Park is a property based initiative which includes the following features:

— Has formal and operational links with a University, other Higher Education Institution or Research Centre;
— Is designed to encourage the formation and growth of knowledge based businesses and other organisations normally resident on site;
— Has a management function which is actively engaged in the transfer of technology and business skills to the organisations on site.

This definition reflects the concern of universities and other technological institutions to develop a separate and unique identity based on the formal relationship of the park with a centre of technological excellence, and an objective of encouraging the transfer of technology and business skills. Thus, the definition is intended to exclude those developments which are promoted solely as locations for high technology firms, but where there is no organisational commitment or objective to stimulate or facilitate access to technology.

4.3. THE DEVELOPMENT OF SCIENCE PARKS IN NORTH AMERICA

The initial concept of a Science Park came from the United States and, currently, the US developments continue to be on a much larger scale than those anywhere else in the world. However, within the United States the best-known developments do not conform to a single consistent pattern and so, for illustrative purposes, we shall discuss three very different but also very successful developments:

these are associated with the MIT in Boston, the Stanford University Industrial Park, and the Research Triangle Park in North Carolina. We shall then conclude this section by setting out the Office of Technology Assessment's (OTA) (1984) five-fold classification of high technology developments in the United States.

Each of these developments at Boston, Stanford and Research Triangle is now, by any standards, a major success. Pizzano (1985), for example, reports that

> In the twenty-eight years since the formation of Research Triangle Foundation 27,000 jobs have been added directly to the region through the location of research facilities in the Park. The Foundation anticipates the creation of 60,000 jobs when the Park is at full occupancy.

If anything, the developments at Stanford and in Boston have been even more rapid. The growth in Boston is clearly associated with MIT through the formation of numerous high technology businesses in the area, as illustrated by Cooper (1973). This stems, in part, from the encouragement which faculty staff received to start their own business — notably, the allowance of one day per week in which they could undertake consultancy. In many cases, as Bullock (1983) points out, consultancy may have led to design and development work, with this being the basis of an embryo business. After a period of time, this 'soft' business became 'harder', when a manufacturing capability was added.

The developments in Boston are most clearly chronicled by Dorfman (1983), who shows that within a 30-mile radius of the centre of the city, there were at that time approximately 250,000 people employed in the electronics and related industries, and that this number had increased by about 75,000 over the previous five years. In her view 'graduates and staff of MIT have provided the single most important source of entrepreneurs in the region'. Perhaps somewhat surprisingly, however, the only evidence cited for this is the rather dated survey by Roberts and Wainer (1968), who found that there were 175 new Massachusetts firms in the high-tech sectors that had been formed by former full-time staff at MIT.

Whilst both Boston and Stanford are centres for the growth of the US electronics industry — indeed, the growth in California has, if anything been more rapid than in Boston. The factors underlying this growth are very different. The real commonality is that both are spawned from leading US universities — the three leading

Departments of Electrical Engineering for almost 20 years have been MIT, the University of California at Berkeley, and Stanford. The differences between the two locations, however, are much clearer. MIT and the Boston area, for example, were leading centres of scientific learning in the inter-war years, whereas the Stanford Research Park was not conceived until 1951. If anything, the growth of the high-tech sector in Boston could be genuinely regarded as a spontaneous development, whereas the Stanford Park was clearly the result of an initiative by Professor Frederick Terman, who set out after the war to make money for Stanford and transform it into one of the premier universities in the United States. A third key difference between the two areas was that the development in Boston occurred at a location which had all the legacies of an old industrial area — derelict buildings and declining employment opportunities in the textile industries — whereas the Stanford site was a genuine 'greenfield'. As Dorfman expresses it, 'in the Bay area high tech replaced apricot and walnut orchards, rather than textile mills'.

There is, however, one crucial similarity between the two areas and that is the role played by a single key firm. In the case of Boston, the key firm was Digital Equipment (DEC), whilst the fortunes of Stanford were closely linked with that of Hewlett-Packard and, later, Fairchild. The growth of these firms over two decades from start-up to major international corporations clearly provided substantial numbers of jobs both directly and indirectly. It is estimated that DEC provided more than 10 per cent of all high-tech employment in the State of Massachusetts, and indirectly provided up to 20 per cent. It appears that in almost all locations in the US where high-tech firms have been important, the contribution of a single firm — Fairchild in Palo Alto, Control Data in Minneapolis and Texas Instruments in Houston — has been crucial. Such firms provide a nucleus of qualified scientists and engineers working in a commercial and rapidly changing environment who become aware of new business opportunities. Thus, a series of spin-outs occur from these firms and, it appears, at a higher rate from an increasing number of small high-tech firms that over time cluster in strategic locations.

Before concluding this brief review of the developments around Stanford, it is worthwhile introducing a note of caution. A survey by Oakey (1984), who interviewed 60 small firms in Palo Alto, found that they had fewer and less important contacts with their universities than a comparable sample of firms in south-east England and in Scotland. In this sense, Oakey's results may parallel those of Cooper (1973) who found that out of the 243 high-tech firms started in Palo Alto during the 1960s, only six had full-time founders who came directly from Stanford. Clearly, it is difficult to evaluate the contribution of these links to the firms, but it does illustrate the risks of generalising about area differences.

In several respects the growth of Research Triangle illustrates some of the points identified in the Boston and Stanford cases, yet the area also has its own unique characteristics. Research Triangle is an interesting example of an out-of-town research, city-type development which is dependent on the establishment by large firms and institutions of major research and development facilities. It has more in common with French technopoles and the Japanese technopolis than with British and German initiatives, which are essentially based on smaller firms. Like Stanford, Research Triangle is a managed rather than a spontaneous development since it was established on the initiative of Governor Luther Hodge at the end of the 1950s. Like Boston, on the other hand, it was an area that had suffered relatively badly from declining employment opportunities in textiles. The Research Triangle was formed by the three universities of North Carolina in Chapel Hill, North Carolina State in Raleigh and Duke University in Durham. Unlike either Boston or Stanford, none of these universities were in the front rank of US institutions and so, perhaps for these reasons, in its early years, development on the Park was slow. It was not until 1965 that the Park took off with the announcement that IBM was to establish a major R & D facility, creating 9,000 jobs. The credibility which this vote of confidence by IBM gave to the Park, leading to major openings by Burroughs-Wellcome and others, is a key lesson for all those contemplating the development of a Science Park.

This brief review, whilst it has concentrated upon the successful examples of Science Parks and related developments, has shown that there is no single model to be followed. Some have grown almost spontaneously (Boston), whereas most of the others are the result of a clear policy initiative. Some have emphasised the high quality of the amenities of the areas (Stanford), whereas others have developed in less attractive climates. Most have stressed links with universities, and where these links are important the particular successes are generally with 'front-rank' universities, although the growth at Research Triangle shows that parks can grow even where such universities do not exist. It is clear that an individual park can be transformed by the decision of a firm to locate there (IBM at Research Triangle, Fairchild at Stanford). Perhaps the only

67

consistent element within the parks which are established as a clear act of policy, and which ultimately become highly successful, is the commitment of key individuals to the scheme (Terman at Stanford, Luther Hodge at Research Triangle).

Whilst the above cases are all very successful, there are many, less well-known, developments throughout the United States. In fact, the OTA (1984) identified five types of developments in different communities:

(1) *High Technology Centres*, such as 'Silicon Valley', Santa Clara, and Boston, which have a strong and expanding base of high technology firms, research universities and venture capital.

(2) *'Diluted' High Technology Centres* in major conurbations — for example, New York, Chicago, or Philadelphia, with larger, broader and more mature economies. To achieve a critical mass and overcome the effects of dilution, high technology firms have been grouped together in large highly visible centres.

(3) *Spillover Communities*. By creating a pleasant physical environment, smaller towns on the edge of high technology centres or 'diluted' centres have succeeded in attracting high-tech firms seeking lower-cost premises in a less competitive labour market, as a spillover from the established centres. Wang, for example, established its new headquarters site at Lowell, Massachusetts, outside Boston.

(4) *Technology Installation Centres* linked to a single isolated major research facility (e.g., Boeing at Seattle, Kennedy Space Centre, Florida). These centres attract suppliers, and can facilitate spin-outs, particularly in the aftermath of a downturn in trade or a reduction in research funding.

(5) *'Bootstrap' Communities*. These lack most of the attributes sought by high technology firms but, by offering low costs and a high quality of life, they seek to attract branch plants of expanding high technology companies as a seeding nucleus to create a new high technology community. Examples include Colorado Springs, Orlando, Pheonix and San Antonio.

It is against this broader background that mainstream US initiatives to encourage high technology industry need to be set. States and cities have developed a broad range of initiatives to strengthen their high technology sector. These include co-ordinating an inter-disciplinary approach involving land use, planning and creation of Science Parks, the development of applied science at the university, vocational and technical training, marketing and promotion to attract firms, venture capital funds and the development of high technology task forces. All these focus local attention and resources on technology-led economic development.

Considerable attention is directed towards attracting inward investment opportunities from other parts of the United States. With many more mobile projects, partly reflecting the size of the continent, and the dynamic evolution of companies, there is a continuing need for high growth companies to establish a network of locations across the United States, providing an important impetus for the development of high technology firms, and the rapid transformation of some local economies. In some cases, the university itself may have embarked on Science Park development, both to enhance the value of its land assets and to attract companies to locate near them, so supporting developments within the university. However, the majority of Science and Research Parks have involved a State or City Authority, particularly in the provision of land and infrastructure and in promotion, generally linked to a business package of promotion of the state or city. The image and reputation of the university, a park-like environment of low density and well-designed office facilities are the main elements used to attract high-tech firms. Typically, American Science Parks are substantial developments mostly in excess of 200 acres, more akin to large very high quality industrial estates, and designed to attract high technology laboratories of large multinational companies.

In parallel with the development of large-scale Science Parks has been the creation of Innovation Centres, to provide incubator facilities for new-start and young companies engaged in exploiting research, much of which may have originated from the universities. Innovation Centres were first established under National Science Foundation grants; ten centres have since been established for an eight-year period. Each Innovation Centre is strongly linked to the university, frequently as part of programmes sponsored by universities. Links are also forged with the private sector to promote the values of capitalism, as well as to develop the university's role in entrepreneurship training and technological innovation. In some universities, this may extend to establishing venture and seedcorn funds for early stage spin-offs and new-start businesses. Subsequently, other universities have established Innovation Centres and incubator facilities, each providing space and management resources to assist the formation and growth of firms exploiting new technology.

In the United States, initiatives exist to promote the high technology sector at all levels — federal, state, city and universities — and are more highly developed than in Europe. It reflects the fusion of two priorities — an emphasis on high technology industry, stimulated particularly by space and military needs, and the importance attached to entrepreneurship and the small business.

4.4. THE DEVELOPMENT OF SCIENCE PARKS IN THE UK

The development of Science Parks in the UK has been stimulated by US experience but, in general, the UK model is much closer to that of the American Innovation Centres than to US-style Science Parks. Whilst the American experience has provided valuable evidence of what could be achieved,the development of Science Parks in the UK, with only a few exceptions, has occurred to mitigate local job losses rather than as part of a coherent policy towards the high technology sector.

4.4.1. The first phase: Cambridge and Heriot-Watt

The first UK Science Parks were established in the early 1970s wholly by the universities and without external partners. At Cambridge, the decision by Trinity College, one of the constituent colleges of the University, to establish a Science Park arose from a University committee, the Mott Committee, set up to review the university's policy towards industry (Segal Quince, 1985). Until that date, very little land had been released by the University or Colleges for industrial development. IBM, for example, was not provided with land because of a fear that Cambridge might become dominated by industry in a similar way to developments in southern Oxford. Crucially, however, the Mott Committee recognised that the University as a whole would benefit from the establishment of research-based, high technology industry in Cambridge. It recommended 'a moderate growth of science-based industry in Cambridge, in order to take maximum advantage of scientific expertise, equipment and libraries available in the area and to increase feedback of all kinds from such industry to local research laboratories'.

Trinity College, having a 130-acre undeveloped site on the edge of the city some two miles from the University, decided to create a prestige environment offering high quality buildings on a well-landscaped site, with the objective of achieving a long-term financial rate of return comparable with that of the College's other commercial investments. Initially, 28 acres were set aside for development by the College itself and by a few tenants taking ground leases. A critical step was the granting of an innovative planning agreement in 1971: the original designation of the site was part of the green-belt. Use of the Science Park was limited to those engaged in the following activities:

— scientific research associated with industrial production;
— light industrial production of a kind which is dependent on regular consultation with either or both of the following:
  (a) the tenants own research, development and design staff established in the Cambridge area;
  (b) scientific staff of the University or of local scientific institutions;
— ancillary buildings and works appropriate to the use of the land as a Science Park.

Construction of the Park began in 1973, with the first tenant moving in within the year. Subsequent progress is shown in Table 4.1. In the first ten years, to 1982, 23 companies had moved on to the Park, occupying 148,000 sq. ft and employing about 500 people. More recently, with the overall growth of high technology industry in Cambridge, the Park has mushroomed and it is now the largest Science Park in the UK. By 1986 it had 68 firms employing some 1,900 people, occupying 530,000 sq. ft of premises.

Table 4.1: Number of lettings on Cambridge Science Park

Years	No. of tenants
1973–8	7
1979–81	11
1982–4	22
1985–6	28

At about the same date as the Cambridge Park was beginning, a second park was established on the new green-belt campus at Heriot-Watt University, which was relocating from the centre of Edinburgh. Its concept and objectives were somewhat different from those at Cambridge. The Principal of Heriot-Watt at the time was

71

Professor R. Smith, who had been at MIT during the 1960s and was strongly influenced by US experience in developing research parks and other collaborative ventures with industry. From the outset, Heriot-Watt was established as a Research Park, with tighter criteria for the selection of tenants than at Cambridge. The basic criteria applied by the University (Monck, 1986) for the selection of tenants is that

> there should be a significant proportion of research and development in the activities to be carried out at the park; that there should be some equilibrium between the discipline employed by the tenant and at least one department of the University; and that there should be a willingness in principle to collaborate with the University when collaboration is possible.

Even in the early 1970s, Heriot-Watt had a strong tradition of applied research and links with industry. The University was one of the earliest to establish an active industrial liaison office, Unilink, to pursue collaborative projects with industry. To provide a focus for its specialist capabilities, it evolved a policy of establishing specialist self-funding technology transfer institutes undertaking applied research work for the Science and Engineering Research Council (SERC), and contract research for industry. The Research Park fitted into this framework, providing separate accommodation for the growing number of research institutes (examples include the Institute of Offshore Engineering and the Chemical Consultancy Service), a limited number of academic spin-out companies, including Edinburgh Instruments, and external companies like Syntex, wishing to establish a research unit.

Perhaps because of its restrictive policy, progress has been very slow. The decision to establish the Park was taken in 1972; physical development began a year later, and the first tenants moved on to the Park in 1975. By 1986, the Research Park had only 23 organisations occupying 270,000 sq. ft on 56 acres, of which eight are Technology Transfer Institutions from the University. Like the Cambridge Park, the Heriot-Watt Research Park has been funded by the University and through the sale of ground leases to tenant companies. Recently, the Scottish Development Agency has funded a small incubator unit for multiple occupancies. Heriot-Watt and Cambridge were then the pioneers in the development of Science Parks and, although they created a lot of interest at the time, more than a decade was to elapse before the next park opened.

4.4.2. Factors underlying the second phase

Several reasons may be advanced for the lack of development of Science Parks in the 1970s. At that time, higher education in Britain was still expanding, and few universities were prepared to commit their land for industrial development. Science Parks are costly to develop, and universities felt there were better uses for resources than speculative property projects. Despite initial interest, progress in the parks at Cambridge and Heriot-Watt was slow. In addition, during the 1970s the enabling technologies (particularly linked to microprocessing and computing) had not developed sufficiently, so the rate of formation of NTBFs was still low, the small enterprise culture not yet having taken root. For these reasons, there was not a clear demand for the provision of high quality industrial units linked to universities until the end of the 1970s.

By the early 1980s, however, matters had changed and, partly in response to these changes, the so-called 'second wave' of Science Parks were founded. Several developments coincided at this time: the collapse of many mature industries leading to a rapid rise in unemployment, particularly in major conurbations; and at the same time, severe financial cut-backs in universities, many of which were located in these urban areas. With little prospect of an immediate revival of the mature industries, high technology offered a ray of hope. Planners pointed to Silicon Valley and Route 128 in Boston as examples of job creation through new technology. In particular, the transformation of the city of Boston, over a ten-year period, from a depressed area dependent upon textiles and engineering to one leading the world in the development of new technologies was seen as particularly relevant. Local authorities, which had begun to concern themselves with economic development in the late 1970s, recognised that the key source of expertise on technological matters was their local university. This led to new links being forged between universities and local government where few had existed in the past.

By the early 1980s, a number of 'enabling' technologies had also reached a stage of offering substantial business breakthroughs, frequently involving radical innovations opening up entirely new products in niche markets. Whereas much of the more traditional incremental applied research was only relevant to large companies, many of the newer developments, frequently involving the combination of several technological ideas, increasingly lent themselves to exploitation by new and small firms. Examples include the development and novel application of microprocessors, microcomputing and software, communications, lasers, industrial design and automation and, more recently, new materials and specific areas of biotechnology. Initial capital requirements were comparatively modest for those already engaged in these developments, yet profit margins could be spectacular. Companies frequently achieved very high growth rates by marketing internationally and finding new applications for their technology. Despite these opportunities, exploitation in the early stages of product development was undertaken more frequently by individuals aware of the commercial potential of their technological innovation, rather than by larger companies. The latter appeared to find it difficult to assimilate radical technologies, often in unrelated and narrow niche markets into their core business areas. The people best placed to exploit technological innovations were those most closely involved in its development.

Several other changes occurred which accelerated the shift in emphasis towards innovation by small firms. Traditionally the primary route for commercial exploitation of research developed by universities and research institutions was by larger companies, often through licensing agreements secured either by the British Technology Group and/or through direct research contracts. The severe recession of the early 1980s led many large companies to cut back on internal R & D, and in some instances even to disband their corporate research laboratories. More frequently, in order to improve efficiency, companies shed peripheral business activities in order to concentrate their resources on 'core business activities'. Corporate policy discouraged diversification through the introduction of new products. Hence, the familiar route by which promising technological developments by large companies were exploited was more limited during the early 1980s recession. On the other hand, the opportunities for establishing businesses to exploit new technological developments became somewhat easier, the opportunities to exploit the new microtechnology being observed by many scientists and engineers. This has been paralleled by a growth in specialised venture-capital institutions, prepared to make substantial selective equity investments in soundly based businesses, including a small proportion of new starts.

There has also been a significant shift in UK government policy since 1979 towards the small firm sector as a whole, backed by the positive encouragement of an enterprise culture. This change in emphasis has been reflected in many of the economic development initiatives pursued by local authorities, shifts in attitude in the higher education sector towards entrepreneurship and the improvement in services to small firms offered by banks, accountants, training provided and 'help agencies'. Changes have also occurred which make it easier for academics and researchers in higher education to establish their own businesses in parallel with their academic work. Furthermore, large companies are also taking an increasingly positive attitude towards the promotion of spin-off companies, whereby employees leave the parent company to establish a business to develop the technologies researched in large-firm laboratories. Where the large firm does not feel threatened by such a development, it may even take a modest equity stake in the infant business.

Whilst these developments were occurring, there was increasing recognition that the provision of suitable premises could act as a constraint on the growth of small firms (Coopers and Lybrand, 1980). Furthermore, knowledge-based businesses have locational and premises requirements which are different from those of both traditional manufacturing firms, the business services sector, and from small firms in general. NTBFs place a greater emphasis on design, development, consulting and training, rather than on product manufacture, and so traditional workshops on general purpose industrial estates are not satisfactory. Similarly, inner city commercial offices which cannot accommodate significant levels of product development and testing activities are also unacceptable. NTBFs require premises in which there is little distinction between offices, development laboratories and production areas. Within an overall shell designed for general office standards, these firms require a high degree of internal flexibility to enable the layout and use of space to change with the growth of the business. Easy access, car parking and quality of the working environment have to be accommodated in the design.

Many of these criteria are incorporated into the design of new purpose-built premises for larger high-tech firms, but for those NTBFs lacking capital and needing flexibility, rented property is essential. In many areas of the UK, such premises did not exist in the early 1980s, so these firms had to adapt existing industrial premises or operate from suboptimal offices. Throughout this decade, so far, it is only in some parts of the south-east of England, where demand was particularly strong, that private developers and the major funding institutions have developed speculative 'high-tech' schemes, which could be let at sufficient rents to provide a commercial return. Elsewhere in the UK, the lack of demand generally in the industrial and office sectors held back rents and the prospects of rental growth, so inhibiting the private sector from investing. Despite the expected higher rates of return from 'high-tech' premises, there has been a virtual absence of provision by the private sector outside south-east England. This reluctance of the private sector to provide suitable premises for technology-based industry meant that public sector organisations, such as local authorities and government development agencies, committed themselves to filling this gap. They have played a leading role in both filling the property gap in general, as well as in the provision of specialist accommodation for the high-tech sector.

Within the higher education sector, changes also occurred in the early 1980s which led to a reappraisal of attitudes towards relationships with industry in general, and to academic spin-outs and Science Parks in particular. Many commentators (for example, EIU (1985), Williams (1985a)) place particular significance on the reduction in university funding announced by the UGC in September 1983. For some universities the UGC cuts required many of the most seriously affected to reappraise their options, including, in some cases, their surplus land holdings, alternative funding arrangements, and their relationships with industry and the local community. For some universities, Science Parks were already being actively considered prior to 1983, but few institutions had the expertise or the means to develop a park on their own. Some had considered the idea of a partnership with a local authority or a development agency, but in many cases, the idea was treated with considerable suspicion. In the aftermath of the cuts, however, there was a greater recognition of the potential benefits of a Science Park to a university as a focus for development and as an indication of commitment to the local community.

Few universities, if any, developed Science Parks exclusively as a way of generating revenue. Those universities with surplus land recognised that plans conceived during expansionary times would have to be shelved, perhaps for ever, and so they could sell land for appropriate purposes. One or two universities in south-east England, where land and property prices were particularly buoyant, saw the financial benefits to their university from developing a Science Park but they remained the exception. Whilst the 1983 cuts caused many universities to rethink their financial strategies, Science Parks were not established as a solution to these problems directly. Instead, they were seen as one element in the diversification strategy adopted by the more enterprising UK universities.

This diversification was, in the end, accepted for several reasons. In line with trends in the United States, increasing emphasis was also placed on allocating public research funds to those centres of outstanding excellence. The peer group review process adopted by the Research Council was, in 1986, reinforced by the UGC's star rating system of academic departments. Subsequently, the UK government announced new funding arrangements for the universities, including suggestions gradually to delineate universities into three categories — research universities (those with centres of excellence); mixed category, with research and teaching functions; and teaching universities, with minimal research work. These changes, together with the proposal to establish up to 30 national specialist research centres (for example, in super conductivity) will have a profound effect on universities' strategies towards their technological departments.

In essence, universities are in competition for funding for applied research. The ability of a university in any field clearly depends on the quality, excellence and, increasingly, on the size of the research team devoted to a particular field. This in turn can be significantly influenced by the extent of collaboration with research teams from industry, whose global resources devoted to a given topic frequently far outstrip those of a single university. Because of the impact of advanced technology on industrial competitiveness, research groups will, in future, increasingly be in competition with each other to develop solutions to problems and facilitate their adoption in new products and services. Some university Vice Chancellors have recognised that their ability to compete depends on collaboration, greater specialisation in applied research, the attraction of industrial research groups to locate close to their research departments to facilitate faster communication of problems, ideas and solutions and establishing a critical mass of expertise in particular topics through clustering. Against this background, a Science Park is a key component in such a strategy. Universities also became increasingly conscious of the need to take positive and visible steps to establish closer collaboration with industry as a way of ensuring greater relevance and uptake of their research output by industry, and hopefully provide employment opportunities for its graduates.

Following the example set in the United States, an increasing number of academics and researchers were establishing new businesses as a way of exploiting their research ideas commercially. In some cases this positively reflected the increasing national emphasis on encouraging an enterprise culture and support for small firms, but in other instances it was a response to more negative developments. Thus, for example, difficulties in securing research funds, diminishing prospects for academic promotion, and an increasing divergence in salaries with counterparts in industry — all have been important factors in motivating academics to commercialise their ideas. Universities recognised that if such firms were located on the campus, this would enable successful applied researchers to remain within the university environment whilst at the same time pursuing their private interests.

Another key factor that influenced universities to establish Science Parks was unemployment, both locally and amongst recent graduates. Universities were vulnerable to criticism when security of employment was guaranteed for 'tenured' members of staff, yet its graduates were experiencing major problems in obtaining work. Some universities in the major urban areas felt that it was necessary to make a commitment to the locality and collaborate with local authorities attempting to regenerate such areas. It led to the backing of several Science Parks in inner city areas by university administrations conscious that their university ought to be seen to be making a clear contribution to the local community.

4.4.3. The second wave: in practice

After the establishment of the Cambridge and Heriot-Watt Science Parks in the early 1970s, ten years were to elapse before the second wave of parks was developed. The catalyst for this was the emergence of a few key individuals in universities, development agencies and local authorities. These individuals recognised the need for change and were aware of developments in high technology in the United States and the contribution that research parks and innovation centres were making. They included, amongst others, Sir Frederick Crawford, the Vice Chancellor of Aston, who had been Professor of Electrical Engineering at Stanford; Warwick University's Vice Chancellor, Professor Butterworth, and his registrar Mike Shattock; Tony Pender, the Chief Executive of English Estates; Edward Cunnington, the Director of the Product Planning and Development Division of the Scottish Development Agency; and Ian Page, the Industrial Development Co-ordinator at Bradford Metropolitan Council. All these individuals were influenced by the experience of John Bradfield, the Bursar of Trinity College, who established the Cambridge Science Park, and in many cases, by what

Table 4.2: Participation of higher educational institutions (HEIs) in Science Parks and related high technology developments, 1987

	Universities	Polytechnics	Other initiatives	No. of Science Parks
HEIs in formal Science Parks	34	5	3	(36)
Universities that admit companies on the campus but on an *ad hoc* basis	3	—	—	—
HEIs associated with 'remote' property developments	4	3	—	—
HEIs known to be reviewing options	5	3	1	(8)
HEIs without any plans	6	19	—	—
Total	52	30	4	(44)

Note: Numbers in brackets indicate total number of Science Parks. Since some parks are joint initiatives between bodies, the row totals do not sum.

they had seen in the United States. They were instrumental in deciding to establish the next group of Science Parks at places such as Aston, Warwick, Bradford, etc.

Table 4.2 shows that by 1987, 36 Science Parks which broadly conform to the UK Science Park Association definition had been established. All except six are linked with universities; and of the remainder, five are in partnership with polytechnics and institutes of further education, and one with a corporate research laboratory of a major company. A full enumeration of the Parks is provided in the Appendix to this chapter.

Most of the main universities and university colleges outside London have become involved in Science Parks as shown in Table 4.2. Of the 52 UK universities (excluding London Colleges), 34 have formal Science Parks, a further three universities have *ad hoc* arrangements for individual companies to locate on their campus (though there is no planned Science Park scheme), and four universities are identified with more remote property developments. Of the remaining eleven institutions, at least five are known to be actively reviewing their options.

Table 4.3 shows that by 1987, 36 Science Parks had been

Table 4.3: The development of UK Science Parks

Date		No. opened	
Prior to	1982	2	Cambridge, Heriot-Watt
	1982	1	Merseyside
	1983	4	Aston, Bradford, Leeds, Glasgow
	1984	8	Warwick, Nottingham, Loughborough, Norwich, Southampton, St Andrews, Manchester, Hull
	1985	6	South Bank, Surrey, Newtech (Deeside), Aberystwyth, Bolton, Durham
	1986	7	Swansea, Stirling, Kent, Brunel, Birmingham, Antrim, Bangor
	1987	5	Aberdeen, Cambridge (St Johns), Cardiff, Keele, Sunderland
Under construction		3	Salford, Sheffield, Belasis Hall (Cleveland)
Total		36	

established in the UK. A further seven proposals are at different stages of development. Oxford had been frustrated by difficulties in obtaining planning permission for five years. At Newcastle, no progress had been made for three years because of the difficulty of finding a suitable site adjacent to the university and polytechnic. At the Universities of York and Essex, plans have been delayed due to a lack of funds; and at the Universities of Reading and Sussex, which had both provided a location for one or two companies on their campuses, alternative options are being considered with their County Councils.

Three universities had established working arrangements with property developments remote from the campus. Bath University has identified with the White House Technology Park, a scheme developed by the district council at Westbury some 20 miles from Bath. Arrangements were made between Imperial College London and Blue Circle in the development of Ribblesdown Science Park on an old quarry site on the southern outskirts of London. Bristol University and Bristol Polytechnic have agreed to assist in the development of a research centre on the edge of Bristol as part of a major 500-acre mixed scheme with housing, a hotel and industrial space. This is being planned by Chesterfield Properties and Hambros Bank. Some polytechnics and larger higher education colleges have also been active in the development of Science Parks. Some, notably South Bank, Sunderland, Sheffield, Bolton Institute of

Higher Education and North East Wales Institute, were the principal institutions associated with the scheme. In other instances they work in partnership with the local university — for example, at Manchester, Liverpool, Newcastle and Sussex (Brighton). Other polytechnics, including Wolverhampton, Plymouth and Dundee, have developed arrangements to support firms on particular business parks. However, up to 1987, 22 of the 30 UK polytechnics had not been actively involved, even in those cities that have developed Science Parks.

There are also indications that several government research institutes are at the preliminary stage of evaluating the relevance of a Science Park. The most advanced is the Ministry of Defence (MOD) Establishment RSRE, Malvern. This follows the creation of Defence Enterprises Ltd, a private sector group financed by City institutions, with an exclusive contract to trawl in nominated MOD research establishments for promising technological developments which could be commercialised for the civilian market.

Another significant development is being pioneered by ICI and English Estates, who are establishing Belasis Hall Technology Park adjacent to ICI's chemical complex at Billingham in Cleveland and within a few miles of their Advanced Material Centre at the Chemicals and Polymers works at Wilton. ICI plan to offer companies not only access to their research facilities, but also provide commercial advice and assistance. Already, several ICI projects have been identified as having the potential for spinning out as separate businesses on to the Park. ICI's development is a model of enlightened self interest for other large companies which have strong technological capabilities, yet are conscious of their social responsibilities to a local area. As yet, this form of corporate venturing, which is now becoming increasingly important amongst many large US companies, has yet to develop in Britain. ICI is hoping that their Technology Park will change this by opening up opportunities for spin-outs by their staff, so leading to a more entrepreneurial attitude throughout the company, as well as making a significant and visible contribution to the local community.

4.4.4. The financing of Science Parks

By the end of 1986, a total £153m had been committed to Science Park developments. Some £92m had been spent on completed parks, £46m for expansion on existing schemes; and £15m is being invested

81

Table 4.4: Financing of UK Science Parks

	No. of parks	% expenditure	£m
Government development agencies	18	20	31
Local authorities	12	23	35
Universities	9	19	29
Tenant companies	6	29	44
Private sector institutions	7	9	14
		100	£153m

in seven new schemes due for completion in 1987–8 (Dalton, 1987). Funding for Science Parks has come from five sources — universities (including bank borrowings), local authorities, government development agencies, private sector institutions and tenant companies themselves. Table 4.4 provides information on the levels of investment by each group and the number of parks where investments have been made. The high level of investment by tenant companies is accounted for by just 21 firms who occupy 31 per cent of the premises.

Table 4.5 shows that at the end of 1986, Science Parks had 391 tenants who together occupied 58 per cent of the premises, 31 per cent of space being for owner-occupation. The remaining 11 per cent of the space was unoccupied — a low voids ratio in property terms in an expanding market.

Table 4.5: Occupancy on UK Science Parks

	No. of firms	sq. ft (000)	% of area
Let to tenants	391	1,114	58
Owner-occupation	21	582	31
Total	412	1,696	89
Unoccupied		212	11
		1,908	100

4.4.5. The role of universities and polytechnics

All Science Parks have been developed with the formal support of the relevant universities or polytechnics. Securing this commitment to a Science Park from the university has, in some cases, been a slow and tortuous process. This reflects a variety of influences, such as the 'democratic' nature of universities, in some cases a fear of property developers (even those in the public sector), a desire to preserve the good name of the university, a distrust of commercial issues, and a desire to permit only 'clean research and development activities'. Ultimately, the universities' response reflects the interests of the Vice Chancellor and senior officers (generally the Bursar and Registrar), and the overall culture and attitude of the university as a whole towards enterprise, industry and the commercialisation of research. In the 'second' wave, some of the most supportive universities have been 'new', small universities formed in the 1960s, often with a strong applied science and technology tradition, and generally those who were hardest hit by the UGC cuts.

In many of these schemes undertaken by development agencies and local authorities, the support of the university has been a crucial factor in securing a suitable site adjacent to the institution. In some cases the land was owned by the university, whereas in others it was reserved by the local authority for expansion by the university. However, the conditions under which the university agreed to release land and co-operate in a Science Park have varied considerably between institutions. In some cases, the university insisted on vetting all tenant applications, limiting the use of the site for research activity and requiring evidence from prospective tenants of collaborative links. Such conditions were in practice more onerous than local authority planning approvals, and may even have precluded financial support from some public sector bodies which are required to act 'commercially' and achieve the Treasury's minimum return on investments.

Few universities have developed Science Parks alone: apart from the Cambridge Science Park and that at Heriot-Watt, only four other parks have been developed by a university, acting as a principal. At Surrey, the University has been able to develop its scheme by selling/leasing land for development; and at Southampton, Brunel and Keele, early development is being funded mainly by the Universities and by bank borrowing.

In the main, then, Science Parks have depended on external partners, generally a regional development agency or a local authority. Where no obvious funding institution existed, plans to develop a Science Park have been frustrated. Thus, some universities in the south of England, such as those at Reading, Exeter, Sussex (Brighton), Essex (Colchester) and East Anglia (Norwich), have found it more difficult to establish a park than northern universities located in areas where there are public sector bodies able and willing to take a lead in such matters.

4.4.6. The role of public authorities

4.4.6.1. Central government

As was shown in Part I of this book, central government has a long history of providing support for R & D, the transfer of technology and its diffusion into industry. More recently, government has promoted the development of specialist information technology (IT) skills training programmes and introduced a series of measures to stimulate the small firm sector as a whole. However, whilst government has welcomed the development of NTBFs, it has introduced few specific measures to support this group of firms. Its small firm policies have not set out to encourage the development of particular types of firms, and there is no regional differentiation in the policies to stimulate innovation. The range of measures to support research and technology make little distinction between large firms, small firms and new starts.

Though Science Parks have been broadly welcomed by government, notably by the Departments of Trade and Industry and Employment (Channon, 1987), no explicit policy has been developed to define the role and objectives of Science Parks in the context of higher education, research, small firm programmes, the diffusion of technology or their wider environmental impact, particularly in inner cities. The main exception has been the support provided by Regional Development Agencies for Science Parks and high technology development in the Assisted Areas of the UK. This support has been in the form of providing purpose-built property to stimulate the development of indigenous high technology industry and to attract mobile inward investment projects.

The most active participant has been English Estates, whose main responsibility is the development of industrial and commercial property in the Assisted Areas of England for the Department of Trade and Industry and in rural development areas for the Development Commission. By 1987, English Estates had initiated eight schemes with universities and polytechnics, two major projects with industrial companies and other high technology developments on industrial estates and rural areas. In the designated regionally assisted areas outside England, the Development Agencies for Scotland, Wales and Northern Ireland have considerably greater

Table 4.6: Science Parks initiated by development agencies

	No.	Sq. ft (000)	Sq. ft under construction (000)
English Estates	9	224	144
Welsh Development Agency	3	86	18
Scottish Development Agency	4	103	25
Irish Development Board	1	43	16
Mid Wales Developments	1	12	10
	18	468	213

powers for facilitating economic development. Each Agency has developed Science Parks to complement existing initiatives designed to improve university–industry links. The extent of all these developments is shown in Table 4.6. In almost all cases, the schemes are funded and managed by the agency, which seeks the 'voluntary' assistance and participation of the HEIs and local authorities. Indeed, the leadership exercised by government Development Agencies has meant that the development of Science Parks in the more deprived parts of the UK has moved ahead of those in the prosperous regions.

4.4.6.2. Local authorities

In recent years, local authorities, particularly those in the larger urban conurbations, have developed a range of local economic initiatives designed to create new employment opportunities (Young and Mason, 1983). One element of this has been the encouragement of small high technology firms to achieve high rates of growth and also the encouragement of existing firms in the locality to introduce new technology to improve their products and processes. In many cases, local authorities have played a key role in encouraging universities and polytechnics to take a more active role in the revival of local economies, including the development of a Science Park or Innovation Centre.

The extent of involvement by an individual local authority has depended on its political composition, the characteristics of the institution of higher education in the area, and the financial resources available. The willingness of a local authority to undertake a programme of economic development does not, however, depend only on party politics. Some Conservative-led authorities have been reluctant to intervene actively in the local economy, but others have been vary active. Some Labour authorities have felt that Science Parks were 'irrelevant' to the creation of new employment in the area and preferred to concentrate resources on community-based projects such as managed workshops, Skill Training Centres, Itechs and more basic Innovation Centres. However, several large inner city local authorities have taken a strong lead in developing Science Parks in their areas, notably Birmingham, Nottingham, Manchester and Coventry. The developments have been funded under Section 137 of the 1972 Local Government Act. In many cases, these areas are also designated 'urban programme' areas and so are eligible for urban development grant assistance (up to 75 per cent) from the Inner Cities Directorate of the Department of Environment.

The role of the local authority in the development of the Science Park will vary: some, like Bradford, Hull, Durham and Bolton, have played an active part in facilitating the development and subsequent promotion, but have not been a main contributor to the funding or management of the scheme; others, like Coventry, Manchester and Birmingham, have contributed substantially to the physical development of the scheme and participated as members of the Science Park company, along with other partners. A third group (for example, Nottingham City Council and Leicester County Council) has planned, financed and managed the scheme without formal participation from other partners.

4.4.6.3. The private sector

Private sector capital has mainly been channelled into firms in the high technology sector rather than into the Science Park *per se*. Only in a handful of cases has the private sector participated in the development of a Science Park, either as owner-occupiers (for example, BOC and Grand Metropolitan PLC at Surrey, Napp Laboratories at Cambridge and Syntex at Heriot-Watt), or, in the case of three of the clearing banks and the Prudential, for a mix of motives including promotional and social reasons. Private property developers and the traditional property-related financial institutions have played almost no part.

The absence of the property institutions, despite their backing and enthusiasm in the early 1980s for high tech and Business Parks along the 'M4 corridor' west of London, was because most Science Parks do not conform to the institutions' criteria for investment. Institutions seek property investments with strong evidence of rental growth, low voids, few planning restrictions on use and, most importantly, long leases (typically 21 years) to well-established companies with strong balance sheets. By 1987, institutional involvement had been minimal: on the Cambridge Science Park, the Post Office Pension Fund had entered a sale and lease-back deal with one company, and 3i's interest in a 1½-acre development has been sold on to three investment funds.

In general, private sector developers had not been involved in Science Parks, principally because of the difficulty in selling on to financial institutions. Their reluctance to finance Science Parks may also have stemmed from a lack of experience in valuing specialised property developments having a high proportion of young technology-based companies, and a lack of evidence on rental levels, yields and growth prospects.

For Science Parks, the clearing banks have played a more important role. This derives partly from the unique role which Barclays played in promoting and financing high technology companies in Cambridge in the early 1980s. They financed many of the high growth companies in the city and so were able to develop a keen awareness of the financial needs of NTBFs. This enabled them to interpret financial propositions more accurately, and to assess risk and monitor the progress of their client companies in a more informed way. Based upon this experience, Barclays established a high-tech unit to train people in nominated 'high-tech' branches as part of a broad thrust to increase their market share in this sector. As part of this strategy, Barclays financed an incubator unit on the Warwick Science Park.

Several other financial institutions have made similar commitments to other Science Parks, although these may have been prompted more by promotional and social reasons than pure commercial criteria. The most significant and imaginative commitment was made by Lloyds Bank who, together with Birmingham City Council, created a £1m venture fund to be invested by Birmingham Technology Ltd in Aston's tenant firms. The role of this venture fund has been crucial in attracting high quality new firms in leading-edge technologies to Aston. The decision by the Prudential Assurance Company to support the South Bank Technopark and the Midland Bank role at Birmingham University, are other indications of private sector involvement in Science Parks.

Despite the above examples, very few Science Parks are led by the private sector. The major exceptions are Surrey, and to a lesser extent Cambridge. The private sector has backed the Surrey Research Park because of its unique setting in green-belt land in

Surrey, where typical land prices for industrial development are over £1m an acre, and current rents are about £12–16/sq. ft. Despite tight planning restrictions, the University has been able to attract a range of private sector organisations. BOC International, for example, has completed a 120,000-sq. ft development on the site; Grand Metropolitan Biotechnology has an incubator building for letting to start-up businesses; and a private property developer is funding the next phase of the Park.

4.5. UK SCIENCE PARKS: AN APPRAISAL

This chapter has described the heterogeneous group of HEI property-related developments in the UK which are broadly classified as Science Parks. The purpose has been to provide an insight into the objectives pursued by the main participants — such as universities, polytechnics, banks and financial institutions, local authorities, development agencies, etc.

If this book is to provide the basis for an appraisal of the effectiveness of Science Parks as instruments of public policy to promote economic development, it is essential to recognise the variety and (potentially conflicting) objectives of the participants. It is also vital to recognise that any assessment undertaken here must be preliminary, since only two parks have been in operation for more than a decade and a majority have existed for less than three years. In principle, the objective of this study is to estimate the added value or additionality which the Science Park provides, which in turn requires agreed assessment criteria which are, in principle, capable of impartial estimation and preferably of measurement.

To some extent the items to be included on the assessment agenda have already been set by MacDonald (1987), who presents a challenging review of the development of Science Parks in the UK. MacDonald questions whether, given their existing institutional arrangements, Science Parks lead high technology firms to create more wealth and employment than would have occurred without the policy initiative. The basis of MacDonald's scepticism is as follows. Firstly, he believes that many politicians have overestimated the contribution which Science Parks can make to the creation of wealth and employment within the short to medium term. In this he is echoing the view of Professor Ashworth, Vice Chancellor of Salford University who, in his 1984 speech to the Confederation of British Industry, scoffed at Ministers who go up and down the country giving the impression that new technology-based companies founded by entrepreneurial university professors and housed in pastel coloured incubator units in Science Parks attached to their universities will play a major role in bringing down next month's unemployment.

Secondly, MacDonald questions whether, in practice, the links between Science Park tenants and the University are as close or as important as those involved in the promotion of parks like to indicate. MacDonald states that 'Boards see links with the University as absolutely fundamental, yet on one of the largest Science Parks the manager insists that no tenant has ever used the University library'.

Thirdly, citing the work of Lowe (1985), MacDonald suggests that the development of Science Parks is not a commercial proposition, at a time when 40 per cent of high technology floorspace in Britain remains unlet. Further evidence for this is found in the report of Debenham, Tewson and Chinnocks (1983), which found that the yields on Science Parks were generally in the range of 1–3 per cent.

Fourthly, MacDonald argues that since technology transfer actually takes place between one high-tech firm and another, rather than with the university, it is particularly unfortunate that greater efforts are not made to encourage closer links between firms on Science Parks.

Fifthly, he argues that there is no reason to believe that high-tech firms are ever likely to be crucially dependent upon the type of information to be found in the science and engineering departments of the local university. Hence one key *raison d'être* of Science Parks is flawed.

Sixthly, and finally, MacDonald argues that the function of the Science Park in acting as a vehicle for academics to commercialise their research is also undesirable, since there are likely to be net social costs in encouraging good academics to become second rate entrepreneurs.

The points raised by MacDonald are a challenge to the promoters of Science Parks to justify their policies. In broad terms, such policies can only be justified if it can be shown that the net social benefits exceed the net social costs. To demonstrate the benefits, it has to be shown not only that, for example, firms have established on the park, but that these firms either would not have been established if the park had not existed, or that they would have had to locate elsewhere — and that the alternative location would have imposed costs upon the firm in such a way as to impair its performance.

The remainder of this book will address the question of estimating the 'added value' of Science Parks. This means that it is necessary to have a clear understanding of the characteristics of firms currently occupying premises on UK Science Parks. If it is possible to show that such firms were growing substantially faster than might be expected, and that they themselves felt that they were benefiting from their location, then this would be persuasive evidence that Science Parks were providing genuine 'added value'. In practice, the problem is to estimate what would have happened to such firms if Science Parks had not existed. This problem has been overcome in several ways. Firstly, the largest ever survey of firms currently located on Science Parks has been undertaken, covering just over one-half of all such firms. In that survey, firms were asked to provide indices of their performance — notably, their growth in employment, output and profitability. They were also asked for their views on the benefits which they obtained from a Science Park location, both at the time when a decision was made to locate there, and also how this has changed since that time.

The performance of a firm, however, depends upon a number of factors such as the size of the firm, its age and the sector in which it operates. It would be somewhat misleading, for example, to compare the performance of Science Park firms, almost all of which were small, with that of the largest 100 quoted companies. Equally, it would be unwise to compare Science Park firms with the average UK small firm (even if there was such a firm, or even an index of such firms), on the grounds that Science Park firms would be expected to perform rather better since they are in the high-tech sectors where performances would generally be expected to be better. Only by comparing the performance and responses to questions of firms in the high-tech sectors both on and off a Science Park can an adequate estimate of the 'added value' of a Science Park be made. For these reasons the empirical work undertaken asks almost identical questions of a group of high-tech firms of a similar age and ownership, but which were not located on a Science Park.

A supplementary issue is whether there are real differences between the performance and responses of high-tech firms from those firms of similar age, but which are in more conventional sectors. Intuitively, one would expect such differences to exist, and this appears to be confirmed in the results from Cambridge City Council (1986), reported in Chapter 3, but it is helpful to identify clearly where they exist. For this reason, many of the questions which are asked in this survey have been asked in previous surveys of firms of a similar age and ownership characteristics (Storey (1982), English Estates (1985), Johnson and Storey (1987)). The results of the survey are reported in Part II.

Appendix

The Distribution of Science Parks in the UK

Largely because of the significant public sector involvement, the distribution of Science Parks does not reflect the distribution pattern of NTBFs. On the contrary, a number of Science Parks have been sited in areas in which NTBFs are underrepresented to provide a stimulus for the region.

Table 4A.1: Regional distribution of Science Parks in the UK

	Assisted area	Non-assisted area	Inner city
South-east	—	5	1
South-west	—	—	—
East Anglia	—	3	—
East Midlands	—	2	1
West Midlands	3	1	2
North-west	4	—	4
Yorkshire and Humberside	3	1	3
North	3	—	1
Wales	3	2	2
Scotland	3	2	1
Northern Ireland	1	—	—
Total	20	16	15

Significantly, 56 per cent of Science Parks are located in the regionally assisted areas of the UK, and 40 per cent are in inner city areas — within an urban environment of a major city in the UK.

The developments

All Science Parks have developed new purpose-designed premises, mostly built speculatively as advanced premises for letting. A few, notably Merseyside Innovation Centre, Aston Science Park and Chilworth Research Park, include refurbished buildings for use by park tenants. The phenomenon of purpose-built premises for owner-occupation has only occurred in six Science Parks: on three schemes at Heriot-Watt, Surrey, and to a lesser extent Cambridge, this has been the dominant method of development.

The style of design has depended on the nature of the site, and the land available for development. The buildings conform to three basic layouts:

(1) multi-tenancy integrated building —
   one storey, e.g. Barclays' Venture Centre, Warwick
   two storeys, e.g. Durham Mountjoy Research Centre
   three storeys, e.g. Southbank Technopark, London;
(2) terraced units each with their own front doors — Listerhill, Bradford;
(3) separate indivisible buildings for single occupation — Cambridge Science Park

The argument for multi-occupancy in an integrated building is that this type of layout achieves greater interchange and sense of community amongst tenants. Multi-occupancy buildings typically include a central reception and waiting area, meeting rooms, canteen (in a few cases) and offices for the Science Park manager and his staff.

These advantages have to be set against the extra costs due to common areas (typically about 12–15 per cent in area) which have to be reflected in the rents. Multi-occupancy buildings are also more complex to administer, involving recharging the tenants for a range of property services (heating, upkeep and lighting of common areas, reception, security, etc.). An effective internal security system is required to enable tenants to come and go at any time of the day or night.

Opinions vary widely about the pros and cons of multi-storey buildings. On limited land areas there is generally no alternative. Whilst this does not appear to inhibit the performance of consultancy, computer software, and design organisations, companies with a significant product development, requiring regular

93

deliveries of components, etc., prefer ground floor premises.

Whilst single-storey terraced units lend themselves less well as incubator facilities, many tenants prefer self-contained units with their own front door, self contained WCs, and easy access for deliveries. From an estate management point of view they are more straightforward to administer, having simpler service charges confined to upkeep of landscaping, external security and insurance. The layout of terraced units can influence tenant interaction on a site.

Science Parks designed to attract larger companies need to offer serviced plots, and self-contained buildings with additional space for expansion. This has been a key feature at Heriot-Watt and at the Cambridge Science Park, which both have sufficient land to accommodate companies that require additional land for growth at a later date.

The growth of Science Parks

On existing Science Parks, additional phases under construction in 1986 have added a further 582,000 sq. ft of space, an increase of 31 per cent during the year. The seven new schemes will have added a further 215,000 sq. ft (11 per cent) in 1987. However, this pace of expansion of over 42 per cent per annum is unlikely to be maintained. Less new parks are forecast to open in future years, and many of the existing parks are constrained by the size of their sites and, in a few cases, by difficulties of raising finance for further phases. The land area set aside for the park varies considerably from as little as half an acre in some inner city developments to 130 acres in out-of-town and rural developments (see Tables 4A.2 and 4A.3). Inner city locations have presented the most serious problems: in several instances, potential developments have been shelved because of the difficulty of finding an appropriate site near enough to the university or polytechnic. In part, the problem is one of land assembly, often compounded by costs of land clearance and reclamation which may make a Science Park an uneconomic proposition, even for public sector agencies. If the park has only a limited land area, further phases of development are not possible, thus inhibiting the expansion of existing tenants, and limiting the scheme to those firms which were at a particular stage of development during the letting phase (often no more than a 9-months to 18-months period). Without a steady development programme, the

Table 4A.2: Size of Science Park — available land area

Size (acres)	Inner city	Out of town	Total
0– 3	7	5	12
4– 10	3	3	6
11– 25	4	6	10
26– 50	—	2	2
51–100	1	3	4
> 100	—	2	2
	15	21	36

Table 4A.3: Size of Science Park versus buildings completed and under construction

Sq. ft	No.
0– 15,000	7
15,001– 30,000	8
30,001– 50,000	9
50,001– 75,000	4
75,001–100,000	3
100,001–200,000	2
200,001–300,000	1
> 300,000	2
Total	36

value of the park for emerging technology-based firms in the locality is thus severely limited.

Science Parks cater, in the main, for young locally based companies in relatively narrow technological sectors. Surveys of all Science Parks carried out in 1985 and repeated in 1986 provide an overall picture of tenant firms in terms of their sector size, age, status and employment. The following tables (4A.4 and 4A.5) are based on an analysis of over 400 tenant firms on Science Parks in December 1986 (Monck, 1986 and 1987).

During the two years of the survey of Science Parks, the resilience and expansion of Science Park tenants has been impressive. During 1986, 19 per cent of tenant firms based on the Science Parks expanded their premises, and 2 per cent moved to smaller units. During the same period, 4.8 per cent of tenants left the Science Park, moving to alternative premises; and 2.9 per cent of tenants ceased trading, compared with 8 per cent amongst conventional small firm tenants in workshop units (Southern, 1986).

Table 4A.4: Previous location of Science Park tenants

New-start companies	42%
Existing firms	58%

Previous location	% of all Science Park firms		
	New-start firms	Existing firms	All firms
From university	17	} 32	17
5-mile radius of park	17		49
30-mile radius of park	6	11	17
Elsewhere in the UK	2	10	12
Overseas	—	5	5
	42	58	100

Current age of firms on Science Parks (% of all park firms)

Under 1 year	30
1–3 years	35
3–5 years	19
> 8 years	16
	100

Employment (% of all park firms)

1– 5 employees	46
6–15 employees	36
16–50 employees	14
> 50 employees	4
	100

Status of tenant firms (% of all park firms)

Single-plant independent companies	64
Head office multi-site companies	3
Subsidiary or branch of UK companies	17
Subsidiary or branch of overseas companies	10
Unit, department or subsidiary of university	6
	100

Size of premises (% of all park firms)

Sq. ft	
0– 1,500	58
1,501– 4,000	21
4,001–10,000	15
> 10,000	6
	100

Sector (% of all park firms)

Computing and software	34
Electrical, electronic and instrumentation	19
Chemical, medical and biotechnology	12
Other — mechanical and environmental	7
Consultancy and technical services	19
Financial and business services	9
	100

Table 4A.5: Property changes by tenants, 1985–6

Property changes	% (1985)
No change	79
Contraction	2
Expansion	19
	100

% expansion by tenants	% of expanding tenants
50	24
100	49
200	17
300	61
400	4
	100

Reasons for leaving the park	
Tenants moving to alternative premises	4.8%
Financial failures during the year	2.9%
Total	7.7%

Part II

The Survey of High Technology Firms

5

The Characteristics of Surveyed Firms

5.1. INTRODUCTION AND OBJECTIVES

Part I of this book provided a review of existing work on the role of science in promoting economic development and of the role which universities and other institutions of higher education (HEIs) might be expected to play. It was noted that in recent years a greater role has been played by smaller firms in promoting technological change, and that this, together with the more active role of HEIs, is the major reason which underlies the growth of Science Parks in the UK in the 1980s. A full understanding of the growth of Science Parks, and in particular those established in the 1980s, can only be achieved through an understanding of the firms on the parks. It is important to know the extent to which they are in sectors which can genuinely be regarded as 'high-tech'. The performance of these businesses is also of great interest since they are often portrayed as major sources of new wealth. The key issue as far as Science Parks are concerned, however, is the extent to which the park adds value to a business.

In Part II of this study, we assemble the statistical information on the basis of which a judgement can be made on the added value of a park. Nevertheless, it must be emphasised that, even when all the evidence has been assembled, it is not possible to conduct a precise calculation on this matter. Rather, it is necessary to weigh the evidence carefully and reach informed, if not necessarily precise, judgements. This assessment is undertaken in Part III of the book.

To provide the basis for these judgements, a survey of all firms located on UK Science Parks was proposed, but it was recognised that this alone would not provide a clear indication of the added value of a park, since there would be nothing with which to compare the responses. Hence it was decided that similar questions should be asked of a group of otherwise similar firms not located on a park. A final comparison was also possible with small independent firms in all sectors, because a number of these questions had been asked in previous surveys which some of the authors have undertaken. From this it was possible to identify the extent to which responses were purely a reflection of sectoral composition and the extent to which they genuinely reflected a Science Park location. This survey, then, had several objectives:

(a) It was designed to provide an authoritative statement about the characteristics of small high technology businesses in the UK, and about the individuals who have founded and currently manage such businesses.

(b) It was intended to highlight both the similarities and the differences between small firms operating in the high-tech sector and small firms operating in the more conventional sectors.

(c) The prime objective, however, was to identify for small businesses in the high-tech sectors the perceived advantages of being located on a Science Park.

5.2. SURVEY METHODS

Several methods could be used to achieve these objectives: for example, the financial performance of the firms could be assessed by the use of information obtained from Companies House, and comparing this with data for a sample of small firms, such as that produced in *Business Monitor*. This method of comparison is that used, for example, by Storey *et al.* (1987) and by Burns and Dewhurst (1986). A second method of comparison would be to use one of the commercial data bases, such as Dun and Bradstreet, for comparing the performance of high-tech firms with those of similar-sized firms in the more conventional sectors. This approach has been used extensively in the United States by, for example, Armington, Harris and Odle (1983). Whilst such comparisons are helpful, they are not able to shed any light on the factors which explain any differences in performance. These can only be obtained by deriving the views of the business owners themselves. Given the sophisticated nature of the issues, it was not thought to be practical to attempt to obtain these views by postal survey techniques, and so it was decided that a direct, face-to-face survey had to be launched.

Whilst face-to-face questionnaires have a number of advantages, they also have several key limitations which need to be recognised. Firstly, such interviews can only provide a subjective view of the issues — a view which may be coloured by a desire to hoodwink the interviewer or, perhaps, at the other extreme, to provide the 'answers' which the respondent thinks the interviewer wishes to hear. Problems also arise because on some occasions, the person interviewed may not have all the relevant information — or perhaps they may not even have been with the business at the time some key decisions were made. Even for individuals who *were* involved at the time, their ability to recall key events is also likely to vary, with some tending to place a rather rosy glow upon historic events. For all these reasons it is unwise to assume that the face-to-face interview is an ideal vehicle for obtaining such insights; and in interpreting the subsequent results, all of these limitations have to be borne in mind.

To overcome some of these problems the following steps were taken. Firstly, two pilot studies were undertaken with tenants at the Aston and Cambridge Science Parks. These parks were selected because they were likely to contain a very different tenant profile, with the Cambridge tenants being generally much longer established, less likely to be independent start-up businesses, but being located on a much less centrally managed park than at Aston. At both of these parks standard questionnaires were administered by Paul Quintas and David Wield of the Open University. The majority of tenants in both locations were interviewed using a questionnaire, many of the questions on which had been shown to yield useful answers in previous surveys of small firms. This questionnaire contained only a small proportion of 'open-ended' questions, and it became clear during these interviews that its use might lead to some factors, specific to high-tech firms, being overlooked. For this reason a smaller number of tenants were questioned using much more 'open-ended' methods.

When the pilot interviews were completed, the study team reviewed the relative success of the two questionnaires and came to the conclusion that the main fieldwork should be undertaken on a questionnaire which combined the best elements of both the pilots. In practice, it was more heavily weighted towards the 'closed' style, but several issues highlighted by the 'open-ended' questionnaire were ultimately incorporated into the main fieldwork.

5.3. DEFINITIONS AND MAIN FIELDWORK

As noted earlier, there is no general agreement as to the definition of 'high technology'. For our general purposes we have chosen to regard all businesses currently located on a Science Park in the UK as being high-tech firms. Science Parks were known to contain firms of a variety of different sizes and ownership structures, but, given that one of the major objectives of this study was to identify the contribution of the park to the firms' performance, it was also necessary to obtain some comparisons with the high-tech firms not on the Science Park. To obtain names and addresses of such firms, several decisions were made. Firstly, the prime focus of the non-Science Park sample would be that these firms were to be primarily independent businesses, not subsidiaries of other firms. Secondly, given that most of the businesses on Science Parks were not only independent, but also had no other branches, the non-Science Park sample should also reflect these characteristics. Thirdly, the selection of non-Science Park firms was also designed to reflect the broad sectoral composition of Science Park firms. Fourthly, it was clear that a high proportion of the tenants of Science Parks consisted of relatively youthful firms, and so it was important that the non-Science Park group reflected these characteristics. Finally, Science Parks are found in most parts of the UK and, if anything, seemed to be more heavily concentrated in the less prosperous areas. It was therefore important that these regional differences were reflected in the survey.

Once the main fieldwork questionnaire had been devised, it was thought necessary that, in order to overcome the problem of potentially misleading responses, it should be administered by staff from the various regional offices of Peat Marwick. It was felt that if business people could see that the questions were being put by informed professional staff, this would reduce the acknowledged likelihood of interviewers being provided with inadequate information. After a one-day briefing session in London on interviewing techniques, a nominated manager in each of the chosen Peat Marwick offices was given a quota of high-tech firms to find in their locality which met the pre-stated criteria according to size, ownership, sector, etc. This operation was co-ordinated by Rory Landman at Peat Marwick in London.

The main fieldwork interviews were undertaken by Peat Marwick staff during the period September to November 1986. During that time, interviews were conducted both with Science Park tenants and with 'comparable' firms not on a Science Park. In addition, an interview was also arranged with the manager of each Science Park in order both to inform the survey team of the background and development of the park, and also to inform the manager of the general nature of the responses of the firms. Since all interviews with the firms were strictly confidential, all these comments were 'unattributable', but the passing on of these general comments was thought to be helpful.

5.4. CHARACTERISTICS OF SURVEYED FIRMS

A total of 284 firms were surveyed, of which 183 were on a Science Park and 101 were not on a park. Unfortunately, it was not possible to obtain complete information from all firms and so many subsequent tables provide the responses from less than the full 284 cases. Nevertheless, we have no reason to believe that, where there are cases missing, this leads to significant biases and so to misleading results. The remainder of this section is devoted to a description of the broad characteristics of the firms involved.

5.4.1. Ownership characteristics

Table 5.1 shows that the objectives of the survey in terms of ownership structure have been achieved. Firstly, the table shows that approximately one-fifth of firms on Science Parks can be classified as start-up firms since they are truly independent firms without any previous trading address. However, there is a further one-third of firms which, although they had traded before starting on the Science Park, were single-plant independents at the time of the survey. Some of these firms will, of course, have a long history of trading before locating on the park, whereas some may have traded from a home address but for all practical purposes be identical to the first group of firms. One-fifth of all firms on Science Parks classify themselves as subsidiaries, generally of larger companies. Finally, there is a quite substantial proportion of businesses (12 per cent) placed in the 'other' category. These are primarily businesses established by the university, the objectives of which are only partly commercial. Science Parks also contain several co-operatives, which are placed in this group.

It will be recalled that the objective of the off-Science Park

Table 5.1: Ownership characteristics of surveyed firms

Ownership	Science Park No.	%	Off-park No.	%
1. Single-plant independent, no previous address	38	21	34	34
2. Single-plant independent with previous address	62	34	36	35
3. Independent with other branches	24	13	21	21
4. Subsidiary	37	20	9	9
5. Other	22	12	1	1
Total	183	100	101	100

sample was to identify primarily high-tech independent firms. That this is achieved is also shown in the table since 90 per cent of such firms claimed to be independent. There was, however, a rather higher proportion of independent businesses, but which had branches elsewhere, than amongst Science Park businesses. As we shall see later, this is a reflection of the fact that generally the off-Science Park sample tends to be rather older and better established than those of the Science Parks.

5.4.2. Age of businesses

Table 5.2: Age of surveyed firms

	Science Park No.	%	Off-park No.	%
1. < 4 years	45	28	12	16
2. 4–9 years	57	35	14	18
3. 10–25 years	43	26	29	38
4. 26–50 years	11	7	14	18
5. > 51 years	7	4	7	10
Total	163	100	76	100

The age of businesses in this survey is shown in Table 5.2. Not surprisingly, most of the businesses are quite youthful, reflecting the fact that small firms tend to be rather younger than medium- or large-sized firms, and the fact that many of the technologies used by the firms are also very new. It will be observed that it was not possible to obtain complete information on the age of all companies, and so data are presented only for 239 firms.

The table shows that despite the attempts to obtain a sample of high-tech firms on and off Science Parks, it is clear that the off-Science Park firms are generally rather older than those on the Science Park. It also shows that whilst 28 per cent of Science Park firms were less than four years old, only 16 per cent of non-Science Park firms were in this age range.

5.4.3. Geographical coverage

At the end of 1986, there were 346 businesses located on Science Parks in the UK, of which 183 or 53 per cent were included in this study. As Table 5.3 indicates, the coverage varied somewhat from one Science Park to another, and no firms were surveyed at Aberystwyth, Birmingham, Heriot-Watt, Kent and St Andrews. A total of 34 businesses were located on these parks and so if these locations are excluded, it can be seen that the overall coverage for the Science Parks where interviews did take place was approximately 59 per cent.

The omission of Heriot-Watt, where there were 18 businesses, and the relatively low coverage of firms on the Cambridge Science Park (35 per cent) deserves some comment. Since Heriot-Watt and Cambridge Science Parks were established very much earlier than the remaining parks it means that the survey does contain an over-representation of 'new wave' Science Parks. This may also partly account for the differences in the age distribution between firms on and off the Science Parks.

Table 5.3, in the final three columns, shows employment in 163 out of the total of 183 businesses surveyed on Science Parks. It shows that these businesses provided employment for 2,024 workers, with no distinctions being made in this table between full- and part-time jobs. Average (arithmetic mean) employment in these firms was 12.4 workers, but this was strongly influenced by the inclusion of the Cambridge firms. If the latter were excluded then arithmetic mean employment was only 9.6 workers.

In terms of employment, the off-park firms are considerably larger than the Science Park firms, with an arithmetic mean employment of 23.3 workers, as is shown in Table 5.4. The table also shows that the off-park firms are disproportionately grouped in the less prosperous northern areas of England.

107

Table 5.3: Science Park locations: survey coverage and employment

	Locations	Number interviewed	Total tenants	Coverage (%)	Employment Total	Employment No.	Av.
1.	Aston	26	35	74	263	23	11.4
2.	Bolton	10	10	80	37	5	7.4
3.	Bradford	16	24	67	166	15	11.1
4.	Brunel	3	9	33	7	1	7.0
5.	Cambridge	24	68	35	683	24	28.5
6.	Clwyd	3	4	75	68	3	22.7
7.	Durham	4	5	80	30	4	7.5
8.	East Anglia	1	4	25	9	1	9.0
9.	Glasgow	6	15	40	55	6	9.2
10.	Hull	9	12	75	62	9	6.9
11.	Leeds	5	11	45	47	5	9.4
12.	Liverpool	7	12	58	25	7	3.6
13.	Loughborough	7	16	44	73	6	12.2
14.	Manchester	6	13	46	43	5	8.6
15.	Nottingham	12	14	85	83	11	7.5
16.	South Bank	16	36	44	88	14	6.3
17.	Southampton	5	15	33	51	3	17.0
18.	Surrey	5	9	56	74	5	14.8
19.	Swansea	4	4	100	8	1	8.0
20.	Warwick	16	30	53	152	15	10.1
	Total	183	346	53	2,024	163	12.4

Table 5.4: Off-park locations: numbers and employment

Region	Number interviewed	Employment		
		Total	Number	Average
Northern	23	607	22	27.5
Yorks and Humberside	11	182	8	22.8
East Midlands	13	175	10	17.5
East Anglia	0	0	0	0.0
South-east	12	243	7	34.7
South-west	25	422	23	18.3
West Midlands	0	0	0	0.0
North-west	3	32	3	10.7
Wales	14	94	2	47.0
Scotland	0	0	0	0.0
Northern Ireland	0	0	0	0.0
Total	101	1,775	76	23.3

5.4.4. Sectoral coverage and functions

The prime functions undertaken by the high-tech firms in this survey are shown in Table 5.5. In classifying firms in this way, it must be remembered that the same firm may undertake a number of functions at the particular location and that it can, in some cases, be difficult to identify a single main function. The classifications in the table should, then, only be taken as broadly indicative of the functions of the surveyed firms.

Recognising these caveats, Table 5.5 shows that out of the 284 firms, a total of 23 per cent classified themselves as being primarily in the computing hardware and systems market, with there being some important differences between those located on and off the Science Parks. Thus, for example, 26 per cent of all Science Park firms are in this grouping, compared with only 17 per cent of those off the park. The next two most important groups are software and microelectronics, both of which provide the main activity for about 35 per cent of all respondents. Again, there are some differences between those firms on and off the park, most notably that 25 per cent of all firms located off the park were primarily in microelectronics compared with only 10 per cent of those located on parks.

The table indicates that despite the efforts to match, in terms of sector, the firms on and off the parks, it is not possible to achieve this perfectly at the level of activity disaggregation presented in Table 5.5. Even so, it should be clear that according to most criteria, the firms in this survey would be classified as being in the high

Table 5.5: Main activities of surveyed firms

Activities	Science Parks	Off-park
Hardware and systems	26.2	16.8
Software	15.3	11.9
Microelectronics	9.8	24.8
Instrumentation	2.7	5.9
Automation	3.8	6.9
Electrical equipment	1.1	3.0
Medical	3.3	1.0
Pharmaceutical	2.7	4.0
Fine chemicals	0.5	0.0
Biotechnology	3.3	5.0
Mechanical	0.5	1.0
Environmental	3.8	6.9
Other manufacturing	0.5	1.0
Design and development	3.8	5.0
Analysis and testing	14.2	2.0
Other technical services	3.3	3.0
Financial and business services	4.9	2.0
Total	100.0	100.0

technology sectors and that almost all sectoral groupings are found amongst those located both on and off Science Parks.

5.5. CONCLUSIONS

In this chapter we have indicated how the surveyed firms were identified, recalling that it was our objective, firstly to identify those characteristics which distinguish small high technology firms from small firms in the more traditional sectors. Our second, and more important, objective was to identify what were the distinguishing characteristics of the firms located on a Science Park compared with otherwise 'comparable' firms located elsewhere. Only in that way was it thought possible to estimate what 'added value' a Science Park provides.

It is never easy to present information on 'comparable' firms satisfactorily, particularly in the small-firm sector. In subsequent chapters it is necessary to subdivide the firms not solely between those located on and off the Science Park, but also in a number of other ways — such as the sophistication of their technology, whether or not they are located in the south of England, whether or not the firm is independent or a subsidiary, etc. Given the inevitable problems associated with this type of analysis, we believe that the

110

firms in this survey do provide an adequate sample of Britain's new high technology industries, providing adequate geographical, technological, sectoral and ownership coverage.

6

Founders of High Technology Firms

6.1. INTRODUCTION

In this chapter we consider the characteristics of individuals or groups of individuals who have established high technology firms, whether these are on or off Science Parks. The particular focus of attention here is the educational qualifications of the founder(s), their work experience, and their motivations in establishing the business. All these elements will affect both the likelihood of the business being formed in the first place and the likelihood of the business succeeding. This chapter in particular provides an opportunity to compare the personal characteristics of those individuals establishing small high technology firms with those establishing small firms in the more conventional sectors. We are able to undertake this comparison because the same questions have been asked in the same format in this study as in several other studies with which some of the current authors have been associated.

In presenting our data, comparisons are made with three other studies of entrepreneurs in a variety of sectors of business in the UK. The first study is reported in Storey (1982) and presents the results of interviews with 301 firms which were new to the County of Cleveland, primarily between 1973 and 1977. Of these firms, 159 were wholly new, the remainder being ones that moved into the county from outside. In this study, all sectors other than retailing were included.

A second study, which asked some identical questions to the present one, was reported in English Estates (1985). This was a survey of 146 small firms occupying 'starter units' in English Estates premises. The vast majority of these firms were in the manufacturing sector and more than half had begun to trade for the first time in the previous two years, and only 12 per cent began trading more than seven years prior to the survey. All the firms surveyed were located in north-east England.

The third study with which comparisons are made is reported in Johnson and Storey (1987). This is a survey of 299 small firms in six contrasting areas of the United Kingdom (London, Glasgow, Teesside, Corby, Reading and Morcambe/Lancaster), and covers all sectors in proportion to their contribution to the total stock of UK small firms. This survey was conducted in 1985 but included all ages of small firms.

6.2. GENDER OF FOUNDER

The present study shows very clearly that the founder of a high technology firm in the UK is almost certain to be a male. Whilst this may not be a surprise, what is equally clear is that although most groups of entrepreneurs are male-dominated, the current group of high technology firm founders has an even lower proportion of females than any of our previous studies. Out of the 284 firms surveyed, it was possible to identify a key founder in 261 cases, but of these, in 256 cases (98 per cent) the founder was male. In some instances the firm may have been established many years ago and now be a large enterprise, perhaps owned by another firm. To take this possibility into account, we also examined only the independent companies, but here also 97 per cent of founders were male.

These results indicate even higher concentrations of male entrepreneurs than in the other studies. Thus, for example, in the Johnson and Storey study, only 68 per cent of founders were male, reflecting in part the fact that female entrepreneurs are much more likely to be found in the service than in the manufacturing sector. It may also reflect the way in which the question was asked, in the sense that it referred to a 'key' founder and a number of businesses may be a husband-and-wife partnership. This is shown in the English Estates study, which showed that whilst only 2 per cent of founders were female, a further 5 per cent were male/female partnerships.

The clear male dominance in the present group of high-tech entrepreneurs therefore provides some justification for the use of the shorthand term 'his business', which will be used throughout the remainder of the text.

6.3. AGE OF FOUNDER

There are two ways of examining the issue of the age of the entrepreneur. The first is to examine his current age at the time of the survey, and the second is to examine his age at the time at which he started the business. Where the vast majority of firms in the survey are relatively new, then these two measures will differ only slightly, but where the surveyed firms can be of any age, as in this case, then it is more useful to look at the age of the founder when the firm was started. This is shown in Table 6.1, which shows the age of the founder at the time at which the current business was started.

Table 6.1: Age of founder at time of business start-up

	< 25	25–30	31–35	36–40	41–45	46–50	51–55	> 55	Total
Cases	11	40	54	49	39	20	12	11	236
Percentage	4.7	16.9	22.9	20.8	16.6	8.5	5.1	4.7	100.0

The table shows that 23 per cent of those starting a high-tech business did so between the ages of 31 and 35 years, and that a further 21 per cent were between the ages of 36 and 40 years. Conversely only 5 per cent were more than 55 years old and only 5 per cent were less than 25 years old.

6.4. EDUCATIONAL QUALIFICATIONS

Over the years there have been a number of surveys of entrepreneurs which have investigated the question of whether higher levels of education are associated with smaller businesses that have a better performance, however defined, than otherwise comparable businesses which are owned by less educated individuals. It must be admitted, however, that the results have been somewhat inconsistent: for example, Gudgin, *et al.* (1979) indicated that graduate-owned businesses appeared to grow rather faster than non-graduate-owned firms. In our previous studies, we have not been able to make this distinction, primarily because of the relatively few graduates in the sample. We have, however, been able to distinguish between those entrepreneurs without any formal educational qualifications and those who have some qualification. Broadly it appears to be the case that this distinction did not prove to be useful in predicting the performance of small or new firms. Probably the most rigorous attempt to explore the nature of this possible relationship is the work of Pickles and O'Farrell (1987), who examined the work history of a representative cohort of Irish men and women. When they examined that proportion of the cohort which became self-employed, they distinguished between those who employed other workers and those who employed no other workers. For both groups it was found that increases in education beyond the elementary level lead initially to an increased probability of becoming self-employed. The most highly educated groups (graduates), however, were less likely to become self-employed than those with educational qualifications immediately below the graduate level. When a distinction was made amongst the self-employed between those with and without employees, it was apparent that the graduate-owned businesses were more likely to be employing other workers.

In contrast to most other studies of entrepreneurs in the UK, the present collection of high-tech firm founders has a high proportion with paper qualifications. Out of the 227 key founders of independent companies in the survey, 77 per cent claimed to have some form of paper qualification. The contrast with other studies could hardly be more clear: for example, the Cleveland study reported in Storey (1982) shows that only 66 per cent claimed to have a paper qualification. The contrast was even clearer when the nature of these qualifications was examined. In the Cleveland study, less than 5 per cent of founders had a degree, whereas in the present grouping more than half of those with a formal educational qualification had a first degree.

Table 6.2 also shows some interesting distinctions between the independent companies established on Science Parks and those

Table 6.2: Educational qualifications of independent companies

| | Science Park | | Off-park | |
	No.	%	No.	%
Qualified	101	75	73	79
Non-qualified	34	25	19	21
Total	135	100	92	100
With first degree	65	64	38	52
With higher degree	53	52	12	16
Number of respondents	101	100	73	100

located elsewhere. The founders of the Science Park firms are equally likely to have a formal educational qualification as those located elsewhere (75 compared with 79 per cent) and are almost equally likely to have a first degree (64 compared with 52 per cent). The real differences occur in the likelihood of having a higher degree, where 52 per cent of qualified Science Park founders had such a degree compared with only 16 per cent of those founders with businesses not on a Science Park.

6.5. MOTIVATIONS IN ESTABLISHING THE BUSINESS

It is broadly possible to distinguish between the positive and negative factors which cause an individual or group of individuals to establish a business. These are usually referred to as 'push' and 'pull' factors. Amongst the most important 'push' factors are the loss of an existing form of employment, but it may also include the recognition that the individual has poor prospects in his existing form of work. Thus, for example, he may not be happy in his relationships with his boss, or he may feel that the company does not value his contribution to the business. In the context of high-tech entrepreneurs, there may be a feeling of frustration, particularly amongst research scientists, when the product or process which they have developed is not commercially exploited by their employer.

The main types of 'pull' factors are where an individual sees a clear market opportunity for a product. This observation can be made by an individual, either from a marketing or from a research viewpoint. Indeed, on some occasions the business idea can derive from some form of leisure pursuit.

Finally the distinction between 'push' and 'pull' factors should not be made in such as way as to suggest that the two are mutually exclusive. An individual, for example, could regard both as being important in influencing his decision to become an entrepreneur. For analytical purposes, however, the distinction does have some validity and we propose to examine these broad motivations here.

In many respects the results from Table 6.3 are very surprising. They show that approximately 20 per cent of new-firm founders in the high technology sectors were unemployed or likely to become unemployed immediately prior to starting their business. In this sense they were motivated by the clearest of all motives for starting a business — the threat of having no work. What is most surprising about these results is that they differ only modestly from those of

Table 6.3: The threat of unemployment to founders of independent businesses

	Science Park		Off-park	
	No.	%	No.	%
Unemployed	22	18	18	20
Not unemployed	102	82	70	80
Total	124	100	88	100

Table 6.4: Main reasons for starting in business

	Cleveland (%)	OSG (%)	Science Park (%)	Off-park (%)
Motivated by negative factors (forced entrepreneurs)	9	15	5	8
Motivated by positive factors	14	29	22	31
Knowledge of specific market	44	25	44	36
Other motivations	33	31	29	25
Total	100	100	100	100

studies of entrepreneurs in other sectors. The Cleveland study, for example, showed that approximately one-quarter of founders were, in fact, unemployed prior to start-up. A similar figure was obtained by Johnson and Storey (1987), yet in both these studies the typical entrepreneur lacked educational skills. If it is correct that individuals with educational qualifications are less likely to be unemployed, or less likely to remain unemployed for any length of time, then it is surprising that there is so little difference between samples of educated and less-educated entrepreneurs in terms of this key 'push' factor.

We investigate these matters further in Table 6.4 by making a broad classification of the broad motivations of entrepreneurs in establishing a business. Again, we make a comparison between the present study, the results of which are shown in the final two columns, and previous studies. Broadly, the motivations are broken down into negative factors such as unemployment or the threat of unemployment, positive factors such as always wanting to start a business, market and related factors such as seeing a clear business

117

opportunity, and then a variety of other elements such as chance events. In these circumstances it is always a highly subjective act on the part of the researcher to classify such complex motivations into single categories. Nevertheless, the exercise does demonstrate that it is indeed market-related factors which dominate in almost all the studies, and that these are mentioned by many more people than the negative factors. Whilst too much reliance should not be placed upon this, it is interesting to note that market-related factors are of particular importance amongst Science Park founders.

6.6. OTHER BUSINESS INTERESTS

Although this chapter has been primarily concerned with the personal characteristics of key founders of independent high-tech businesses, it is not reasonable to assume that this is their only business interest. Table 6.5 shows that at the time of the survey, 24 per cent of the key founders of independent businesses on Science Parks owned other businesses. For key founders of independent businesses not on a Science Park, 31 per cent owned other businesses. In the vast majority of cases the key founder has an ownership interest in only one or two other businesses.

Table 6.5: Business ownership amongst key founders of independent companies

	Science Park		Off-park	
	No.	%	No.	%
Owned other business	29	24	27	31
NOT owned other business	93	76	61	69
Total	122	100	88	100
Number of businesses owned				
1	11	41	11	42
2	8	30	11	42
3	4	15	3	12
>3	4	15	1	4
Total	27	100	26	100
Date of establishment of other businesses				
Before	11	41	7	27
After	11	41	16	62
Same time	2	7	0	0
Before/after	3	11	3	12
Total	27	100	26	100

Given that the Science Park businesses are generally newer than those located off the park, it is perhaps not surprising that 62 per cent of the latter group of key founders established their other business interests after the one being surveyed. What is perhaps more surprising is that 42 per cent of Science Park founders with another business interest established this *after* establishing the business which is now located on the Science Park. Bearing in mind that the majority of Science Park businesses are less than ten years old, it suggests that these key founders have already begun to diversify their portfolio of business interests.

6.7. PART-TIME EXPERIENCE

A number of businesses begin on a part-time basis. Thus, for example, 22 per cent of the new firms in the Cleveland study began on a part-time basis, and it is frequently argued that starting on such a basis provides a relatively low-risk way of accumulating experience of both the market and of the problems of business management. If the Belgian experience, reported by Bragard, Donckles and Michel (1985) is typical, then an even higher proportion of continental businesses begin on a part-time basis than in the UK. The Belgian researchers report that 30 per cent of their sample began in this way.

Table 6.6: Part-time business activity among independent firms

	Science Park		Off-park	
	No.	%	No.	%
Part-time activity	39	31	19	21
Never part-time	86	69	71	79
Total	125	100	90	100
Duration of part-time				
< 6 months	4	12	1	6
6–11 months	8	24	4	22
1–2 years	11	33	9	50
> 2 years	10	31	4	22
Total	33	100	18	100

From Table 6.6 it can be seen that there appear to be some differences between Science Park and non-Science Park firms in terms of their likelihood of being started on a part-time basis.

119

Amongst the non-Science Park independent firms, 21 per cent of founders started on a part-time basis — a figure very close to that derived from the Cleveland study. On the other hand, 31 per cent of the founders of Science Park independent firms started on a part-time basis — a figure much closer to that derived from the Belgian studies. It seems likely that many of the businesses located on the Science Parks were begun by university academics on a part-time basis, and this is reflected in the lower part of the table, which shows that virtually two-thirds of them were in operation for more than two years prior to the business being established on a full-time basis.

6.8. PREVIOUS EMPLOYMENT HISTORY

Previous research into entrepreneurial backgrounds has identified several important features: firstly, that entrepreneurs tend to come from families with a business tradition; secondly that they tend to establish businesses in the industry in which they were formerly employed; and thirdly, that an individual is significantly more likely to establish a firm if previous working experience is in the small-firm sector than if it is in the large-firm sector. In the current sample of high-tech entrepreneurs, we are able to test the latter two hypotheses.

Table 6.7 shows two elements of the employment history of the key founders of independent businesses in this sample, but in undertaking the analysis it examines not only the nature of the entrepreneur's employment immediately prior to this business, but also his prior employment history. The table shows that the key founders of Science Park independent businesses are much more likely to have been employed in the public sector than those founding similar businesses which are not on Science Parks, with 33 per cent of Science Park key founders being employed in the public sector immediately prior to starting their business (Job 1) compared with 19 per cent amongst non-Science Park key founders. This is primarily because of the high proportion of Science Park founders employed in the local university. When, however, a rather longer time-perspective is adopted, an interesting picture emerges. Amongst the non-Science Park founders, only 19 per cent of whom were employed in the public sector immediately prior to starting the business, there appears to have been considerable public sector employment experience. Thus, for example, 30 per cent of this group were employed in the public sector three jobs prior to this

Table 6.7: Employment history of key founders of independent firms: 1

Sector of previous employer

		Science Park		Off-park	
		No.	%	No.	%
Job 1:	Public Sector	38	33	16	19
	Private sector	77	67	69	81
	Total	115	100	85	100
Job 2:	Public Sector	23	26	18	29
	Private Sector	64	74	45	71
	Total	87	100	63	100
Job 3:	Public Sector	12	20	13	30
	Private Sector	48	80	30	70
	Total	60	100	43	100

Size of previous employer in terms of employment

		Science Park		Off-park	
		No.	%	No.	%
Job 1:	1–50	31	35	33	46
	51–500	25	28	12	17
	500+	33	37	26	37
	Total	89	100	71	100
Job 2:	1–50	14	23	11	21
	51–500	20	33	19	37
	500+	27	44	21	41
	Total	61	100	51	100
Job 3:	1–50	13	30	8	22
	51–500	10	23	9	25
	500+	20	46	19	53
	Total	43	100	36	100

business (Job 3) and this is a higher proportion than for Science Park founders, only 20 per cent of whom were employed in the public sector in Job 3.

Similar patterns are apparent from a study of the lower part of Table 6.7, which shows that for non-Science Park founders employment in a small firm with less than 50 workers was the most common immediately prior to starting the business. This was the case for 46 per cent of respondents, although 37 per cent were employed in large firms with more than 500 workers. Non-Science Park founders therefore appear to conform with the conventional wisdom that entrepreneurs are likely to come from a small-firm background.

This is less clearly true for Science Park key founders, 37 per cent of whom were employed in an organisation with more than 500 workers, compared with 35 per cent in an organisation with less than 50 workers. Again, we attribute much of this difference to the strong presence of ex-university employees amongst the Science Park sample. Even so, it has to be recognised that although no fully adequate national data are available, it is probably broadly true that only about 20 per cent of the UK work-force is employed in organisations with less than 50 workers, so that any proportion substantially in excess of 20 per cent indicates that small firms are producing more than their 'share' of entrepreneurs.

The lower half of Table 6.7 illustrates a very important result in the study of entrepreneurship. It shows that whilst most entrepreneurs, particularly those establishing their businesses off a Science Park, were employed by a small firm immediately prior to starting their business, a majority (53 per cent) were employed by a large firm in their third job prior to starting the business. It suggests that a number of entrepreneurs have some experience of working for a large firm. They then move out of that firm into a medium-sized firm, and finally into a small firm before starting their business. Support for this proposition is shown by the fact that amongst non-Science Park key founders, in Job 3 large firms are dominant, but that for Job 2 both large and medium-sized firms are dominant. Analysis of Job 1, as we noted above, shows small firms to be the most important.

The pattern is less clear for founders of Science Park firms, although the relative importance of large firms does decline, the closer the individual gets to establishing the business.

6.9. SECTORAL PATTERN OF EMPLOYMENT HISTORY

In this section we examine the sectors of employment from which the high-tech entrepreneurs are drawn, the results being shown in Table 6.8. The table also makes the now familiar distinction between those businesses located on a Science Park and those located elsewhere, and it also investigates whether the entrepreneur switches sector when he changes job prior to starting the business. Again, Job 1 is the most recent job before starting the current business and Job 3 is the least recent job.

Table 6.8 shows very clearly that the most important sector producing high-tech entrepreneurs is electrical engineering, with

Table 6.8: Employment history of key founders of independent firms: 2

Sector of previous employer	Science Park			Off-park		
	Job 1	Job 2	Job 3	Job 1	Job 2	Job 3
	(per cent)			(per cent)		
Chemicals	6	9	6	10	5	4
Mechanical engineering	4	11	6	4	3	11
Computer hardware	2	0	0	5	4	9
Instrument engineering	3	1	0	5	3	4
Electrical engineering	17	24	22	34	37	33
Other manufacturing	12	11	23	7	15	9
Total manufacturing	44	56	57	65	67	70
Professional services	34	23	17	21	18	11
Software	2	1	4	1	0	0
Public services	5	2	2	2	3	9
Other services	11	15	12	12	5	9
Total services	52	41	35	36	26	29
Others	4	3	8	0	7	0
Total	100	100	100	100	100	100

approximately one-third of all founders of off-park firms being formerly employed in this sector immediately prior to starting in the business (Job 1). For off-park founders, the dominance continues when previous employment is examined, with 37 per cent of entrepreneurs in second job prior to starting the business being employed in the electrical engineering sector, and 33 per cent in the third job prior to the current business. As we shall show shortly, the key founder of the business being surveyed could have been a business owner in his previous job, so it cannot always be inferred that these are employment sectors immediately prior to the entrepreneur establishing his first business. Instead, the data refer only to employment prior to establishing the current business.

The dominance of the electrical engineering sector is much less apparent amongst founders of Science Park firms. Amongst this group, 34 per cent of all key founders immediately prior to start-up were employed in the professional services sector which includes universities. In fact, it is interesting to note that the services sector is a much more important source of employment for those individuals who established a business on a Science Park than for those establishing a business elsewhere.

Finally, Table 6.8 also shows that for both groups of entrepreneurs there are indications that as they get closer to establishing the current business, they are gradually moving away from employment in the manufacturing sector. Thus, 57 per cent of Science Park founders had their Job 3 in the manufacturing sector, compared with only 44 per cent for Job 1. A similar, though much smaller, change occurs amongst non-Science Park founders, where there is a change from 70 to 65 per cent.

6.10. CAREER DEVELOPMENT OF ENTREPRENEURS

It is frequently argued that the managerial experience which an individual brings to a business is crucial to success. Indeed, it is almost tautological to state that the performance of a small firm depends crucially upon the owner, since in many small firms the business is the owner. Table 6.9 investigates the career development of those founding a high-tech business and shows that immediately prior to establishing the business (Job 1), 74 per cent of Science Park founders occupied a managerial position. An almost identical proportion of off-park founders (75 per cent) also held a managerial post.

Table 6.9: Career experience of key founders of independent firms

Management experience	Science Park			Off-park		
	Job 1	Job 2	Job 3	Job 1	Job 2	Job 3
	(per cent)			(per cent)		
Management position	74	64	50	75	57	46
No management position	26	36	50	25	43	54
Total	100	100	100	100	100	100
Business ownership experience						
Owner or part owner	29	13	12	22	12	2
Not owner or part owner	70	87	88	78	88	98
Total	100	100	100	100	100	100

The upper half of the table shows, however, that relatively few individuals consistently occupied managerial positions throughout their career. Thus, for example, when the third job prior to establishing the current business (Job 3) is examined, only about 50 per cent of both groups occupied a management position.

In some cases the management post which the individual occupies is that of owner or part owner of a business. The extent of this is shown in the lower half of the table, where it is shown that 29 per cent of founders of businesses located on a Science Park were in business either as an owner or part owner in their previous job. For off-park founders, the comparable figure is 22 per cent. It therefore appears to be broadly true that about three-quarters of founders of high-tech businesses have gained some managerial experience in their job immediately prior to starting this business, with about one-quarter obtaining this as an owner or part owner.

Finally, the table also shows that whilst perhaps one-quarter of founders owned a business immediately prior to starting the current business, very few have been involved with several businesses. Thus, for example, only 2 per cent of non-Science Park founders and 12 per cent of Science Park founders were owners or part owners of a business in Job 3.

6.11. CONCLUSION

This chapter has examined the background of the key founder of high-tech businesses with two main objectives in view: firstly, that of highlighting the extent to which high-tech entrepreneurs differ from individuals establishing businesses in the more conventional sectors; and secondly, that of examining whether there are differences between individuals establishing a business on a Science Park, and those not on a Science Park.

We conclude that the high-tech entrepreneur is more likely to be male than his counterpart in the more conventional sectors, but is likely to be of a similar age. Not surprisingly, he is likely to be very much better educated, with founders of firms located on Science Parks having significantly higher academic qualifications than those located off Science Parks.

More surprisingly was the importance, even within this highly educated group, of the motivation of fear of unemployment in establishing the business. Perhaps the most interesting research result which was identified was that whilst many entrepreneurs, immediately prior to starting the business, may have worked in a small firm, many have had experience in a large firm. There may even be a pattern amongst such individuals of starting work in a large firm, moving to a medium-sized firm and then to a small firm.

It is often at that point that the business idea is implemented, so that the next move is to start the firm. Finally, there is no reason to dispute the conventional wisdom of entrepreneurial studies that individuals generally form businesses in the industry or trade in which they were formerly employed.

7

The Technological Characteristics of Firms: Technology Transfer

7.1. INTRODUCTION

The next two chapters explore the technological aspects of Science Park firms. Part I of this study presented a set of arguments which point towards the key role of new technology-based firms in the regeneration of advanced economies. As will be recalled, it was argued that economic regeneration depended on the development of technically innovative products and manufacturing processes. The argument follows that the future of advanced industrial economies lies in high value-added activities and so the emphasis must be on knowledge-based industries operating at the scientific and technological 'leading edge'. Universities and other HEIs are seen as reservoirs of knowledge and expertise, and as education and training resources, to help the growth of new technology-based industries. The UK, whilst it may be 'world class' in basic scientific discovery (although this is increasingly being questioned), is believed by many to have a poor record in the application and commercialisation of the fruits of scientific research. There is thus pressure on HEIs to link themselves more closely to industry, and to place greater emphasis on development and application.

For many analysts and policy makers, these developments point to the need for new initiatives harnessing the high value-added resource of universities and linking them to companies in order to promote new technology-based product and process innovations. Science Parks are one initiative intended to foster such developments.

The key concept at the centre of the Science Park phenomenon is *technology transfer*, which includes the concept of *knowledge transfer*. At its most accessible level, technology transfer would involve the physical transfer of discreet lumps of hardware developed in the university or HEI to the firm. However, it might also involve the development and transfer of techniques, the solution to specific technological problems, and the transfer of specialised knowledge. In many cases the knowledge or techniques being transferred will be embodied in individuals. Such individuals may move physically into firms as founders, directors, R & D staff or students on specific projects. Alternatively, they may work on a consultancy basis from the HEI. To make matters worse from the point of view of understanding technology transfer and attempting to perceive and record its existence from outside, the importance of informal contact, personal networks and serendipitous exchanges is often emphasised as being an important feature of technology transfer.

This chapter will identify the nature of Science Park firms in terms of the nature, orientation and level of their technological activities. It will look in detail at the industrial sector and activity of firms, and at how these are changing over time. Special attention is paid to identifying the indicators which point towards the relative technological sophistication of firms: what is meant by 'high tech', and what advantages does being a high technology company confer? As in other chapters, the population of firms surveyed is sub-divided in several ways. A distinction is made between those on and off Science Parks, between independent and non-independent businesses, and between those located in the south and the north of Britain.

7.2. WHAT IS 'HIGH TECHNOLOGY'

Before reviewing the empirical evidence from the research, the concept of 'high technology' is briefly discussed. Defining what is and what is not high technology is problematic. The term 'high tech' is now common (and thus devalued) currency, appearing on consumer products from running shoes to vacuum cleaners, deodorants to cheeseburgers. Reading the property pages of magazines or newspapers leaves the strong impression that high tech is simply an architectural style or a narrowly defined set of building methods and materials. Nevertheless, much emphasis is placed on high technology industries, and so a workable definition would seem to be essential.

Alternative phrases to that of 'high tech' provide rather more specific meaning. These include: knowledge-based, new technology-based, leading-edge, and R & D intensive industry.

Precise definitions of these terms are not easy to find, and agreement between writers is even rarer; but they do point towards possible factors which might be definable. Many recent studies of new technology-based industry include a section intended to define high technology (see, for example, Markusen *et al.* (1986) and Hall *et al.* (1987)). A range of defining characteristics has been suggested and writers generally plump for indicators which have the fewest disadvantages as they see it. These indicators fall into two groups: firstly, measures of resource inputs to high technology activity, such as R & D effort, R & D expenditure, and the employment of qualified personnel; and secondly, measures of output or performance of high technology firms, such as growth rates, value added, patent records and technological innovations. Indicators based on firms' R & D expenditure expressed as a percentage of turnover are known to be an unreliable indicator in the case of new industries and new small firms. Young firms with little or no income will inevitably appear more R & D intensive than established firms with high levels of income. Additionally, R & D activity is itself notoriously difficult to measure, especially in small firms which do not have clearly demarcated R & D departments or functionaries.

The broadest definitions of high tech identify whole industrial sectors as such, which can lead to curious anomalies. Thus, for example, various different approaches place the Vehicles sector (Industrial Order IX) in the top five industrial sectors. This sector includes activities as disparate as 'manufacturing, assembling, modifying and repairing . . . spacecraft' and 'manufacturing and assembling . . . bicycles' (Henneberry, 1984, p. 148). Clearly, such sectoral classifications are too broad to be useful for anything beyond a first approximation.

Sectoral classification also presents problems of comparison between sectors — how does one compare the relative innovativeness of, say, a firm involved in peptide synthesis with another firm whose field is image processing. Measures are needed which draw on other factors, such as the relative closeness of the firm to the leading edge of current knowledge and practice (current knowledge may of course be separated by years or decades of development time from industrial application).

Fortunately, this study does not require a definition of 'high technology' since the subject matter is chosen for us — that is, firms located on Science Parks. Further, if these firms were selected to locate on Science Parks, with the implication of being close to leading edge university research and highly qualified staff, then the

129

findings of this study will help characterise this form of high technology development in the UK in the late 1980s.

The survey, then, did not obtain independent verification of the subject firms' technological level. Instead, it uses a range of indicators to approximate the technological level of the subject firms. There are two types of possible measures:

(1) those that concentrate on inputs to a firm that are assumed to relate to innovation, such as measures of R & D expenditure and numbers of qualified scientists and engineers employed, and indications of links to university R & D; and

(2) those which concentrate on performance or output characteristics of firms, such as growth performance, measures of innovation and of patents.

Clearly the importance of high technology firms and the reason why they are currently of such interest is related to their performance: they are expected to perform better than the average firm on a number of indicators. The input measures may, however, give a clue to the potential performance of a firm, in the absence of output information (if, for example, the firm is too new to have actually produced anything).

The presentation of the survey results relevant to technology begins with a deceptively simple question: what do the firms do, and in which industrial sectors are they located?

7.3. INDUSTRIAL SECTORS AND ACTIVITIES OF THE FIRMS

The presentation and discussion of the survey results relating to technology begins by developing the brief examination of the industrial sectors and the areas of activity outlined in Chapter 5. Since 'high technology' is often defined in terms of industrial sectors, the sectoral distribution of the firms surveyed will provide an important indication of their scope and characteristics. However, it is necessary to supplement the sectoral analysis with an examination of the types of activities in which the firms are involved. Thus, for example, firms in the 'computer hardware and systems' sector may be manufacturing microcomputers or designing and assembling turnkey systems using bought-in hardware. The survey therefore included a detailed set of questions around the activities in which firms are engaged.

130

The task of categorising firms into industrial sectors appears to be simple at first sight. However, many firms may not fit easily into one category: they may be involved, for example, in both instrumentation and software development, or provide design and development services whilst also being involved in hardware production. One of the companies surveyed functions as a technology transfer agency, whilst developing its own biotechnology product. Fortunately, the majority of firms are more amenable, and so have been characterised by their principal sectors, each firm being allocated to the one sector which best fits their operation. The resulting aggregate picture gives a good first approximation as to the sectors of performance of the firms.

Table 7.1: Sectoral distribution of firms

	All firms (per cent)	Science Park firms (per cent)	Off-park firms (per cent)
Computer-related:			
Hardware and systems	23	26	17
Software	14	15	12
Microelectronics	15	10	25
Instrumentation	4	3	6
Automation	5	4	7
Electrical equipment	2	1	3
Medical	3	3	1
Pharmaceuticals	3	3	4
Fine chemicals	0	1	0
Biotechnology	4	3	5
Mechanical	1	1	1
Environmental	5	4	7
Design and development	4	4	5
Analysis/testing	10	14	2
Technical services	3	3	3
Financial/Business services	4	5	2
Other	1	1	1
Totals	100	100	100
Number of firms	284	183	101

Note: Each firm has been assigned to its principal sector, which will tend to underestimate the internal diversity of firms.

Table 7.1 gives a picture of the 284 firms surveyed, developing that shown in Chapter 5. The three columns show the sectoral distribution of (1) all firms surveyed, (2) Science Park firms, and (3) off-park firms. It can be seen that there is a concentration in computing and microelectronics: over half of all firms are in computer hardware and systems, software or microelectronics. Added to this, sectors such as automation and instrumentation also involve a great deal of computing and microelectronics, and so the dominance of Information Technology (IT — which includes microelectronics, computing and telecommunications) is obvious. For comparison, the medical, chemical and biotechnology sectors account for only 10 per cent of firms. Those firms involved in technical services, analysis and testing, and design and development, represent 17 per cent of all firms. It is also likely that many of these firms are providing services linked to, or are themselves reliant upon, IT.

Some significant differences can be seen between the Science Park firms and the off-park firms. Off-park firms tend to be more involved in microelectronics, and less in computer hardware and systems, compared to Science Park firms, and Science Park firms are far more heavily involved in analysis and testing. Amongst the sectors with lower populations, off-park firms are more likely to be found in instrumentation, automation, electrical equipment, biotechnology and environmental sectors. Science Park firms predominate in business services.

There is no significant difference in sectoral distribution between independent firms and subsidiary firms. Minor exceptions to this are analysis and testing, where subsidiary firms are dominant. Conversely, in the computer hardware, software and microelectronics sectors, independent firms are more important. Sectoral differences between firms located in the south of England and those in the rest of the UK (called 'the north' here for convenience) were also not significant. More southern firms are involved in automation, design and development, and biotechnology; and more northern firms were found in environmental, business services, and in electrical equipment (where there were no southern firms at all), but the broad pattern was similar.

The foregoing does not, however, tell us what the firms actually do — what activities they are involved in, and what the nature of their business is. If, for example, firms are in the computer hardware and systems sector, do they manufacture hardware, or do they buy in products which they assemble into systems? As a second example, firms in the automation sector may produce hard products, or they may design, install and implement turnkey systems using bought-in products, thus acting as hands-on consultants. It is therefore necessary to move beyond the sectoral analysis and look

Table 7.2: Principal on-site activities of firms disaggregated by site type[a]

	Science Park firms	Non-Science Park	Independent firms	Subsidiary firms	Science Park independents	Off-park independents
Manufacture	14	27	20	15	13	29
Production	6	6	7	1	8	6
Design/ development	21	14	19	15	24	14
Research	6	5	5	10	6	3
Marketing/sales	8	6	6	12	5	6
Warehousing	12	10	11	12	10	11
Servicing/repair	11	11	9	18	9	9
Analysis	5	7	7	3	6	7
Consultancy	5	5	6	0	6	6
Training	4	2	3	4	4	2
Software	4	1	4	0	5	2
Others	5	6	5	10	4	5
Totals[b]	100	100	100	100	100	100

Note: a. Figures are percentage of firms recording each activity, in each site type.
b. Not all figures necessarily sum to 100 because of rounding errors.

in depth at the types of activities in which firms are involved.

Respondents were initially asked to identify the principal activities undertaken by the firm in the premises occupied. Table 7.2 shows the results. The categories emerged from respondents' own descriptions of their principal activities. The columns show the percentages of firms involved in each activity for (1) Science Park firms, (2) off-park firms, (3) independent firms, (4) subsidiary firms, (5) Science Park independent firms, and (6) off-park independent firms. It can be seen that there is general similarity between Science Park and off-park firms, with some notable exceptions. Off-park firms are twice as likely to be involved in manufacture on site as park firms, which is a predictable result, given the restrictions that many parks place on manufacture. Science Park firms are more involved in design and development on site, and are marginally more involved in software development and production.

Rather greater differences can be seen, however, between independent firms and subsidiary firms. This is interesting, given that the sectoral analysis above revealed differences between firms on and off parks but not between independent and subsidiary firms. Column 3 of Table 7.2 shows that independent firms are more heavily involved with on-site manufacture and production than are subsidiary firms (column 4). Interestingly, however, significantly

Table 7.3 Most important firm activities as a source of income: 'arrival' and 'current' compared

	Science Parks		Off-park		Independent firms		Subsidiary firms	
	On arrival	Current	On arrival	Current	On arrival	Current	On arrival	Current
Product-related	81 (23)	86 (22)	52 (26)	59 (25)	106 (24)	117 (23)	27 (26)	28 (25)
Software	52 (15)	65 (17)	29 (14)	31 (13)	62 (14)	76 (15)	19 (18)	20 (18)
Consultancy	73 (21)	75 (19)	33 (16)	32 (14)	87 (19)	87 (17)	19 (18)	20 (18)
Contract research	27 (8)	27 (7)	7 (4)	10 (4)	26 (6)	31 (6)	8 (8)	6 (5)
Contract development	32 (9)	36 (9)	22 (11)	28 (12)	47 (11)	55 (11)	7 (7)	9 (8)
Contract design	20 (6)	22 (6)	15 (8)	19 (8)	32 (7)	38 (7)	3 (3)	3 (3)
Subcontract production	4 (1)	5 (1)	10 (5)	11 (5)	14 (3)	16 (3)	—	—
Testing and analysis	14 (4)	14 (4)	11 (6)	12 (5)	21 (5)	22 (4)	4 (4)	4 (4)
Licence income	10 (3)	15 (4)	4 (2)	8 (3)	9 (2)	16 (3)	5 (5)	7 (6)
Training	24 (7)	28 (7)	7 (4)	14 (6)	24 (5)	34 (7)	7 (7)	8 (7)

Services	8 (2)	8 (2)	8 (4)	8 (3)	7 (2)	11 (2)	4 (4)	4 (4)
Other	6 (2)	8 (2)	3 (2)	3 (1)	14 (3)	8 (2)	2 (2)	3 (3)
Total mentions	351	389	201	235	449	511	105	112
Total firms	160	160	94	94	207	207	47	47
Percentages	(100)	(100)	(100)	(100)	(100)	(100)	(100)	(100)

Note: Figures are numbers of mentions; figures in parentheses are percentages of total responses in each column. Only firms answering both 'arrival' and 'current' are included.

more off-park independent firms are involved in manufacture on site than is the case with Science Park independent firms (29 compared with 13 per cent).

In the 'softer' activities, Science Park independent firms are the more likely to undertake design and development on-site, but subsidiary firms are more heavily involved in research. Somewhat surprisingly, a high percentage of subsidiary firms stated that marketing is a major activity from their present site. Similarly, twice the proportion of subsidiary firms are involved in servicing compared with independent firms.

The foregoing present a broad picture of the main activities undertaken by the firms on site. More detailed analysis reveals further differences. Firms were asked to state the three most important activities from which income is derived, and additionally, to state these both for the firm's current position, and when the firm first arrived at the present site. Table 7.3 shows the most important activities firms are engaged in, and from which they derive income, for Science Park firms, off-park firms, independent firms and subsidiary firms. The table gives the position at arrival on the present site, in comparison with their current position. In order to ensure that the data is consistent and picking up actual trends within firms, only those firms which responded to both 'arrival' and 'current' activities have been included. This avoids the problem of the time series data being affected by the inclusion of additional firms in the 'current activities' columns.

It should be remembered that firms were invited to identify the three most important activity areas which provide a source of income (although on average firms mentioned 2.3 activities). This table therefore provides a comparison with the main activities undertaken on site, shown in Table 7.2. The total number of mentions and the total number of firms are given at the foot of each column. Disregarding for a moment the changes between 'arrival' and 'current', it can be seen that there is remarkable similarity between park and off-park firms, with products, software, consultancy and contract design being the major sources of current income. Rather more off-park firms mention products, and fewer mention consultancy or contract research as sources of income. Five times the proportion of off-park firms compared to Science Park firms mention subcontracting as an important source of income. It is interesting to note that contract research, contract development and contract design, taken together (R & D), account for approximately 23 per cent of all mentions in all firm types (i.e. all columns of the table), except in the case of subsidiary firms, where they account for 16 per cent of activities. If consultancy activities are added to contract R & D, these account for around two fifths of all major activity. These findings should be interpreted with caution, however, since no weighting was attached to these 'three most important mentions'. Thus, a respondent's third mention, although given equal weight in Table 7.3, may have less significance in reality. Nevertheless, the table does reflect the spread of important activity and aggregate differences between firm types.

The data provides information on changes in firms' activities between arrival at the present site, and current activities. Analysing the changes occurring over time shown in Table 7.3, several points emerge. The totals at the foot of the table show that the number of activities mentioned by firms increased between 'arrival' and 'current', for all firms. The increases are 10 per cent for Science Park firms, 16 per cent for off-park firms, 14 per cent for independent firms, and 7 per cent for subsidiary firms. This suggests that firms have diversified over time, increasing their range of activity. What, then, is the nature of these changes?

Activities related to products have decreased slightly for both on and off-park firms, but so too has consultancy, with contract research, contract development, and contract design virtually unchanged. Software activity has increased slightly in Science Park firms, but decreased off-park. In those activities which are mentioned less frequently overall, some significant changes can be seen. Income from licenses has increased for all categories of firm, rising from ten to fifteen mentions for Science Park firms, four to eight for off-park firms. Training as a source of income has doubled for off-park firms (from seven to fourteen mentions), and increased in independent firms from twenty-four to thirty-four mentions.

Table 7.4 presents a much simplified view of activity changes for Science Park and off-park firms, divided between southern and northern locations. The stars represent activities in which there has been an above-average increase in mentions (i.e. average increase for each column). The zeros show those activities which have remained static or have declined, and the blanks are areas that have shown average increases. It should be remembered that the table does not indicate different magnitudes of responses between activities, but is intended simply to show those activities which have increased or decreased over time.

It can be seen at a glance that across all categories of firm, licensing and training show above-average increases, and product related

Table 7.4: Changes in activities over time: Science Park–off-park; North–South comparison

	Science Park		Off-park	
	South	North	South	North
Product-related				
Software	*	*		
Consultancy			O	O
Contract research	O		*	*
Contract development	O	*	*	
Contract design	*		*	O
Subcontract production	—	*		O
Test/analysis	O	O	O	*
Licence income	*	*	*	*
Training	*	*	*	*
Services	*	*	—	O
Other	O	O	O	O

Note: Changes are between 'arrival' and 'current' activities as sources of income, identified as 'most important'.

Key:
*	= Above-average increase in activity
O	= Static or declining level of activity
—	= No recorded activity
Blank	= Average increase in activity

activity has increased only marginally. Other activities depict quite dissimilar shifts when different firm types are compared. Most notably, software shows above-average increases in Science Park firms but not in off-park firms. Of the 'softer' activities, consultancy has decreased as a source of income in off-park firms and contract research has increased significantly off-park whilst decreasing in southern Science Parks. Contract development has similarly decreased in southern Science Parks, but increased significantly in northern Science Park firms and in off-park firms, most notably in the south. Contract design has decreased in northern off-park firms, but increased significantly (from a lower base) in southern off-park firms, and to a lesser extent, in southern Science Park firms. Other unspecified service activity has increased on Science Parks, whilst decreasing off-park. Testing and analysis presents interesting differences: a static 1 per cent of all southern firms mentioned this category, whereas in the north 8 per cent of off-park and 5 per cent of Science Park firms mentioned this activity. Only in northern off-park firms was any increase recorded.

Thus, the balance of changes between 'hard' and 'soft' activities does not appear to support the Bullock hypothesis unequivocally (i.e. a shift from 'soft' to 'hard' over time — Bullock, 1983) for this group of firms. Only on southern Science Parks is there a shift away from contract research and contract development, but this is not accompanied by a significant rise in product-related activity. It is worth noting, however, that income from licences has increased significantly for all types of firm, and subcontracting production has increased in northern Science Park firms.

7.3.1. Summary of sectors and activities

As a first approximation of the *sectoral* character of the firms, we have seen that there is considerable concentration within the microelectronics and computing sectors, with Science Park firms more heavily involved with computer hardware and systems, and rather more off-park firms involved in microelectronics. Additionally, many other smaller sectors incorporate IT products or rely on IT systems, such as instrumentation and automation. Analysis and testing is the next single largest category, but this is dominated by Science Park firms (14 per cent of Science Park firms compared with 2 per cent of off-park firms). There is a range of other sectors represented, each of which involve less than 5 per cent of all firms. The pharmaceutical, medical, biotechnology and fine chemicals sectors together represent 10 per cent of all firms. Business services involve 5 per cent of Science Park and 2 per cent of off-park firms.

In terms of the activities firms undertake on site, off-park firms are twice as likely to manufacture in their premises as Science Park firms, with the latter being more involved with design and development, and software production and development. Overall, independent firms are involved in manufacture on site to a greater extent than subsidiaries, but off-park independent firms are significantly more involved in manufacture than are Science Park independent firms.

The survey results build up a more detailed picture of the activities from which firms derive income, and how these have changed over time. This analysis shows that the number of activities has increased between their arrival at the site and currently, suggesting some diversification over time. Product-related activity has increased only marginally, whilst licensing and training has increased significantly. 'Softer' activities are in general increasing, although on southern Science Parks there is a shift away from contract R & D. Overall, there is little evidence of any shift from 'soft' to 'hard' activities.

139

7.4. THE TECHNOLOGICAL LEVEL OF FIRMS

The problems of defining 'high' technology have been discussed above. According to most definitions, the majority of firms in this survey would be classified as 'high tech' and, as will be shown, their performance, as a group, is very different from run-of-the-mill firms of a similar age. The particular characteristics for which Science Parks select firms are that they are high technology, R & D-intensive, knowledge-based, or leading-edge businesses. Whilst Science Park firms are assumed to have these characteristics, it is clear that, in practice, there is a grading of technological sophistication. Within this high-tech grouping it is important to distinguish between those at the technological frontiers and those in a less advanced position. In the study, firms were asked to rate their own technological level, and these responses were compared with other indicators of technological content.

7.4.1. Measurement and indices

Firms were asked to rate the technological content and the relative novelty of their products, and/or the knowledge input to their services, in terms of being 'leading-edge', 'advanced', or 'established' technology/knowledge. In the analysis of their responses, firms were divided between leading-edge and merely high-tech according to their own rating. Those firms stating that their product contains leading-edge or advanced technology, or is entirely novel; or firms stating that the service they supply is based on leading-edge knowledge, were all classified as being leading-edge firms. Firms stating that their product contains established technology or has little technological content, or their product is not particularly novel or firms that provide a service which is not unique, were classified as being high-tech firms. Following these criteria, 84 firms (30 per cent) out of the total sample of 284 were rated leading-edge and 183 (64 per cent) high-tech. The remaining 17 firms (6 per cent) are omitted from the following analyses, since they occupied an 'intermediate' status.

Table 7.5 shows that a higher proportion of Science Park firms rate their technical activities as a leading-edge than the off-park sample firms. The difference in self-rating between on- and off-park firms is statistically significant: a higher percentage of Science Park firms perceived themselves to be close to the technological leading

Table 7.5: Technological level (self-rated) on/off park

	Science Park	Off-park	Total
'Leading-edge'			
Number	64	20	84
Percentage	39	20	
'High-tech'			
Number	102	81	183
Percentage	61	80	
'Totals'			
Number	166	101	267
Percentage	100	100	

Note: Significant at the 1 per cent level; 17 'intermediate' firms omitted.

edge than did off-park firms. If such significant differences occur between park and off-park firms, might a similar variation be observed between firms of different ownership status? Comparing independent firms and subsidiary firms, no statistical difference is found, however. The difference in rating does not, then, occur between firms of different status, but between firms on and off parks. If we look at independent firms only, on and off park, the proportion of leading-edge-rated firms is almost identical to that shown in Table 7.5: two-fifths of Science Park independent firms are rated leading-edge compared with one-fifth of off-park independent firms.

Interesting differences emerge when locations are disaggregated between those in the southern part of England (south of a line from Bristol to the Wash) and the rest of the UK, which we will call the 'north' for convenience. Table 7.6 shows the percentage of leading-edge and high-tech firms located on southern and northern parks, and also the off-park firms similarly disaggregated. It can clearly be seen that significantly more southern Science Park firms than northern ones perceive themselves as being leading-edge, but all Science Park firms rate higher than all non-park firms. The percentage of southern park firms rating high-tech is significantly lower than all the other site categories. There is also a considerable variation between individual parks (not tabulated); from 6 per cent of firms rating leading-edge on one park to over 50 per cent of firms on six parks. We were concerned that the inclusion of the Cambridge Science Park might skew the results for the southern parks, since Cambridge is the oldest and largest park surveyed.

Table 7.6: Locational differences in 'leading-edge'/'high-tech' firms

	'Leading-edge'		'High-tech'		Totals	
	No.	%	No.	%	No.	%
Science Parks, south	26	48	20	37	46	85
Science Parks, north	39	30	84	65	123	95
Off-park, south	8	19	32	74	40	93
Off-park, north	11	19	47	81	58	99

Note: Percentages do not sum to 100 because 17 'intermediate' firms are omitted.

Even after removing the Cambridge firms, however, 47 per cent of southern park firms were self-rated leading-edge, significantly more than in other site types.

These results suggest that Science Park firms consider their technology to be more leading edge than the off-park sample, which was chosen to contain comparable firms. A higher percentage of southern park firms rate leading-edge than northern park firms, but there is little difference between independent firms and subsidiary firms. How, then, does this self-assessment accord with other data in the survey which indicates the technological levels of firms?

A range of questions was intended to provide an indication of the technological capability of firms. These include information on the inputs to R & D, such as the percentage of staff employed by firms that are qualified scientists and engineers (QSEs), the level of expenditure on R & D, the R & D strategy of the firm, and research links with universities and other higher educational establishments. Other indications of technological level focus on measures of outputs, such as the launch of new products, and 'intermediate outputs' such as patents.

The first of these indicators is the percentage of qualified scientists and engineers (QSEs) employed by firms. The mean percentage of total employees that are QSEs turns out to be high for all firms: 43.7 per cent for leading-edge firms and 39.5 per cent for high-tech firms, a difference which is not significant. Table 7.7 gives a breakdown of QSE employment. The left-hand column shows the percentage of leading-edge or high-tech firms which have no QSEs employed. It is interesting to note that 14 per cent of leading-edge firms (10 firms) have no QSEs employed. This may be explained by the firms being staffed entirely by directors or relying on consultants. The five remaining columns show QSE intensity

Table 7.7: QSE employment levels of 'leading-edge' and 'high-tech' firms

Per cent QSEs	0	1–20	21–40	41–60	61–80	81–100	Total
'Leading-edge' firms	10 (14)	7 (10)	14 (20)	20 (29)	12 (17)	7 (10)	70 (100)
'High-tech' firms	90 (20)	25 (17)	30 (20)	19 (13)	21 (14)	23 (16)	148 (100)

Note: Percentages (in parentheses) represent the percentage of firms recording each level of QSE employment (QSEs as percentage of total employment).
Significant at 10 per cent level.

Table 7.8: R & D expenditure as a percentage of turnover, 'leading-edge'/'high-tech' firms

	R & D expenditure as percentage of turnover						
	0	1–20	21–40	41–60	61–80	81–100	Total
'Leading-edge' firms	5 (10)	14 (29)	13 (27)	9 (19)	6 (13)	1 (2)	48 (100)
'High-tech' firms	21 (17)	64 (53)	15 (12)	8 (7)	10 (8)	3 (3)	121 (100)

Notes: Percentages (in parentheses) represent the percentage of firms recording each level of R & D expenditure.
Significant at 2 per cent level.

increasing from left to right. For leading-edge and high-tech firms, the percentage of firms with each level of QSE employment is shown. More high-tech firms employ 1–20 per cent QSEs (that is, the lowest level) than leading-edge firms, but significantly more leading-edge firms record 41–80 per cent QSEs. Paradoxically, more high-tech firms than leading-edge have the very high level of 81-100 per cent QSE employment. Thus, although there are differences between the firm types, the leading-edge firms do not show up as being unequivocally more QSE-intensive.

A second indication of the technological capability of firms is the financial resources invested in R & D. These are expressed as a percentage of turnover, and shown in Table 7.8. The left-hand column shows the percentage of firms with zero R & D expenditure, and it is again curious that 10 per cent of leading-edge firms have no R & D budget (those firms refusing to supply information or answering 'not applicable' are not included in this figure). The remainder of the table shows R & D intensity increasing from left to right, with the figures referring to the percentage of firms recording each category of R & D expenditure.

There is a significant difference between the R & D intensity of leading-edge and other high-tech firms. Leading-edge firms are generally concentrated in the middle and lower levels of R & D expenditure, with other high-tech firms at the lower levels. Some 34 per cent of leading-edge firms spend more than 40 per cent of their turnover on R & D compared to 18 per cent of other high-tech firms.

Table 7.9: Thrust or direction of R & D

	No significant research	Product improvement	Extend existing products	Complementary products	Radical new research	No. of firms
'Leading-edge' firms	6 (7)	41 (50)	54 (66)	46 (56)	35 (43)	82
Other 'high-tech' firms	22 (13)	101 (57)	115 (64)	104 (58)	52 (29)	179

Note: Percentages (in parentheses) represent the percentage of firms mentioning each R & D aim. Firms mentioned more than one category, so percentages sum to more than 100.

A further indication of the technological capability of firms is given by their view of the thrust of their R & D activity: to what aims is it directed? Table 7.9 shows the range of responses from leading-edge and other high-tech firms, each firm mentioning more than one R & D aim. Figures are the percentage of firms in each category (leading-edge or high-tech) which mentioned each R & D aim. As can be seen, the main difference between the firms is in the 'no significant research' and 'radical new research' areas, where the leading-edge firms do appear to be more concentrated. However, these responses are themselves unverifiable, and doubts must be raised over the claims around 'radical new research' in small firms which are close to the market.

The seemingly paradoxical 7 per cent of leading-edge firms which do 'no significant research' may actually be a realistic response, given that many of the largest UK electronics companies would claim to be development- rather than research-oriented. Overall, however, the general responses to these questions point to a degree of internal consistency in the leading-edge firms' view of their technological capability.

7.4.2. Technological level and HEI links

Links with the local university or HEI are fundamental to the Science Park ethos and these are more fully discussed in Chapter 8. Nevertheless, in the present context we now examine whether such links figure more prominently in the factors affecting locational choice for leading-edge firms as opposed to other high-tech firms. Firms were asked to identify factors which were important in their choice of location.

Table 7.10: Reasons for choice of site related to the HEI: leading-edge and other high-tech firms

| | All firms | | Science Park firms | |
	'Leading-edge'	Other 'high-tech'	'Leading-edge'	Other 'high-tech'
Key founder at local HEI	14 (17)	30 (17)	6 (14)	14 (21)
Access to HEI facilities	37 (46)	58 (32)	25 (60)	32 (48)
Recruitment of graduates	17 (21)	26 (14)	7 (17)	18 (27)
Prestige of HEI	22 (27)	43 (24)	17 (41)	25 (37)
Prestige/image of site	48 (59)	98 (54)	30 (71)	50 (75)

Note: Figures refer to the number of firms mentioning each factor. Figures in parentheses represent the percentage of all firms in that column mentioning each factor (firms mentioned more than one factor, so percentages cannot be summed). The table presents only that 19 per cent of responses to the question on reasons for choice of site which relate to the HEI, plus prestige and image of site.

Table 7.10 shows the locational choice factors which relate to the HEI. It compares leading-edge and other high-tech firms, for all firms and for Science Park firms only. The first row of the table shows that a smaller proportion of Science Park 'leading-edge' firms mentioned a key founder at the HEI as being a relevant factor in location choice than any other category of firm. A marginally higher percentage of leading-edge firms mentioned 'access to university facilities' than did other high-tech firms, but overall this was the second most frequently mentioned reason. The 'recruitment of graduates' category offers a curious paradox: across all the firms surveyed, more leading-edge firms than other high-tech ones thought this factor relevant, but on Science Parks, more other high-tech companies mentioned this factor. Marginally more leading-edge firms than other high-tech firms, both on and off-park, considered the 'prestige of HEI' to be relevant, but in the 'prestige and image of site' category, there is no clear difference between leading-edge and other high-tech. Roughly double the proportion of firms thought the prestige of the site to be relevant, compared with those mentioning the prestige of the HEI. Overall, then, it was the prestige and image of the site which was the most frequently mentioned factor influencing choice of location.

How do these reasons for location choice translate into actual links between firms and the HEI? Do leading-edge firms show a higher degree of research linkage with the local HEI in practice? A subsequent question invited respondents to state what links with the HEI had occurred since locating on their present site. Table 7.11 shows that there are only minor differences between leading-edge and other high-tech firms in terms of their HEI links, but that informal links with academics were the most frequently mentioned overall.

In general, leading-edge firms do score higher percentages, most noticeably in their 'employment of academics', but the differences are not very great. Interestingly, on Science Parks, more other high-tech firms mentioned 'informal links with academics' than did leading-edge firms. Informal links have been associated by Segal Quince (1985) with the successful NTBFs in the Cambridge area, and would thus be expected to have importance for leading-edge firms. The fact that this result is not obtained in the current survey indicates the hazards of generalising about UK Science Parks from the experience of Cambridge alone. Respondents were also asked to select the three 'most important' links with the HEI. The results for Science Park firms only are shown in Table 7.12. Significantly, more other high-tech firms thought that informal links with academics were among the three most important links with the HEI than did leading-edge firms. In the more formal linkages, more leading-edge firms thought the employment of academics and access to equipment important than did other high-tech firms.

Overall, the above indicators together suggest that there is some,

Table 7.11: Links with the HEI

| | All firms | | Science Park firms | |
	'Leading-edge'	'High-tech'	'Leading-edge'	'High-tech'
Informal links with academics	50 (69)	95 (66)	29 (71)	45 (76)
Employment of academics	29 (40)	47 (33)	17 (42)	20 (34)
Sponsorship of research	15 (21)	23 (16)	9 (22)	8 (14)
Access to equipment	31 (43)	56 (39)	19 (46)	25 (42)
Number of firms	73	143	41	59

Note: Figures refer to the number of firms mentioning each factor (except last row). Figures in parentheses represent the percentage of all firms in that column mentioning each factor (firms mentioned more than one factor, so percentages cannot be summed).

Table 7.12: The most important links between Science Park firms and the local HEI

	'Leading-edge'	'High-tech'
Informal links with academics	18 (44)	37 (62)
Employment of academics	16 (39)	15 (25)
Sponsorship of research	4 (10)	7 (12)
Access to equipment	15 (37)	17 (28)
Number of firms	41	60

Note: Figures refer to the number of firms mentioning each factor. Figures in parentheses represent the percentage of all firms in that column mentioning each factor (firms mentioned more than one factor, so percentages cannot be summed).

but nevertheless qualified, support for the identification of a leading-edge group of firms. In particular, their generally higher R & D expenditure as a percentage of turnover and a higher percentage employment of QSEs suggest a higher level of R & D effort, arguably a prerequisite for technological capability. Science Park leading-edge firms' greater emphasis on formal links with the HEIs offsets their rather surprising lower level of emphasis on informal links with academics compared with that given by other high-tech respondents.

7.4.3. Technological level and outputs

Having considered the inputs to R & D, this section compares the outputs of leading-edge and other high-tech firms. One measure of output is the level of patenting activity in firms (although there are problems using patents as an indicator, notably sectoral differences in the use of patenting). Table 7.13 shows that a higher percentage of leading-edge firms than other high-tech firms took out one or more patents in the preceding two years, with the difference more pronounced in the earlier, rather than the more recent, year.

Table 7.13: Patenting performance of leading-edge/high-tech firms

	% of firms with one or more patents	
	Last year	Previous year
Leading-edge	35	31
High-tech	27	21

This finding raises the question as to what kinds of activities leading-edge and other high-tech firms are involved in, in which industrial sectors they perform, and how these differ. Table 7.14 shows the broad classification of firm activities on a comparable basis to that of Table 7.2. Table 7.14 shows that fewer leading-edge firms are involved with manufacture and production — 22 against 27 per cent of other high-tech firms. The next largest group is those firms involved in 'design and development', with little difference between leading-edge and other high-tech firms. High-tech firms are more likely to be involved in 'analysis' or 'service and repair' activities. The finding which is least consistent with the concept of leading edge is 'warehousing and distribution', in which, curiously, a higher percentage of leading-edge firms is involved.

Using the same classification of industrial sectors as in Table 7.1, Table 7.15 shows that there are also some sectoral differences between leading-edge and other high-tech firms. Some 49 per cent of leading-edge firms are in IT-related sectors, compared with 56

Table 7.14: Main activity of firm on present site, leading-edge and other high-tech compared

| | 'Leading-edge' | | 'High-tech' | |
	No.	%	No.	%
Manufacture/production	21	22	66	27
Design and development	21	22	46	19
Research	5	5	12	5
Marketing/sales	7	7	17	7
Warehousing/distribution	14	15	22	9
Servicing/repair	5	5	30	12
Analysis	3	3	14	6
Consultancy	7	7	9	4
Training	3	3	7	3
Software	4	4	6	2
Other	4	4	16	7
Totals	93	100	245	100

Table 7.15: Industrial sectors of leading-edge and other high-tech firms

| | 'Leading-edge' | | 'High-tech' | |
	No.	%	No.	%
Computer related:				
Hardware and systems	19	23	44	24
Software	15	18	23	13
Microelectronics	7	8	34	19
Instrumentation	2	2	8	4
Automation	3	4	10	6
Electrical equipment	1	1	4	2
Medical	4	5	2	1
Pharmaceuticals	2	2	6	3
Fine chemicals	0	0	1	1
Biotechnology	5	6	6	3
Mechanical	1	1	1	1
Environmental	3	4	9	5
Design and development	6	7	6	3
Analysis and testing	12	14	13	7
Technical services	2	2	5	3
Financial and business	2	2	9	5
Other	0	0	2	1
Totals	84	100	183	100

Note: Each firm has been classified into one category. X-tab. is not significant.

149

Table 7.16: Most important activities as a source of income

	'Leading-edge'		'High-tech'	
	Initial	Current	Initial	Current
Products	49	61	58	68
Software	39	49	37	43
Consultancy	49	58	47	53
Contract research	25	31	15	20
Contract development	35	40	24	29
Contract design	22	26	21	28
Subcontract production	1	3	11	14
Testing and analysis	16	15	14	18
Licences	13	21	13	18
Training	16	23	25	35
Service and repair	3	4	5	6
Other	4	3	7	5

Note: Figures are percentage of firms (high-tech/low-tech) recording each activity. Firms mentioned more than one activity, so percentages cannot be summed.

per cent of other high-tech firms. Leading-edge firms are rather more involved in software, medical, biotechnology, design, development and analysis and testing; whereas, perhaps surprisingly, significantly more other high-tech firms are involved in the microelectronics sector.

It will be recalled from Table 7.3 that an analysis was presented of those activities from which the business derived income. Table 7.16 shows this range of activities, for both leading-edge and other high-tech firms, distinguishing, as before, between 'current' and 'on arrival'. It is clear that currently, products are a source of income for 61 per cent of leading-edge and 68 per cent of other high-tech firms. This suggests, in relation to the above discussion on manufacture and production on site, that leading-edge firms are more likely to be manufacturing elsewhere, and warehousing and distributing from the site in question. We will return to this point below. The principal areas from which leading-edge firms are much more likely than high-tech firms to derive income is in 'contract research' and 'contract development'. 'Consultancy' is an income source for over half of all firms, with little difference between leading-edge and other high-tech firms.

Computer software has been included as a separate category, although software is clearly a product. Indeed, one respondent insisted that software production should be classed as manufacture (others maintained that 'all software development is R & D', or even 'research'). Thus, a separate category is useful. Almost half of leading-edge firms obtain income from software (Table 7.16), although from Table 7.15, it appears that only 5 per cent listed software production as a 'main activity' on site. Some 43 per cent of other high-tech firms obtain income from software, but only 3 per cent regard software production as the main activity.

There is a significant difference between the two groups of firms in the 'subcontracting production' category, with the percentage of other high-tech firms recording this almost five times as high as for leading-edge firms. This is perhaps understandable since leading-edge firms are unlikely to be earning much income from providing subcontracting facilities such as jobbing engineering.

A high percentage of all firms obtain income from software (49 per cent of leading-edge and 43 per cent of other high-tech firms in Table 7.16), but very few firms (5 and 3 per cent respectively) regard software production as a principal activity on site. This may suggest that much software is bought in to the firms as packages and marketed or developed externally by subcontractors, or licensed out to provide income.

In terms of changes over time, Table 7.16 again shows that there is *little* evidence of leading-edge firms moving from 'soft' activities, such as consultancy, to 'hard' activities such as manufacture, the pattern suggested by Bullock for high technology development in the US (Bullock, 1983). In fact virtually all activities have increased and soft activities have increased at approximately the same rate as hard activities.

The picture that emerges is that leading-edge firms, in comparison with other high-tech firms, are:

— rather more involved in software, medical, biotechnology, design, development, and analysis and testing
— less involved in the microelectronic sector
— less likely to obtain income from products
— less likely to manufacture on site
— increasingly more likely to obtain income from licences
— more likely to gain income from contract R & D
— more involved in warehousing and distribution on site
— less likely to be involved in servicing and repairs on site
— less likely to obtain income from training
— less likely to obtain income from testing and analysis

151

7.5. CONCLUSION

This chapter has looked at the technological aspects of Science Park firms, and a similar group of firms located elsewhere, for comparison. It first looked at the industrial sectors and the activities in which firms are involved. There is a clear concentration of firms within the microelectronics and computing sectors, within which Science Park firms are more involved with computer hardware and systems than off-park firms, but the latter are more likely to be involved in microelectronics. Overall, more than half of all firms are primarily located within the microelectronics and computing sectors with, in addition, other sectors such as instrumentation and automation also using IT. Some 14 per cent of Science Park firms are primarily in analysis and testing, compared with only 2 per cent of off-park firms. A range of other sectors each contain less than 5 per cent of firms, with the pharmaceuticals, medical, biotechnology and fine chemicals sectors together accounting for around 10 per cent of all firms.

The final part of the chapter examined the technological level of the survey firms. The firms were divided into leading-edge and other high-tech according to their own assessment, and this assessment checked against other indicators. A small intermediate group were excluded. A significantly higher percentage of Science Park firms rated their technology leading-edge than did off-park firms. The alternative indicators in the data suggest that there is only qualified support for the leading-edge firms' selection. Nevertheless, a range of differences in the performance characteristics of leading-edge and other high-tech firms was found. Most importantly, the survey could find no evidence that leading-edge firms which had located on Science Parks had stronger informal links with academics, than other high-tech firms, even though this has been emphasised in studies of Cambridge. We also found that there was little evidence amongst firms surveyed, of a clear movement from 'soft' to 'hard' products.

8

The Technological Characteristics of Firms: Performance and Impact

8.1 INTRODUCTION

The previous chapter considered the activities undertaken by firms in this survey, and it distinguished principally between those which considered themselves to be at the frontiers of knowledge and those which, by their own admission, felt themselves to be less technically sophisticated. This chapter develops the analysis by considering R & D inputs and outputs. It will be recalled from Part I that the complexity of the relationship between R & D inputs and outputs was acknowledged and that at least part of the *raison d'être* of Science Parks was to improve the 'productivity' of research by obtaining a greater quantity of output from a given level of input. For this reason it is essential to understand the factors affecting this productivity, such as the competitive environment which faces the firm, and to identify measures of output such as patenting or new product launches.

A second topic of interest is the impact which the Science Park has upon the wider economic environment. This is examined in two ways. The first is by reporting the extent to which surveyed firms felt influenced by the immediate presence of an HEI and the benefits which this presence provides to park tenants. Secondly, it examines the impact which all firms in the survey had upon the wider economic community both in selling their own products and purchasing those of others.

8.2 R & D INPUTS AND OUTPUTS

This section examines firstly the *inputs* to the innovation process which are committed by firms — the resources in terms of equipment, facilities and human expertise which firms invest in the R & D process. It then looks at the *outputs* from firms' R & D. The purpose of R & D is to develop new products and processes, but since only 14 per cent of Science Park firms manufacture on site, process innovations will not be important. Attention is therefore concentrated on product innovation.

Patents are a second measure of output from R & D, which provide a useful indicator of innovativeness. They are, however, only an intermediate output, and there are problems with using patents as an indicator of cross-sectoral innovative activity (see Pavitt (1982), Taylor and Silberston (1973)). Nevertheless, the extent to which firms on and off Science Parks patent is a useful comparison in this context.

8.3 R & D INPUTS

8.3.1 Qualified scientists and engineers

The proportion of qualified scientists and engineers (QSEs) employed in a firm (as a percentage of total employment) is one indication of R & D effort and intensity. Technological capability and innovativeness has been linked to the percentage of QSEs employed, in many studies, with one recent study even defining 'high technology' sectors in terms of the percentage of QSEs employed (Markusen *et al.*, 1986). Hence the proportion of QSEs to other employees in a firm can be used as an indicator of 'R & D intensity': the higher the percentage of QSEs, the greater the R & D effort. Table 8.1 shows the percentage of QSEs employed in Science Park and off-park firms, so that R & D intensity in terms of percentages of QSEs increases from left to right. The figures refer to the number of firms with each level of R & D intensity, and that figure is also expressed (in parentheses) as a percentage of all firms either on or off-park.

It is clear that Science Park firms have significantly higher R & D intensity in terms of QSEs employed than off-park firms. Fewer park firms employ *no* QSEs (17 against 23 per cent for the off-park firms), and of those firms that do employ QSEs, park firms are more likely to employ a higher percentage of qualified staff. These differences are statistically significant at the 1 per cent level.

Looking at regional differences between sites, Table 8.2 shows

Table 8.1: Percentage QSEs in firms on and off parks

	Zero QSE employment	QSEs as a percentage of total employment					
		1–20	21–40	41–60	61–80	81–100	Total
On parks	27	12	30	29	31	28	157
	(17)	(8)	(19)	(19)	(20)	(18)	(100)
Off parks	18	21	16	13	4	5	77
	(23)	(27)	(21)	(17)	(5)	(6)	(100)

Notes: Figures are number of firms (percentages in parentheses) recording each level of employment. Significant at 1 per cent level. Percentages do not sum exactly to 100 due to rounding.

Table 8.2: QSE employment: locational comparison

	Zero QSE employment	QSEs as a percentage of total employment					
		1–20	21–40	41–60	61–80	81–100	Total
Science Parks South	5	4	10	8	8	10	45
	(11)	(9)	(22)	(18)	(18)	(22)	(100)
Science Parks North	22	8	21	21	23	18	113
	(20)	(7)	(19)	(19)	(20)	(16)	(100)
Off-parks South	5	10	9	6	2	2	34
	(15)	(30)	(27)	(18)	(6)	(6)	(100)
Off-parks North	13	11	6	7	2	3	42
	(31)	(26)	(14)	(17)	(5)	(7)	(100)

Notes: Figures are number (percentage) of firms in each category, recording each level of QSE employment. Significant at 1 per cent level. Percentages do not sum to 100 because of rounding errors.

that Science Parks in the south generally employ a higher percentage of QSEs, and are less likely to employ no QSEs, than are parks in the rest of the UK. On this measure, southern parks are thus more R & D intensive. In the off-park sites, northern firms are more likely to employ no QSEs, and generally record lower QSE levels.

Table 8.3 shows R & D intensity as defined above, but for independent firms alone. Figures refer to the number (percentages) of independent firms both on and off Science Parks, which have the various levels of QSE intensity. The differences between the Science Park and non-Science Park firms are statistically significant at the

Table 8.3: Percentage QSEs in independent firms, on and off Science Parks

	Zero QSE employment	QSEs as a percentage of total employment					
		1–20	21–40	41–60	61–80	81–100	Total
On-park firms	16 (14)	9 (8)	23 (20)	22 (20)	23 (20)	20 (18)	113 (100)
Off-park firms	17 (24)	19 (27)	14 (20)	12 (17)	4 (6)	5 (7)	71 (100)

Notes: Percentages (in parentheses) represent the percentage of firms in each site type recording each level of QSE employment. Not all figures sum to 100 because of rounding. Significant at 1 per cent level.

1 per cent level. Independent Science Park firms have significantly fewer firms with zero QSEs, and a significantly higher proportion of independent Science Park firms employ the highest percentages of QSEs (61–100 per cent). Only in the category 1–20 per cent QSEs does the independent off-park firm have greater representation. Thus, on this measure, it would appear that Science Park independent firms are more R & D intensive in terms of percentage of QSEs employed.

8.3.2 R & D effort — expenditure

The percentage of QSEs employed is only one measure of R & D input. A more conventional measure of inputs to R & D is financial, with gross levels of R & D investment being expressed as a percentage of turnover. As can be seen in Table 8.4, for those off-park firms with some R & D expenditure, expenditure tends to be a lower percentage of turnover than for park firms. Thus, for example, 28 per cent of park firms recorded very high percentages of R & D expenditure (over 40 per cent of turnover) compared with only 15 per cent of off-park firms.

This apparently greater R & D intensity may reflect the fact that a number of Science Park firms are quite young, and do not have any substantial income, thus inflating the ratio of R & D expenditure to turnover. It may also be the case that in smaller Science Park firms, R & D expenditure is assumed to be 'total running costs', if no production or marketing is yet undertaken. This may distort the

Table 8.4: Level of R & D expenditure in Science Park and off-park firms

| | O | R & D as a percentage of turnover | | | | | |
		1–20	21–40	41–60	61–80	81–100	Totals
Park firms	16	38	20	11	12	5	102
	(16)	(37)	(20)	(11)	(12)	(5)	(100)
Off-park firms	11	41	9	6	5	0	72
	(15)	(57)	(13)	(8)	(7)	(0)	(100)

Notes: Figures in parentheses represent the percentage of firms in each type of site which record each level of R & D expenditure. Note not all figures sum to 100 because of rounding errors.

comparison with larger established companies which can more easily draw boundaries around the 'R & D department' and thus R & D expenditure.

To summarise, then, there do appear to be differences in R & D intensity between on- and off-Park firms, but these should not be exaggerated, and may partly reflect differences in the age of the two samples.

8.4 R & D OUTPUTS

8.4.1 Patents

Patents are often used as an indicator of technical development, although there are problems with cross-sectoral comparisons. The propensity to patent varies between sectors, between firms and between countries (Taylor and Silberston, 1973; Pavitt, 1982). Despite the above reservations, patents can provide a limited indicator of technological developments. The current survey, however, has the disadvantage that the firms are often very new, and may not yet have reached patenting stage. Furthermore, about 15 per cent are involved in software, production of which cannot be patented.

Overall, 28 per cent of firms on Science Parks have lodged a patent in the last two years, compared with only 19 per cent of firms not on a Park. However, there is considerable difference between southern and northern Science Parks in terms of patenting. Some 41 per cent of southern Science Park firms have taken out one or more

Table 8.5: Patenting activity

| | Science Park | | Off-park | |
	South	North	North	South
No patents	32 (59)	100 (78)	47 (81)	35 (81)
One or more patents	22 (41)	29 (23)	11 (19)	8 (19)
Totals	(100)	(100)	(100)	(100)

Notes: Percentages (in parentheses) represent the percentage of firms in each site type with/without patents in the last two years — significant at the 5 per cent level.

patents in the last two years, compared with 23 per cent of northern park firms. Table 8.5 shows that it is firms located on Science Parks in the south that were most likely to patent. For off-park firms there are no regional differences.

To test the extent to which these results depend upon differences in age of firm, a more detailed analysis of patenting activity was undertaken, based on information on patents filed in the last twelve months (up to Summer 1986), and patents filed in the previous twelve months. Firms which were less than one year old were omitted from the 'last twelve months' category, and firms less than two years old were left out of the 'previous twelve months' category. Exceptions were made in the case of younger firms which *had* taken out patents: these were included. In this case it was found that a marginally higher percentage of park firms patented in the last twelve months than off-park firms.

The hypothesis that patent activity was being held artificially low because firms were engaged in activities which cannot be patented was also tested. Hence, firms engaged in software and financial and business services as a main activity were excluded. Table 8.6 shows that the proportion of eligible firms which have patented has risen marginally, so that over one-third of Science Park firms took out one or more patent last year, against 22 per cent of off-park firms. Even so, the tendency of these firms to patent does not appear to be significantly affected by being located on or off a Science Park; when the previous year is taken into account, the final column shows that 20 per cent of Science Park firms took out one or more patents compared with 19 per cent of off-park firms.

158

Table 8.6: Patenting activity in selected firms[a] on and off Science Parks

	Firms with one or more patent last year[b]	Firms with one or more patent previous year[c]
Science Park	34 (34)	16 (20)
Off-park	17 (22)	13 (19)

Notes: a. Firms whose principal activity was software or business services were excluded.
b. Firms less than one year old omitted.
c. Firms less than two years old omitted.

Table 8.7: Patenting activity in last year and employment of QSEs in selected firms[a]

	Zero QSE employment	QSEs as a percentage of total employment					
		1–20	21–40	41–60	61–80	81–100	Totals
No patents	17 (16)	16 (15)	22 (21)	24 (22)	16 (15)	12 (11)	107 (100)
One or more patents	1 (3)	6 (15)	15 (36)	5 (13)	6 (15)	7 (18)	39 (100)

Notes: a Not including software and business services firms. Very young firms not included. Figures are the number of firms (percentages in parentheses) at each level of QSE employment. Significant at 11 per cent level.

8.4.1.1 Patents and R & D effort

Having established the extent of patenting activity, attention now turns to the question of how R & D activity affects patenting. Do those firms with the highest R & D effort produce the most patents?

8.4.1.2 Patenting and QSE employment

To examine the relationship between patenting and QSE employment, account has to be taken of the relative youth of many of the firms, and the fact that activities such as software development are not patentable. Table 8.7 shows patenting activity in the last twelve months related to QSE employment, for those firms which were over one year old. Firms which are engaged principally in software

159

and business service activities are omitted. On this basis, patenting performance in the last twelve months does appear to correlate weakly with QSE employment. Interestingly, this analysis excludes 13 of the 14 firms which had no QSE employment but which did record patents. One explanation for this may be that, contrary to conventional wisdom, very young firms may record patents.

8.4.1.3 Patents and R & D expenditure

Those firms with high levels of R & D investment might be expected to be those which tend to patent since R & D expenditure is a measure of input, and patents a proxy measure of output. Some 174 firms provided information on both R & D expenditure expressed as a percentage of turnover, and on patents. Of these firms, 19 per cent of those with one or more patent recorded no R & D expenditure at all. Of those firms known to have some R & D expenditure, only 17 per cent have recorded one or more patent (25 out of 147 firms).

Table 8.8: Patents in the last year related to R & D expenditure as a percentage of turnover

| | R & D expenditure as a percentage of turnover | | | | | |
	Zero	1–20	21–40	41–60	61+	Totals
Firms with no patents	14 (16)	46 (52)	15 (17)	6 (7)	8 (9)	89 (100)
Firms with one or more patent	5 (16)	8 (26)	4 (13)	5 (16)	9 (29)	31 (100)

Notes: Software and business service firms omitted. Firms less than one year old omitted. Significant at 5 per cent level.

As with the previous section, it is important to eliminate those firms which are primarily engaged in software or business services, and those which are less than one year old, in order to exclude those which cannot be expected to have patented in the twelve months prior to the survey. Table 8.8 presents these results, which show a positive relationship between R & D expenditure levels and patenting (significant at the 5 per cent level). Patenting activity broadly increases with R & D expenditure as a proportion of turnover. Again, however, those firms which have patents but no R & D expenditure are something of an anomaly.

We may conclude from this that:

(a) The majority of firms which patent have some R & D expenditure, but having no R & D expenditure does not preclude patenting.

(b) Increased R & D effort in terms of expenditure as a percentage of turnover does appear to be associated with patenting activity. This is particularly significant when very young firms, and firms involved primarily in activities which are not patentable, are eliminated from the analysis.

8.4.2 New product launches

For the majority of Science Park firms undertaking R & D, the ultimate purpose is the launch of new products (remembering that process innovation is not likely to be significant in Science Park firms), although some firms undertake contract R & D for client companies. Only twelve firms in our survey (4 per cent) undertake R & D and design as a main activity, and so it is valid to relate R & D effort to product launch for the sample as a whole. Measures of R & D effort include levels of employment of R & D staff, and levels of R & D expenditure.

8.4.2.1 Employment of QSEs and new employment launches

Out of 284 firms surveyed, 234 provided information on new product launch, together with data on the employment of QSEs. Firms were asked how many new products they had launched in the last two years, either within their existing market or in a new market. Some 143 firms (61 per cent) had launched at least one new product in the previous two years. There does not appear at first sight to be an association between QSE employment and new product launch.

Thirty firms, one-fifth of those launching new products, had done so whilst employing no QSEs at all. Additionally, there is no correlation between increasing levels of QSE employment (as a percentage of total employment) and product launch. This latter finding may be explained by the fact that many firms are newly established, and have not yet brought products to the market.

The data was therefore analysed with all firms under one year old removed. The result for the remaining 178 firms launching new products in existing markets is shown in Table 8.9. It can be seen again that 25 firms having no QSEs still managed to launch new products, but that overall, firms which employ more QSEs record

161

Table 8.9: New product launches in existing markets, related to QSE employment, for firms over one year old

	Zero	1–20	21–40	41–60	61–80	81–100	Totals
			Percentage QSEs employed				
No new product	7	3	8	6	6	11	41
launched	(17)	(7)	(20)	(15)	(15)	(27)	(100)
One or more	25	23	27	26	25	11	137
new products	(18)	(17)	(20)	(20)	(18)	(8)	(100)

Note: Significant at 5 per cent level.

rather better levels of product launches than those with few QSEs, except in the final column. This latter result is the most surprising, showing that only half of those firms with the highest proportion of QSE employment (i.e. over 81 per cent) have launched new products in existing markets.

8.4.2.2 R & D expenditure and new product launches

Eliminating those firms which are less than one year old from the analysis, Table 8.10 shows R & D expenditure related to product launches in new markets for 143 firms. It can be seen that eight out of 24 (33 per cent) firms with zero R & D expenditure have product launches. It is also apparent that despite eliminating firms established for less than one year, the firms with relatively high levels of R & D expenditure are not notably more likely to introduce new products in new markets. One-half of the firms with over 80 per cent of turnover invested in R & D have launched no new products, and for those firms spending over 60 per cent of turnover on R & D, only 55 per cent have launched new products.

Table 8.10: New product launches in new markets, related to R & D expenditure as a percentage of turnover

	Zero	1–20	21–40	41–60	61+	Totals
		R & D expenditure as a percentage of turnover				
No new product	16	20	7	7	5	55
launched	(29)	(36)	(13)	(13)	(9)	(100)
One or more	8	45	19	10	6	88
new products	(9)	(51)	(22)	(11)	(7)	(100)
launched						

Note: Significant at 10 per cent level.

Thus, when firms established for less than one year are eliminated from the analysis, it is apparent that:

(a) firms with zero R & D expenditure are not inhibited from launching new products in existing markets;

(b) more than two-thirds of firms which launch new products expend between 1 and 40 per cent of turnover on R & D; and that

(c) higher levels of R & D expenditure do not correspond to higher levels of new product launch. Of those firms spending in excess of 40 per cent of turnover on R & D, fewer than expected launch new products. This is most noticeable in new markets.

8.4.2.3 Patents and new product launches

Those firms which have patented might be expected to be also those which have brought new products to the market. Table 8.11 clearly supports that hypothesis and is significant at the 1 per cent level. This does not mean, of course, that the launching of new products or patenting are mutually exclusive activities. Of the 214 firms with no patents, 55 per cent had launched new products. Of the 172 firms with new products, 69 per cent had no patents. This suggests that patenting alone is not a perfect indicator of technological development, although a lack of patents may suggest that the products are not particularly novel.

Table 8.11: New products and patent activity over the past two years

	No new products	One or more new products	Totals
No patents	96 (45)	118 (55)	214 (75)
One or more patents	16 (23)	54 (77)	70 (25)
Totals	112 (39)	172 (61)	284 (100)

Note: Significant at 1 per cent level.

Table 8.12: Competition and product launch

Number of competitors	Firms which have launched new products		Firms which have not launched new products		% of firms with new products at each level of competition
	No. of firms	% of firms	No. of firms	% of firms	
0	17	12	14	16	55
1	6	4	2	2	75
2	10	7	11	12	48
3	23	16	14	16	62
4	20	14	7	8	74
5	8	6	9	10	47
6	16	11	7	8	70
7–12	23	16	9	10	72
13–20	6	4	4	4	60
21–40	4	3	3	3	57
41–100	6	4	4	4	60
100+	4	3	5	6	44
		100		100	

Note: Some 62 per cent of all firms have launched new products in the last two years.

8.4.2.4 Competition and new product launches

In Chapter 2 it was noted that some commentators have argued that a competitive market is a stimulus to innovation, whereas others have argued that oligopolistic conditions are a greater stimulus. To test these hypotheses, all firms were asked to indicate the number of firms with which they competed on a regular basis. This is fully examined in Chapter 10. However Table 8.12 compares the level of competition, in terms of the number of competing firms, with respondent firms' propensity to launch new products. The right-hand column shows the percentages of firms at each level of competition that have introduced one or more products in the last two years. This figure should be compared with the overall figure of 62 per cent. It is apparent that this percentage does not increase as competition rises (i.e. down the table). This suggests that there is little support for the view that competition in the market place (as measured here) is a powerful stimulus to innovation. It should be noted, of course, that the *number* of competing firms is only one indication of the intensity of the competitive environment (IBM, for example, has been described as being not 'the competition', but 'the environment' by rival computer manufacturers).

Even when the size of competing firms is taken into account,

Table 8.13: Size of competing firms and product launch

Size of competitors	Firms which have launched new products		Firms which have not launched new products		% of firms with new products at each level of competitors' size
	No. of firms	% of firms	No. of firms	% of firms	
Large	51	39	25	29	67
Medium	32	24	19	22	63
Small	35	27	23	27	60
All	5	4	11	13	31
Med. & Sm.	2	2	1	1	67
Lg. & Sm.	4	3	5	6	44
Lg. & Med.	1	1	1	1	50
Total	130	100	85	100	

there does not appear to be any clear relation between the size of competing firms and propensity to launch new products. Table 8.13, however, shows that there is a tendency for those firms which have primarily large competitors to launch new products, compared with firms with other sizes of competition. Thus, 39 per cent of firms which have launched new products compete with large firms, compared with 29 per cent of firms with no new products. Large firm competition does not therefore inhibit product launch, and may encourage it.

8.4.2.5 Competitive advantage and new product launches

Table 8.14 compares those firms which have launched new products in the last two years with those which have not, in terms of their assessment of where their competitive advantages lie. The various categories of firms' source of competitive advantage are listed. Firms were asked to identify the three categories in which they felt they competed most effectively. The responses of firms which have launched one or more new products in the last two years can be compared in the table with those firms which have not launched new products. The responses appear very similar between the two types of firm, with the most often-mentioned categories being 'flexibility to respond to customers' needs', 'performance and reliability', and 'unique product or service'.

The final column shows the percentage of firms in each category of competitive advantage which have launched one or more new product in the last two years. These figures should be compared with the overall figure of 62 per cent. It can be seen that the categories

Table 8.14: Firms' competitive advantages related to new product launch

Criteria	Firms with no new products n	Firms with no new products %	Firms with one or more new products n	Firms with one or more new products %	% with new product
Design	21	7	34	8	62
Unique product/service	40	13	59	14	60
Leading-edge technology	23	8	26	6	53
Performance/reliability	57	19	70	16	55
Delivery/availability	21	7	21	5	50
Sales channels	4	1	5	1	50
Reputation/image	27	9	44	10	62
Price	23	8	38	8	62
Marketing/promotion	6	2	10	2	63
Flexibility/response	54	18	77	18	59
Overall quality	2	1	10	2	83
Other	26	9	41	9	61
Total		100		100	

Note: Percentages do not sum to 100 due to rounding errors.

of competitive advantage which have a lower than expected percentage of firms with new products are 'delivery and availability' and 'sales channels', and, to a lesser extent, 'application of leading-edge technology'. The only category in which those firms that have launched new products are significantly overrepresented is in the 'overall quality' category: 83 per cent of firms mentioning this category having launched new products.

8.4.2.6 New product launches: summary

This section on product launches has yielded the following conclusions:

(1) The employment of QSEs is not a prerequisite for launching new products. The likelihood of a firm launching a new product is not associated with increasing QSE employment levels.

(2) Firms with zero R & D expenditure are *less* likely to introduce new products than those with positive levels of expenditure. Low and middle levels of expenditure on R & D are associated with high rates of new product introduction, but high levels of R & D expenditure are associated with low

rates, especially for the introduction of new products in new markets. This may reflect the youth of these firms.

(3) The number of competing firms in a market did not appear to be associated with different rates of product launch.

(4) The likelihood of a firm bringing a new product to the market was strongly correlated with its likelihood of having filed a patent in the last two years.

(5) The likelihood of new product launches was higher for firms that compete with large firms, rather than for those who either competed with small firms or who felt they did not encounter any competition.

(6) Those firms who felt that their competitive strengths were in the overall quality of the product were more likely to introduce new products than those who felt their competitive strengths lay elsewhere.

8.5 LINKS WITH HIGHER EDUCATIONAL INSTITUTIONS (HEIs)

The linkage between Science Park firms and the host university or HEI is fundamental to the concept of Science Parks. The HEI is seen as a major resource which firms may tap into and draw upon, and also from which new technology-based enterprises might spring. HEIs vary in the range of expertise and strengths which they offer. In different universities certain departments strongly relate to industry, whilst others do not. Those closest to industry might be expected to be the engineering and electronics disciplines, or they might be service-oriented disciplines such as management or occupational health and safety.

The form of linkages between individual firms and the HEI might include:

— the transfer of people, including founder-members of firms, key personnel and staff into employment in firms;
— the transfer of knowledge (often embodied in the above personnel);
— contract or sponsoring research in the university by researchers and students;
— contract development, design, analysis, testing, evaluation etc.;
— access to university facilities such as libraries, and especially journals;

167

— less formal interchange with academics which may lead to the important exchange of information, or provide access to a network of people and resources.

The value of informal contact is difficult to assess, but commentators such as Segal Quince (1985) place great emphasis on the importance of informal contacts in the growth of the 'Cambridge phenomenon', although McDonald (1987) has questioned the generality of this finding. It is clear that for small, start-up firms with very limited resources, the availability of university facilities and expertise should provide considerable advantages. Small firms would find it difficult to keep up with journal subscriptions alone (one university technological department's journal budget might exceed £30,000 per annum), irrespective of the cost of installing large computers or specialist equipment.

What, then, are the nature and extent of linkages between Science Park firms and the host HEI, and how do these compare with off-park firms? A range of questions was asked in this survey, which attempted to find out how far firms use the university as a resource, and what level of importance they placed upon certain types of linkages.

8.5.1 Choice of site

Firms were asked which were the most important three factors in their choice of location on their present site. These responses were prompted by a card containing 19 factors which might have influenced location decisions, but many interviewees added additional factors. Of all the responses to the question on the factors influencing choice of location, 19.2 per cent related to the local HEI. There is a marked difference, which is to be expected, between park and off-park firms: 24.9 per cent of responses from Science Park firms related to the HEI, compared with only 7.2 per cent of responses from off-park firms. There was also a difference between responses from southern firms and northern firms. Table 8.15 shows this in detail. Interestingly, whilst northern Science Park firms mentioned HEI links slightly more than southern park firms, for off-park firms the position was marginally reversed, with southern firms mentioning HEI links more often.

Table 8.16 shows the advantages which interviewees mentioned as being important reasons for their choice of site, and which related

Table 8.15: Percentage of location reasons that relate to the local HEI

Firm type	%
All Science Park firms	24.9
Southern Science Park firms	21.8
Northern Science Park firms	25.9
All off-park firms	7.2
Southern off-park firms	9.0
Northern off-park firms	6.0
All firms	19.2

Table 8.16: Reasons for site choice related to HEI

	Key founder worked in HEI	Access to HEI facilities	Recruitment of new graduates	Prestige of university link	Prestige/ image of site
Science Parks South	7 (13)	23 (43)	7 (13)	17 (31)	40 (74)
Science Parks North	32 (25)	63 (49)	32 (25)	46 (36)	95 (74)
All Science Parks	39 (21)	86 (47)	39 (21)	63 (34)	135 (74)
Off-park North	6 (10)	8 (14)	0 (0)	1 (2)	16 (28)
Off-park South	1 (2)	7 (16)	5 (12)	3 (7)	11 (26)
All off-park	7 (7)	15 (15)	5 (5)	4 (4)	27 (27)

Notes: Percentage of firms in each site type in parentheses.

to the local HEI. The final column, 'prestige of site', is included for comparison, since it is the single most frequent response from all firms. Several interesting points emerge from this table. 'Access to university facilities' was important to almost half of northern Science Park firms, and somewhat fewer in the south. Access to HEI facilities was significantly less important for non-park firms but was still the most important HEI factor. The fact that a key founder worked at the local HEI was important for 21 per cent of all park firms, with 25 per cent of northern park firms mentioning this factor compared with 13 per cent of southern park firms.

The opportunity to recruit new graduates from the HEI was also thought important by 21 per cent of Science Park firms, with

169

northern park firms again mentioning recruitment significantly more frequently than those in the south. Interestingly, whilst no northern off-park firms thought this important in locational choice, one-eighth of southern off-park firms mentioned this factor. This may reflect differences in the northern and southern graduate labour market, but does not explain why northern park firms should be more concerned about this issue than those in the south.

The 'prestige of being linked to the university' was predictably much more important for park firms than off-park firms, the only surprising factor being that 7 per cent of southern non-park firms thought this important. However, comparison with the final column, 'prestige and overall image of the site', is most interesting. More than twice as many Science Park respondents thought this important as those mentioning the 'prestige of the university'. Fully three-quarters of all Science Park firms mentioned the site prestige and image, with no difference between north and south parks. It is also interesting to compare this percentage (74 per cent) with that of the off-park firms mentioning 'prestige of site'. Some 27 per cent of off-park firms mentioned this, again with no difference between north and south. This percentage might be seen as a measure indicating the basic importance of any off-park site. The 'added value' perceived by Science Park tenants of their location can then be seen to be considerable, given the difference between these two percentages.

Overall university-related facilities do not appear to be major factors influencing locational choice. Of 34 'other' factors added by interviewees, only three related to the university/HEI, and only one, 'the university attitude to industry' was thought a most 'important factor' by one northern Science Park firm. It should be remembered, however, that these tables indicate the most important factors which influenced locational choice: lack of emphasis on the university does not preclude important links with the HEI which develop when the firm locates on site. These issues are now examined.

8.5.2 Links with local HEI

Respondents were also asked to identify the three most important links with the HEI of which they had made use. They were also able to volunteer any additional links. The top half of Table 8.17 focuses on links primarily related to R & D and personnel, whilst the lower half focuses on use of non-research facilities, and the university as a customer.

Table 8.17: Links with the HEI

	Science Parks			Off-park		
	South	North	All	South	North	All
Informal contact	67	57	60	42	47	45
Employment of academics	24	30	28	30	26	28
Sponsor research/trials	19	12	14	19	12	15
Access to equipment	35	40	38	21	36	30
Test/analysis in HEI	17	10	12	7	17	13
Student projects	17	25	22	14	31	24
Graduate employment	22	33	30	28	31	30
Training by HEI	2	5	4	5	9	7
Teaching programme	7	5	5	5	14	10
Other formal links	4	—	1	—	—	—
Use of facilities:						
Computer	11	22	19	9	5	7
Library	44	49	48	16	21	19
Recreation	15	36	30	14	2	7
Conferences	11	17	15	7	16	12
Dining	15	25	22	9	3	6
Audiovisual	9	10	10	5	3	4
Other	4	6	5	2	3	3
University as customer	7	18	15	12	19	16
No response	7	19	15	30	22	26
Number of firms	54	129	183	43	58	101

Note: Figures are percentage of firms mentioning each factor as being one of three most important links with the HEI. The final row shows the total number of respondent firms. Firms mentioned more than one factor, so percentages sum to over 100.

The most obvious and perhaps surprising observation is how apparently similar off-park firms' responses were to those of on-park firms. This is particularly clear in the R & D and personnel links in the top half of the table. Nevertheless, park-based firms clearly place a greater emphasis on 'informal contacts with academics', which may (or may not) be significant channels of communication facilitating information transfer. They also appear to place greater emphasis upon access to equipment. In other R & D and personnel categories, however, off-park firms rate their HEI links as highly as Science Park-based firms. In some areas, such as the sponsorship of trials, student project work and teaching programmes, a higher percentage of off-park than park firms rate these amongst their three most important links.

Comparing north with south, it is noticeable that more northern

171

firms, both on and off parks, rate their links with students as being greater than southern firms. This is perhaps surprising, bearing in mind the relative tightness of the graduate labour market observed in the south. Access to specialist equipment is slightly more important for northern firms, whilst sponsoring trials and research is more important for southern firms, both on- and off-park. North–South differences in terms of 'the employment of academics on consultancy/part-time basis' are more complex. This is seen as an important link by more northern than southern Science Park firms, but by more southern than northern off-park firms.

Moving now to the lower half of the table, differences between on and off-park firms are far more pronounced. Not surprisingly, Science Park firms rate the use of facilities such as computing, library and recreation provision far more highly. This difference is, in a large part, related to the fact that some of these facilities are not available to those outside the university Science Park complex. Also notable is the difference between northern and southern Science Park firms. More northern park firms rate the facilities offered by the HEI as important. This is particularly noticeable in computing, recreation and common room/dining provision. A surprisingly high percentage of southern off-park firms rated their local HEI recreation provision as important.

The local HEI is also a customer to 15 per cent of surveyed firms, with park location seemingly making no difference to this link. Indeed, in the south, off-park firms rated this link more highly than park firms. It is therefore possible to identify the links with HEIs which are location-dependent. There is informal contact with academics, access to equipment, use of the library, the computer, common room and recreational facilities.

Important caveats need to be inserted into any interpretation of these results. The bald tabulations provide us with no insight into the importance or value of the links, or the depth of relationships established. There may also be a bias in the sense that the off-park firms, being older and better established, have had a greater opportunity to create such links. Indeed, it is a very important result to find that almost one-third of off-park firms had a significant link with an HEI.

8.5.3 HEI links: summary

The survey provides several important results. More than twice as many Science Park firms thought the general 'prestige and image of the site' to be an important factor in their choice of location than those mentioning the 'prestige of the university'. Less than half the Science Park firms thought 'access to HEI facilities' to be an important consideration in their choice of location. Overall, only one-quarter of Science Park firms' responses to the question on factors affecting choice of site related to the HEI.

Turning to actual R & D and personnel links with the HEI, it is striking how similar are the responses of off-park firms to those of Science Park firms. Whilst more park firms have 'informal contact with academics' than off-park firms, in the more formal links such as the employment of academics, sponsoring trials, student project links and the employment of graduates, off-park firms have equal or greater numbers of links.

Comparisons between north and south appear to suggest that northern firms on a Science Park have stronger formal contacts with the university than southern park firms. Additionally, northern park firms place a greater emphasis on the use of HEI facilities.

8.6 LINKAGES WITH THE WIDER ECONOMY: THE LOCATION OF CUSTOMERS, SUPPLIERS AND SUBCONTRACTORS

There are three principal information sources in the survey which show the ways in which Science Park firms (and similar off-park firms) are linked to the wider economy. These focus on information about customers, suppliers, and subcontracting. Information on the location of customers shows whether firms are linked to local, national or international markets, and thus their potential for growth. This is fully discussed in Chapter 10. Currently we shall discuss information on the location of suppliers, which again shows the extent of linkages with the local, national or international economy, and thus location of employment- and wealth-creation in 'upstream' supplier industries. The use of subcontractor firms for assembly and manufacture is a key area for Science Park companies who may be restricted in these activities. Our information shows the extent of subcontracting, and gives an indication of the potential for job- and wealth-creation downstream from Science Park firms.

In our review of suppliers, we examine the local links (up to ten miles), the regional links (11–50 miles), the national links (rest of the UK), and finally, linkages overseas. The information covers

Table 8.18: Suppliers' locations

Location in miles	Science Park		Off-park		New firms in all sectors
	Initial	Current	Initial	Current	
'Local' 0–10	21	22	17	15	60
'Regional' 11–50	11	12	20	20	14
'National' 50+	48	47	52	55	30
Abroad	17	17	8	9	5
Total	100	100	100	100	100

Note: Figures are the mean percentage of suppliers from each location. Columns do not add to 100 due to rounding.

both current links and former links based on retrospective information on the situation at the time the firm began operations on its present site.

8.6.1 Suppliers

Table 8.18 summarises the location of suppliers, giving the mean percentage of supplies from each location. Science Park firms are marginally more dependent on local (up to ten miles) sources of supplies than off-park firms. Conversely, off-park firms are more dependent on regionally sourced supplies (i.e. from 11–50 miles) than park firms. Both on- and off-park firms are heavily dependent upon UK supplies from outside their region, more than half of all firms buying in more than 40 per cent of their supplies from the 'rest of the UK'.

Of the 33 per cent of Science Park firms and 29 per cent of off-park firms which import supplies, the Science Park firms are notably more dependent on imports, over half of importing Science Park firms sourcing more than 40 per cent of their total supplies abroad, against a quarter of off-park firms.

The final column of the table compares these results with those obtained from a survey of wholly new firms in Cleveland (Storey, 1982), and which may be regarded as being of a more conventional sectoral structure. It shows that the currently surveyed firms, both on and off parks, are much less dependent upon local suppliers than the Cleveland firms. Thus, the latter group obtained only 5 per cent of supplies from abroad, compared with Science Park firms which obtained 17 per cent, and are therefore much more dependent upon imports.

8.6.2 Subcontracting output

One indication of the linkages between high-tech firms and the wider economy is the extent of subcontracting by these firms. This is particularly important for Science Park firms, which may be restricted in their production activity by industrial use regulations, since manufacture and routine production may be prohibited on the parks. Subcontracting production may therefore represent a significant 'downstream' multiplier of Science Park firms' activity. This has implications for evaluating the contribution of Science Park firms to the economy, both in terms of wealth- and employment-creation.

Table 8.19: Subcontracting by park/off-park firms

		Zero subcontracting	Subcontracting as % of total output (by value)		
			1–20	21–60	61–100
Science Park firms:	no.	69	47	14	44
	(%)	(40)	(27)	(8)	(25)
Off-park firms:	no.	49	35	13	7
	(%)	(47)	(34)	(13)	(7)

Table 8.19 shows Science Park firms' subcontracting compared with the off-park group. It can be seen that there are significant differences between on- and off-park firms. Some 47 per cent of off-park firms do no subcontracting, compared with 40 per cent of park firms. Furthermore, where off-park firms do subcontract, they are more likely to subcontract a lower percentage of their total output. Finally, a much higher percentage of park firms subcontract a high percentage of their output, with 25 per cent of Science Park firms subcontracting 61–100 per cent and (not shown in the table) 22 per cent subcontracting 81–100 per cent. This is, to a large extent, a predictable result. Science Park firms are less likely to have

productive capacity themselves and, of course, many have low levels of output, being very new ventures. Conversely, the off-park firms are more likely to have productive capacity (22 per cent of off-park firms gain significant income from products compared with 18 per cent of Science Park firms).

The above results contrast with the 'Activities' results (Table 7.3), where subcontracted production was a more important source of income for off-park than Park firms. This may be explained by the fact that Table 8.19 looks at subcontracting as a percentage of 'output', not 'income'. Science Park firms are less likely to undertake subcontracted production from customers as a source of income, but are more likely to subcontract production out to external manufacturers.

8.7 CONCLUSION

This chapter has continued the examination of the technical aspects of firms located on Science Parks, together with a 'comparable' set of firms located off a park. It was found that although all firms had high levels of qualified scientists and engineers employed, Science Park firms employ a higher percentage of QSEs than off-park firms. Indicators of the outputs from R & D, such as patents and new products were then discussed in relation to inputs. Detailed analysis suggests that patenting activity is not, in the main, affected by Science Park locations. Levels of employment of QSEs were not found to be associated with new product launch. A complex relationship was found to exist between R & D expenditure levels and new product launches: the majority of firms which launched new products in the last two years spent between 1 and 40 per cent of turnover on R & D, but zero R & D expenditure did not preclude a product launch, and high levels of R & D expenditure did not correlate with higher levels of new product launches. Taking patenting and new products together, firms that patent also tend to launch new products, and vice versa. This suggests that for this group of firms, patenting activity is a good indicator of product launches.

Having looked at R & D inputs and outputs, product performance in relation to competition was examined. Firms with few competitors were found to have lower levels of product launches (a predictable association since a low level of competition is a function of having no product), but product launch did not increase with larger numbers of competing firms. Competition with large firms does not appear to inhibit product launch amongst respondent firms, particularly those which perceive their competitive advantages to lie in the overall quality of their product.

Linkage with the local university or HEI is fundamental to the Science Park ethos. However, less than half of Science Park firms surveyed thought that access to university facilities was important in their choice of location. Moreover, twice as many Science Park firms thought the 'prestige and image of the site' was important in location choice compared with those mentioning the 'prestige of the university'. Overall, only one-quarter of responses to the question on choice of location related to the university or HEI. When actual research links with the HEIs were examined, it is only in terms of informal links with academics that Science Park firms record a higher percentage of responses than off-park firms.

The majority of survey firms' sources of supplies tend to be located in the national market, but Science Park firms are more linked to local suppliers than off-park firms, which in turn are more linked to the national market. Science Park firms are notably more dependent on imported supplies than are off-park firms. In terms of subcontracting, Science Park firms tend to subcontract more, and at greater intensities, than off-park firms.

This chapter has presented a considerable amount of detail and it is therefore worthwhile to highlight two points. The first is that a key characteristic of firms in this sample is their launching of new products, and the survey results show that this is positively correlated with patenting, competition with a small number of generally large firms, and where the firm itself places an emphasis upon quality. Of perhaps equal interest are the results on HEI links. In very broad terms they suggest that whilst firms locating on Science Parks perceive there to be considerable prestige in the location, the extent of formal or informal links with the HEI are rather more limited than might be inferred from the Segal Quince study of Cambridge.

These results suggest the need to reappraise the comparative advantage of a Science Park location. They indicate two alternatives. The first is that less emphasis should be placed upon direct or indirect links with the local HEI, since that can apparently be cultivated by firms located elsewhere. Instead, park management should be looking outward to promote the overall development of the firm, rather than inward to promote links with the university. Alternatively, the results indicate that the level of HEI linkage developed by off-park firms has not

177

significantly been bettered by Science Park firms, and that if such links are to be increased, Science Parks will need to adopt a more pro-active strategy.

9

Property and Management of Science Parks

9.1 INTRODUCTION

This chapter considers, firstly, the property needs of high technology firms, and secondly, the management function on Science Parks. The property section starts with a report on the overall premises arrangements of firms in the survey. It continues with an analysis of the factors that lead to firms' decisions to locate on or off a Science Park. Finally, the firms' future premises requirements are reviewed. The second section examines the role of management on Science Parks. It shows that there are wide variations in the provision of such services, but that broadly speaking, tenants prefer those parks on which site management services are provided.

9.2 PROPERTY

9.2.1 Size of premises

Table 9.1 compares the size of premises on and off Science Parks, for all firms in the survey, and shows that Science Park firms occupy smaller-sized premises than off-park firms. On Science Parks 60 per cent of the sample occupy less than 2,000 sq. ft compared with 34 per cent of off-park firms. Whilst the difference in age of tenants on and off Science Parks is clearly a factor, it does not fully explain this difference.

Table 9.2 shows that 39 per cent of tenants on Science Parks were new firms on arrival, compared with 46 per cent amongst off-park firms. For firms under four years old, the proportion of new starts

179

Table 9.1: Size of premises

Sq. ft	Science Park No.	%	Off-park No.	%
0– 1,000	57	32	18	19
1,001– 2,000	50	28	14	15
2,001– 5,000	43	24	30	31
5,001– 9,000	17	9	16	17
9,001–50,000	13	7	14	15
> 50,000	–	–	4	4
	180	100	96	100

Table 9.2: Relocated and new-start businesses

Business age in years	Science Park New starts No.	Relocation No.	Total No.	Off-park New starts No.	Relocation No.	Total No.
0– 2	43	11	54	8	2	10
3– 4	22	40	62	19	15	34
5– 9	4	37	41	11	18	29
10–25	1	16	17	6	18	24
> 25	–	4	4	2	1	3
	70	108	178	46	54	100
% of firms	39.3	60.7	100	46.0	54.0	100
Average age in years	2.1	6.7	4.9	6.2	9.6	8.1

on and off Science Parks increased to 57 per cent and 61 per cent respectively. These results confirm the importance of Science Parks in providing facilities for start-up firms. However, the survey provides no evidence to suggest that a greater proportion of high-tech firms on Science Parks are start-ups.

9.2.2 Terms of occupation

Table 9.3 shows that Science Parks predominantly provide leased accommodation. Overall, only 5 per cent of firms own their premises on Science Parks (Monck 1986); the current survey includes just 1 per cent owner-occupiers. By comparison a quarter

Table 9.3: Analysis of owned and leased premises

Own or lease	Science Parks No.	%	Off-park No.	%
Owner-occupier	2	1	23	25
Lease	136	83	64	69
Licence	26	16	6	6
	164	100	93	100
Lease length				
Greater than 3 years	43	30	49	70
3 years or less	103	70	21	30
	146	100	70	100

of off-park firms own their own premises, the majority of whom are mature companies who have generally occupied leased premises elsewhere before purchasing. About 65 per cent of owner-occupiers are more than nine years old.

Differences in ownership are primarily a function of age: young firms in general lack the capital to enable them to finance the purchase of premises, and need the flexibility provided by leased premises. The difference is also due to differences in estate management policy. Many Science Park designs do not easily lend themselves to the sale of individual units, particularly if their occupants are in terrace units or in multi-occupancy buildings. Leased units also provide for greater control by the landlord over tenant selection, building design and overall upkeep of the Science Park.

9.2.3 Previous location

More than two-thirds of on- and off-park firms who have occupied other premises before moving to their present site have relocated from within the same city. This is shown in Table 9.4, which illustrates that Science Parks, like other industrial premises, serve a predominantly local market, and in general are not in competition with each other for tenants. It also shows the very similar prior location patterns of on- and off-park firms.

Table 9.4: Analysis of previous locations of firms

Previous location	Science Parks		Off-park	
	No.	%	No.	%
Same city	70	68	36	69
Same county	18	17	10	19
Elsewhere in UK	15	14	6	12
Abroad	2	2	—	—
	105	100	52	100

Table 9.5: Key location factors

	Science Park % mentioning factor as 'most important'	Off-park % mentioning factor as 'most important'
1. Prestige and overall image of site and premises	59	18
2. Access to universities' facilities	33	0
3. Already located in area	32	22
4. Cost of premises	22	49
5. Prestige of being linked to university	18	1
6. Good transport and communication links	18	17
7. Key founder lived locally	17	11
8. Key founder worked in university	16	5
9. Scope for attracting graduates	7	0
10. Key founder worked locally	4	62
11. Availability of skilled labour	4	15

Note: This table shows 'most important' factors and cannot be directly compared with Table 7.10 or 8.16, which identify 'mentions'.

9.2.4 Location factors

An understanding of the factors that led companies to select their current premises provides an insight into important features perceived by on- and off-park firms. As noted in Section 8.5.1 all firms were asked to indicate those factors that influenced them in selecting their current premises, and to indicate the three which were most important. Table 9.5 sets out the main factors in order of importance for firms on and off the Science Park. For Science Park tenants the *most important* were 'prestige and image of the site' (59 per cent of firms), 'access to university facilities' (33 per cent), and 'previous location in the area' (32 per cent). In contrast, for off-park firms, the most significant factors were 'key founder lived locally' (62 per cent), and 'cost of premises' (49 per cent): prestige and image of the site was only significant amongst 18 per cent of off-park firms, and access to university facilities was scarcely mentioned. For Science Park firms, the cost of premises was only significant for 22 per cent. Thus, it can be concluded that firms on Science Parks felt that the generally higher costs of premises were more than offset by the enhanced value of the location in terms of prestige and image of the site, access to the university, and the benefits of being associated with the university. This is particularly significant when it is realised that Science Park rents are frequently comparable to city centre office rents and 50–60 per cent higher than those of equivalent industrial premises.

Whilst the location factors for high technology firms not on Science Parks are similar to those normally identified by small firms in general, Science Park tenants perceive other factors to be more critical. However, some caution is needed when interpreting these results. The rationalised answers given by firms after the location decision was made may differ from those factors considered at the time of the decision. It could be argued, for example, that because Science Park premises are generally more expensive than alternative accommodation, firms may rationalise their decision by highlighting other factors. However, as noted later in this chapter, few firms on Science Parks plan to leave in order to find lower cost premises, suggesting that the rental premium for a Science Park location is acceptable.

9.2.5 Future property requirements

As will be shown in Chapter 11, a particular feature of young high technology firms is the existence of a high proportion of firms growing rapidly in terms of turnover and employment. A consequence of this growth is the need for premises to accommodate the additional work-force. About one half of respondents (51 per cent on Science Parks and 52 per cent off Science Parks) indicated their intention to move to a new site or to take additional premises in the next two years. This is broadly in line with earlier information collected on Science Park firms by the UK Science Park Association: during each of two years, 1985 and 1986, managers reported that some 18–20 per cent of their tenants moved to larger premises, generally on the

Table 9.6: Location of alternative premises

| | Science Park | | | | Off-park | | | |
	New site No.	Additional site No.	Total No.	%	New site No.	Additional site No.	Total No.	%
On this site	18	27	45	(28)	2	4	6	(7)
Within 10 miles	19	4	23	(14)	28	5	33	(37)
Elsewhere	5	8	13	(8)	4	4	8	(9)
Movers	42	39	81	(51)	34	13	47	(52)
Non-movers	—	—	79	(49)	—	—	43	(48)
Total			160	(100)			90	(100)

Science Parks (Monck, 1985, 1986).

There are major differences between firms on and off Science Parks regarding the location of any additional premises, as shown in Table 9.6. Of the firms on Science Parks, 45 (28 per cent of respondents) expected that their extra premises requirements would be met by staying on the park; 18 firms expected to move to larger premises and 27 expected to take an additional unit. Twelve firms said that they would take an additional site, four locally and eight more than ten miles away. Only 5 firms (15 per cent) expected to leave the Science Park altogether. Thus, the majority of current firms look to the Science Park as the prime provider of additional space. In contrast, the majority of off-park firms do not expect their additional premises needs to be met by their present location. Only six out of 47 movers (7 per cent of all respondents) expected that their extra premises needs would be met on their present site. A further nine firms anticipated remaining on their present sites and taking additional premises elsewhere. The majority, 32, (36 per cent of off-park firms), anticipated moving to a new site, 28 of which stated that this would be within a ten-mile radius.

The likelihood of a firm moving is more strongly related to the size of its current premises than to the age of the firm. A high proportion of firms (60 per cent) in small premises of under 2,000 sq. ft are likely to require extra premises, whereas this proportion falls to 30–35 per cent as the size of premises increases to 9,000 sq. ft. Firms in smaller premises on Science Parks are more likely to expand by remaining on the park than those in larger premises. In contrast, amongst the off-park group, firms in larger premises are more likely to expand on site rather than move to alternative

Table 9.7: Reasons given by firms for considering alternative or additional premises

		Science Park		Off-park	
		No.	%	No.	%
(a)	Positive reasons:				
	More space required	71	(89)	37	(82)
(b)	Negative reasons:				
	Wrong location				
	Market	8		8	
	Technical	4		1	
	Production	1		—	
	Other	2		1	
	Cost too great	6		6	
	Wrong premises/need to rationalise	6		11	
	Total	27	(33)	27	(60)
(c)	Other factors:				
	Temporary premises	—		2	
	Wish to purchase	3		2	
	Unconnected with location	5		—	
	Total	8	(10)	4	(9)
	Number of firms providing records	80		45	
	% of firms indicating they intend to move	90		87	

premises at another location. The level of technology also appears to influence firms' future premises requirements. Amongst leading-edge firms, 59 per cent on Science Parks and 71 per cent off parks expect to expand, compared with only 46 per cent on Science Parks and 48 per cent of the remainder of the sample.

Firms indicating an intention to move were also asked to identify the main factors that influenced their plans. The results are summarised in Table 9.7. As expected, a high proportion of firms (89 per cent on Science Parks and 82 per cent off Science Parks) indicated that they would require more space. In addition, a number of firms also indicated 'negative' reasons for needing alternative premises. Significantly, only 33 per cent of 'movers' on Science Parks, compared with 60 per cent of off-park firms, gave negative reasons. These included 'wrong location', 'too great a cost' and 'wrong premises'. This suggests that despite the higher rental levels, Science Park-based firms are more satisfied with their location and property decisions than off-park firms. It helps to explain why a higher proportion of firms on Science Parks expect to expand by remaining on site, whereas off-park firms expect to relocate elsewhere.

9.3 ON-SITE MANAGEMENT AND LINKS WITH OTHER BODIES

An important distinguishing feature of Science Parks is the emphasis placed in the UK on the existence of a 'management function which is actively engaged in the transfer of technology and business skills to the organisation on site' (UKSPA definition of a Science Park). Even so, the way in which this management function is discharged varies considerably between Science Parks. There are wide variations in the level of staffing to support the science park, the background of the personnel and the experience and duties which they are expected to perform.

The purpose of this section is to explore the extent and role of the management function on Science Parks. It also analyses the links established by tenants on and off Science Parks with the HEI, and the wider business community.

9.3.1 Management of Science Parks

The majority of Science Parks in the survey employ either a full-time resident manager or rely on the university's industrial liaison officer to interact with tenant firms. A full-time manager is present in twelve of the 20 parks, three of which involve a team of two or more staff. In the main, the resident staff consisted of a single manager with secretarial and property service back-up.

It is generally the case that tenants on those Science Parks which have been funded by a development agency or by a local authority have business and technological services provided in the first instance by the university's industrial liaison officer. The extent of their involvement with tenants, and with the management of the park as a whole, varies widely between parks. In some instances, particularly where the university and the industrial liaison officer were integral to the scheme from the outset, there is considerable involvement. However, for many industrial liaison officers, the major constraint on their greater involvement with Science Park tenants is time and pressure from other priorities within the university. Rarely does the university set aside sufficient resources for the industrial liaison officer to manage the interface between the university and the Science Park.

The roles and responsibilities of managers also vary widely between parks. This reflects the differing aims and objectives of the parks' sponsors and financial backers, the skills and resources of the sponsoring institutions, the organisation and structure of the park, and the availability of appropriate funds for an on-site management presence.

The different objectives of Science Parks are reflected in the background of the managers. Eight full-time managers have been appointed directly from industry, split approximately evenly between research and technology, sales and marketing, general management, and finance and accounting. On four Science Parks managers are from the university, in three cases from science and technology departments and one from a business faculty. Six Science Parks have on-site management provided by the university's industrial liaison officer, who, in five cases, has been recruited from industry. Almost all the managers and industrial liaison officers have had a degree in science or engineering and have worked for technically orientated businesses.

Except at Aston and Southbank Technopark, who employ specialists, few Science Park managers have a strong background and experience in finance, accounting and the preparation and monitoring of business plans. In several cases, Science Parks have established working arrangements with locally based accounting firms to provide financial advice and assistance in the preparation of business plans to tenants and prospective tenants. On other Science Parks, business advice to tenants is available from one of the sponsors of the Science Park: for example, some local authorities have established business advice centres, and at English Estates their Business Support Service has a special remit to support science park tenants on a pro-active basis.

9.3.2 The value of the management support function on Science Parks

Tenants on Science Parks were asked about the role and value of the management function. Because of the range of responses obtained, they have been summarised to provide an overall indication of the

Table 9.8: Value of the management function on Science Parks

| | Firms | |
	No.	%
Passive or not required	88	54
Helpful	16	10
Very helpful	59	36
	163	100

Table 9.9: Analysis of value of management function on Science Parks

Type of management back-up	No. of tenants interviewed	No. of tenants indicating 'helpful/ very helpful'	%
Team approach	54	35	65
Resident manager	41	20	49
University industrial liaison officer	46	16	35
No formal back-up	22	4	18
	163	75	46

value that tenants place on the provision of management services. According to Table 9.8, almost half the tenants believed that the manager had been helpful or very helpful.

Table 9.9 shows that the highest proportion of tenants (65 per cent) who found a Science Park management function 'helpful' were on parks where a team approach had been adopted towards tenant support. On the nine science parks with a resident manager, 49 per cent of the tenants found the support useful. Where the park depended on the university industrial liaison officer, the proportion of companies reporting a helpful response was 35 per cent. The parks with no formal management had the lowest proportion of tenants (18 per cent) who claimed they had been 'helped'.

Thus, there appears to be a relationship between the proportion of tenants who found the management function helpful or very helpful, and the nature of the management support available. Superimposed upon this is the fact that many of the more recently established parks have only a limited number of tenants. Here management support arrangements may be expected to develop more fully over time as the number of tenants increases, as less attention has to be devoted to establishing the park.

9.3.3 Management support and HEI links

Most Science Parks have developed procedures to help tenants to integrate and develop links with their associated academic institutions. Even so, the level of encouragement and positive assistance varied widely between parks. In some cases considerable emphasis was placed on developing rapport between tenants themselves and with relevant academics through the establishment of tenant clubs, seminars, other organised events and personal introductions to academics so as to encourage links. Though time consuming, park managers recognised that some 'social engineering' was necessary to bring together academics and park tenants, neither of whom may be aware at the outset of their common interests. Several managers reported that it was necessary to establish a minimum level of interaction to demonstrate the benefits of a network. From a small nucleus of contacts a more extensive set of contacts and networks can then be established.

In Chapter 8, these links between firms and HEIs were explored. The analysis indicated a broad similarity of many links between firms on and off the park. However, it was pointed out that informal links with academics, access to equipment, use of the library, the computer, common room and recreation facilities, were much more likely to happen with Science Park than off-park firms. The needs and opportunities for links being established, however, depends on a wide range of issues, including the availability of management time, the level of technical self-sufficiency of the firms, the relevance of academics in an HEI to the firm's work, the research and development strategy of the firm, and its need for complementary technical skills outside its main discipline. It has to be admitted that the survey was unable to assess whether there was great potential for further developing links for firms on Science Parks, or in determining the contribution that the on-site management has made, or could play, in the future to foster new links.

9.3.4 The provision of shared services

The value and the provision of common services — for example, reception, secretarial, telex, photocopying and book keeping — depended mainly on the number and characteristics of park tenants. These services were generally available where parks employ their own on-site manager.

In some cases, for example at Bradford, Durham and Loughborough, a secretarial company offering reception and secretarial services to tenants has been encouraged to set up on the park. The level of uptake appears to depend on the building layout and the mix of tenants, and was most effective in multi-occupancy buildings with common entrance and reception areas. The use of such services was dependent on number, age, profile and size of tenant firms, with the greatest use being made by start-up firms. As they grew beyond five or six employees, tenants increasingly preferred to become self-contained rather than continue to rely on external services. Where there was an effective central receptionist and a significant uptake of shared services, there appeared to be a more integrated, friendly and dynamic atmosphere within the park. It seems that common services improve the contact and rapport between management and tenants, and result in greater social contact between tenants.

9.3.5 The provision of business advice

The survey identified a wide variation between Science Parks on the extent of management advice offered to tenant firms. In some instances almost no advice was available, but in the majority of parks, particularly those with on-site managers, advice was available on request. Even so, utilisation of this service, even by those facing serious managerial difficulties, was in some cases surprisingly limited. In part this may be because of a lack of time on the manager's part, but it also appeared to be due to a lack of awareness on the part of both tenant and manager. In several cases where a manager had established social contact and maintained a general interest in a tenant's developments, there was a reluctance to enquire too deeply into the tenant's affairs unless specific assistance was invited by the tenant. Thus, unless called in by the tenant, the manager was sometimes unaware of some of the difficulties being faced by his tenants.

The issue of the relationship between the Science Park manager and the tenants is therefore complex. On many of the parks, the manager's primary role is to market and manage the park, and is likely to be perceived by many of the tenants as the landlord. Perhaps, more critically, unless the Science Park manager has succeeded in demonstrating his abilities in advising businesses, tenants may not realise the value and quality of the help available. In addition, if in-depth advice is to be provided to tenants, it is a time-consuming activity which is often difficult to blend in with the other responsibilities of developing, marketing and managing the park as a whole. The nature of some of the problems being faced by tenants also requires the manager to possess a range of consulting and counselling skills, particularly in the areas of finance and accounting. These skills are essential if he is to be credible to tenants and help them to face up to the strategic and financial decisions that need to be addressed as a business develops.

9.4 CONCLUSIONS

This chapter has assessed the locational and facilities-related issues for high technology firms. It has shown that Science Parks have catered for a high proportion of younger and smaller high-tech firms, the majority of which are on shorter leases than off-park firms. Because of differences in age, a higher proportion of off-park firms own their premises.

Some 70 per cent of high technology firms which relocate move to premises in the same city, although Science Parks attract a greater proportion of companies from other parts of the UK or from overseas. Even so, Science Parks (as with most other industrial property) service an essentially local need and are not, in general, in competition with each other.

Firms locating on Science Parks place particular emphasis on the 'prestige and image of the site and premises' and, to a lesser extent, access to the university. This contrasts starkly with high-tech firms locating elsewhere, which appear to place greater weight upon the general convenience of the location, and its low cost.

There appears to be strong evidence that Science Park firms are more satisfied with their location than high-tech firms located elsewhere. A much higher proportion of Science Park firms expect to expand at their present location. Furthermore, a much higher proportion of non-Science Park firms mentioned negative factors as a reason for moving than was the case for firms considering a move from the Science Park. Thus, despite the higher rents charged, firms on Science Parks are more satisfied and expect the park to provide the additional accommodation that they require for their expansion.

The survey also provides strong support for further improving the quality and quantity of on-site management and business advice. It shows that where this is provided, it is generally valued by tenants. It also shows that where shared services are provided, this leads to improvements in cohesion between tenants themselves and between tenants and management. It also appears that the increased availability of business advice, selectively and judiciously supplied, can be much appreciated.

10

The Management and Financing of High Technology Firms

10.1 INTRODUCTION

The management and financial problems associated with the growth of small firms have been extensively documented. Making the transition from an entrepreneurially to a professionally managed firm does not come easily to many firms. In recent years, there have been outstanding examples of firms which have achieved rapid growth and success — Apple Computer is a prime example. For every such firm that is successful, however, many others become enmeshed in the problems of identifying markets and managing and financing growth.

This chapter reports the responses of firms to questions about the types of management problems encountered and the constraints inhibiting their growth. Specific questions were asked as part of the structured questionnaire, but the opportunity was also taken for qualitative discussion with owners about these issues. Based on these responses, the markets in which the firms operate are first examined, including their location, types of customers and competitiveness. This is followed by a look at where firms go for advice and assistance and consideration of the nature of the constraints faced by independent high-tech firms, particularly the key issue of financing. In conclusion, the nature of the management development issues with which the firms will have to contend if they are to achieve their long-term growth objectives are reviewed.

The discussion concentrates on independent firms overall. The analysis of the research findings showed very little difference between the experience of firms on-park and off-park in respect of marketing, financial and management issues. However, where significant differences among independent firms do occur as a result of location these are indicated.

10.2 MARKET CHARACTERISTICS

10.2.1 Market demand

A major difficulty facing new and young firms as they seek to grow
is that of identifying and developing markets for their products.
Shortage of demand, along with lack of funds, is often given as the
major stumbling block to development in the early years of a firm's
life. Marketing is often especially difficult for technologically
innovative companies, particularly when they are addressing new
needs and markets. Among the sorts of problems which these
companies typically have to face are:

— difficulties in forecasting market demand for innovative
  products for which users may have little or no frame of
  reference;
— the uncertainty of selecting the right initial market for a new
  technology where there is the potential for multiple applications across a variety of industries;
— the need to educate potential users;
— hesitation by potential customers to buy early-generation
  technologies;
— technological obsolescence.

The firms in this survey, however, did not appear to experience
the above types of problems to the extent that might have been
expected: for instance, when Storey (1985b) asked similar questions
in Cleveland, shortage of demand was the most commonly
mentioned difficulty in the firm's first year of operation. However,
this was not a major problem for many high technology firms in the
current survey — particularly those located on Science Parks. This
was mentioned as a problem in 26 per cent of cases and was far from
being the most serious problem mentioned. An examination of the
firms' products, markets and competition, together with their recent
growth achievements, supports this picture of relative buoyancy of
demand.

10.2.2 Products

The nature of the activities undertaken by the companies is fully
discussed in Chapter 7. It is interesting that when firms began,

about 40 per cent were still at the basic-ideas stage. Subsequent product development activity was strong, however, with on average more than two new products being developed by Science Park firms in each of the last two years. Thus, these firms had relatively new products to offer to the market.

The products and services developed were generally considered by the firms to have a significant technology base. In about one-third of cases, the product or services were considered to be based on 'leading-edge' knowledge or technology: standard services or products with little technological content were rare. Most of these companies were actually developing new technology applications and not relying on 'me-too' products — a factor which differentiates them from the generality of small firms.

10.2.3 Customers

The customer base of the Science Park firms also presents a much stronger profile than is either normally expected among new small firms, or is often perceived for new technology-based firms. The typical development pattern for new enterprises, particularly those with a technology base, has been typified as an initial heavy dependence on contract research and development activities, often undertaken for just one or two clients. Over time, this dependence on a limited number of customers is lessened as companies start to standardise procedures and processes and the client base is expanded. This progression of moving from contract- to product-oriented work is often characterised as a 'hardening process'. As Chapter 7 showed, however, this was not the typical pattern for the firms surveyed. While this was demonstrated in some cases, a move in the opposite direction was also evident — from product sales to contract work.

Similarly, the 'typical' pattern of heavy dependence on a limited number of customers was not demonstrated. Almost 80 per cent of independent companies were selling to more than ten customers and one-third of firms had in excess of 50 customers (see Table 10.1). There was also a good spread across size of customers with only 7 per cent selling exclusively to small firms. The remaining 93 per cent were either selling to firms of all sizes or just to medium-sized and large firms (see Table 10.2).

Other encouraging characteristics of the companies' customer base were its diversity and the significance of the private sector.

Table 10.1: Number of customers — all independent companies

Number of customers	%
< 10	22
11–50	45
51–100	16
> 100	17
Total	100

Table 10.2: Size of customers — all independent companies

Size of customers	%
Large	38
Medium	10
Small	7
All sizes	45
Total	100

Table 10.3: Sales by type of customers — all independent companies

Category of customer	%
Private sector	73
Nationalised industry	7
MOD	2
Other central government	6
University/colleges	6
Other	6
Total	100

Over 70 per cent of sales were made to the latter (see Table 10.3), demonstrating clearly that small high technology-based businesses are not reliant on the public sector. Central government surprisingly accounted for only 8 per cent of sales. It is however possible that these figures underestimate the effective size of government business, as it is likely that a certain proportion of the private sector business represents subcontracted activity originating from the public sector. Nonetheless, the limited success of independent companies in penetrating the large and potentially lucrative central government market is disappointing and possibly reflects a reluctance by government departments to purchase technology-based products and services from the small-firms sector.

10.2.4 Location of markets

Independent technology companies have much wider market distribution throughout the UK and abroad than is typical of other small companies. Over three-quarters of the companies sell more than 50 miles away, accounting for around half their turnover; and around 45 per cent of companies also sell abroad, representing 12 per cent of turnover (see Table 10.4). Science Park firms have a slightly greater sales bias to local customers (15 per cent within ten miles) compared with off-park firms (9 per cent). This pattern is reversed in the regional market (11–50 miles) which accounts for 25 per cent of off-park sales compared with 18 per cent for Science Park sales. The differences are not particularly significant and may be partly explained by the older age of off-park firms. In general, the customer locational profile is very similar for all firms.

Table 10.4: Location of customers — all independent companies

A. Percentage of companies selling within distance range

Distance range	Start-up	Now
Local — < 10 miles	35	38
Regional — 11–50 miles	47	55
National — elsewhere in the UK	68	79
Abroad	27	45

B. Companies' turnover percentage by distance range

Distance range	Start-up	Now
Local — < 10 miles	21	19
Regional — 11–50 miles	15	16
National — elsewhere in the UK	53	53
Abroad	11	12
Total	100	100

The market location for high technology firms overall contrasts sharply with other types of firms, however. In the Cleveland survey (Storey, 1982), which looked at new firms in all sectors, 70 per cent of sales were made locally within a ten-mile radius and over four-fifths in the Northern Region overall. Only 3 per cent of sales went abroad. This is not really surprising: the high technology market is international, and the opportunities for technology-based products are not geographically constrained.

10.2.5 Competition

With their international dimensions, the markets in which small high-tech firms operate are inevitably competitive, but for many of the firms surveyed the number of competitors was not excessive. This probably reflects the fact that they have identified a specific market niche. Thus, for instance, 13 per cent of independent companies claimed to have no competitors and a further 30 per cent had only between one and three competitors (see Table 10.5). As noted in Chapter 8, the number of competitors is not necessarily indicative of the quality and strength of competition, but the fact that over 60 per cent could only identify up to six competitors does suggest that competition was not intense.

The areas in which all firms competed successfully were discussed in relation to Table 8.14. In Table 10.6, however, three characteristics stand out clearly as providing competitive advantages for independent firms:

(1) the uniqueness of the product or service,
(2) the performance and reliability of the product or service,
(3) the ability to respond to customers' needs.

These strengths provide an enviable basis for competing in any market. The ability to respond quickly to customers' needs is perhaps the least surprising competitive attribute claimed and is the classic advantage of small independent firms over larger competitors. In addition, the ability to provide unique products and services (given that a market exists for these offerings) is very encouraging and bears out the observation made above that the firms have been successful in identifying discrete market segments in which to operate. Again, this is a dimension along which small firms can effectively compete against larger rivals. Small firms can flourish by identifying and exploiting market segments which, because of limited size, or complexity of servicing, large volume-based competitors avoid.

It is thus encouraging to see that the firms surveyed evince

Table 10.5: Number and size of competitors — all independent firms

A. Number of competitors

Number	%
None	13
1–3	30
4–6	27
7–10	10
11–20	7
21–50	6
> 50	7
Total	100

B. Size of competitors

Size	%
Large	34
Medium	24
Small	28
All sizes	14
Total	100

Table 10.6: Competitive strengths and weaknesses — all independent firms

Criteria	% of cases	
	Strength	Weakness
Design	8	2
Unique product/service	14	3
Leading-edge technology	7	3
Performance/reliability	16	3
Delivery/availability	5	8
Sales channels	1	19
Reputation/image	9	9
Price	9	16
Promotion/marketing	2	25
Flexibility/response	18	6
Overall quality	6	1
Others	5	5
Total	100	100

strengths in those areas in which their natural potential for competitive advantage lies. Given these advantages, together with the width and depth of their customer base, the companies appear well placed to achieve the strong growth they are seeking. But is the position really so rosy? It is worth considering this further.

10.2.6 Marketing essential to support continued growth

It would appear from the foregoing analysis that independent high-tech firms are well on track for continued sales growth. However, to balance against these favourable indicators are two areas which firms identified as being by far their greatest competitive weaknesses — namely, promotion and sales channels. This was despite their apparent marketing and selling success and the fact that, at least initially, shortage of demand was not generally identified as a problem. This suggests that the firms are not achieving the full potential which they believe is available to them and which will need to be realised for their longer-term growth.

The challenge facing these small firms is therefore that of maximising their true potential. It was noted earlier that, unlike most other small firms, technology-based companies have been successful in developing markets nationally and, to some extent, overseas. However, in terms of the international competition which they face, further penetration will often be required, particularly in export markets. Although some success has been achieved overseas, this only represents 12 per cent of turnover. Given the short product life-cycles of many technology-based products, there is a requirement to reach a large international market quickly to exploit fully the profit potential of the product. This in turn means that they need to develop effective marketing and selling mechanisms to achieve this.

While many of the firms claimed to have marketing skills in their management team, it appears that this is often just part of management's general experience. These key individuals are often stretched in many directions and do not have sufficient time to spend on marketing and selling activities. The problem of management time constraints is discussed later in this chapter and has important implications for growth.

It is likely that many of the firms will need to strengthen and formalise their marketing and selling activities if their growth momentum is to be maintained. They have started with a solid customer base but will need to become more pro-active and aggressive in marketing and promotion. This in turn means acquiring the necessary marketing and selling resources and attitudes to ensure that the business develops the necessary marketing orientation. Market research and marketing planning, which are not generally undertaken at present, will need to be introduced. This will help ensure that product development is guided by market opportunities. The high technology market-place is characterised by rapid change and diversity; technological development is a perishable commodity. The firms seeking to grow will need to maintain their product development activity. Their product sales profile five years hence is likely to be very different from the one which exists today.

10.3 SOURCES OF ADVICE AND ASSISTANCE

The ready availability of external advice and support can be of crucial importance to the small technology business in its formative years. There are many sources of advice and assistance available to small firms. In Table 10.7, the main sources which were identified by respondents are summarised, both at start-up and subsequently, and are considered below.

Table 10.7: Sources of advice — all independent companies

Source of advice	% of responses	
	Start-up	Current
Central Government	13	20
Local Government	3	4
Other public sector	1	1
Enterprise agencies	14	11
Universities	6	5
Banks	21	16
Accountants	21	20
Solicitors	9	8
Other private sector	3	4
Other sources	9	11
Total	100	100

10.3.1 Private sector advice

Despite the growth in public sector agencies, the function of which is to help with the establishment and growth of new businesses, it is private sector organisations — accountants, banks and solicitors — which are most frequently consulted, both at the start of the business and once the business has become established. Thus, for example, of all the organisations mentioned as being contacted by independent companies prior to starting their business, 21 per cent were accountants, 21 per cent were banks and 9 per cent were solicitors. These percentages were fairly consistent between groups of respondents, even when a distinction was made between before and after start-up.

10.3.2 Public sector advice

Among the public sector organisations consulted, the Department of Trade and Industry was mentioned most frequently, followed by the Small Firms Service/Enterprise Agencies. Interestingly, these two groups tended to exhibit differences between start-up and after start-up, with the Department of Trade and Industry being much more likely to be contacted once the business was established. On the other hand, Small Firms Services/Enterprise Agencies tended to be contacted at or prior to start-up, with their role subsequently diminishing.

10.3.3 University advice

A disappointing feature of the advice sought was the lack of use of university-based services to assist the new entrepreneur — such as Business School advice — as well as technical and professional services. Even among independent Science Park companies, use of these facilities was very modest indeed. Similar comments apply to the use of services provided by local authorities.

10.3.4 On-site advice

In the case of some Science Parks, the park management was able to provide advice of where and how to best secure the help needed. As noted in Chapter 9, a few of the parks are actually in a position to provide management support and help directly. This is true only in a minority of cases and the extent of on-site management and its capacity to devote time to providing in-depth business advice to tenant companies varies from park to park. This was reflected in the replies from tenants who were asked about the assistance they received from the Science Park management.

10.4 INITIAL PROBLEMS ENCOUNTERED

In Table 10.8 the incidences of problems experienced by businesses in the first year of operation are listed. Many problems are common to all new businesses, such as shortages of skilled labour and obtaining payment from large debtors; but by far the most significant problem mentioned by over half of the independent firms was the constraint of management time. This critical problem is considered below, together with the perennial problem for new firms of obtaining finance, which was faced by almost one-third of firms.

Table 10.8: Problems experienced by independent firms in first year of operation

Type of problem	% complaining
Shortage of skilled labour	23
Government bureaucracy	26
VAT registration	4
Debtor payment	35
Shortage of demand and markets	26
Shortage of key management skills	29
Obtaining finance	32
Time constraints on management	52

10.4.1 Sources of finance at start-up

The problem of obtaining finance was one of the major difficulties faced by firms at start-up. In this respect, a new technology-based firm is no different to any other small business: it will often have an inexperienced management team with a limited track record and may well be seeking to address new markets with new products. In these circumstances the only way to get started is by the founders providing the finance personally and as Table 10.9 shows, the most important source of funds for new companies in the survey was personal savings. This was the most important source in 55 per cent of all cases, and only the clearing banks represented another significant source (17 per cent of cases).

This confirms the findings of the Bolton Committee (Bolton, 1971) that self-financing is the dominant characteristic of funding in the small-firms sector. It is also entirely consistent with Storey's findings in Cleveland (Storey, 1982) where personal savings were

Table 10.9: Most important sources of finance — all independent firms

Sources of finance	% of responses Start-up	Now
Personal savings	55	20
House mortgage	2	1
Existing business	6	4
Retained profit	—	26
Clearing bank	17	25
Venture capital	3	8
Private equity	2	3
Public agency	4	4
Grant	1	3
Loan Guarantee Scheme	2	3
Other	8	3
Total	100	100

found to be the most important source of finance for 56 per cent of new independent firms. The Cleveland firms, however, were more successful in obtaining bank loans and overdrafts: this was the most important source of finance in 27 per cent of cases. This indicates the greater difficulty of technology-based firms in obtaining start-up capital from conventional banking sources. In Table 10.10, the potential finance sources which were unsuccessfully approached by companies at start-up are shown. This demonstrates the reluctance of banks to lend in this sector, with failed bank loan applications representing 30 per cent of all cases, and venture capital institutions in 45 per cent of cases.

Table 10.10: Other forms of finance investigated

Type of finance	% investigating
Venture capital	45
Bank loans	30
Loan Guarantee Scheme	14
Grants	7

Note: Some companies tried two or more other sources.

There are undoubtedly additional factors which are peculiar to high technology companies which make fund raising more difficult. These include:

— the difficulty of assessing the technological risk — that is, the increased likelihood of a development project not achieving its objectives or of the technology becoming obsolete or superseded before an adequate return can be made;

— the requirement for ongoing R & D to keep the technology up to date, thereby perpetuating the risk;

— the difficulty for potential lenders of actually understanding the business, and therefore the risk; and

— the fact that investments in technology-based companies are often long-term, which in itself increases the risk factor.

Given these additional drawbacks, together with the fact that most banks are short of the skills required to assess the risks involved, explains the banks' reluctance to provide finance to companies in this sector.

Another potential source of capital virtually unused at the outset was venture capital, representing the most important source in only 3 per cent of cases. This in fact reflects the current policy of most venture funds which are looking for:

— minimum equity investments of, typically, £250,000;
— management with a proven track record; and
— high growth/return potential.

It is difficult for new technology firms with often little more than ideas or unproven products and services to compete against the lower risk opportunities available to the venture funds.

10.4.2 Current sources of finance

In Table 10.9 the main sources of finance at the time of the survey are also listed. This shows a major shift in funding away from personal savings at start-up, and towards retained earnings and bank finance. Retained profits were the most important source in 26 per cent of cases, closely followed by clearing banks. Personal savings dropped to 20 per cent although in small companies the distinction between 'personal savings' and 'retained profits' is not always clear-cut. What is clear is that internal sources (savings and retained earnings combined) were still vital, representing the most important source of finance for 46 per cent of companies.

It is noticeable, however, that increasing use of third party funding had occurred since start-up. The greater use of clearing banks has just been noted and the use of venture capital, although still low as the most important source in 8 per cent of cases, had grown. The evolution of funding sources demonstrated by the survey follows an expected pattern. As firms become established and can demonstrate management capability and the ability to exploit their products and services commercially, then external funding sources become increasingly available. This can be characterised in three stages:

(1) *The seed stage*. At this stage a start-up business raises money to prove the idea and diminish the technological risk. In our sample this money was mainly provided by the founders and by profits retained from cash-generating business activities such as consultancy.

(2) *The venture stage* is the stage at which prototypes are developed, market research is conducted and production is set up. Because the amounts required are more substantial at this stage, it is financed by a mixture of retained profits, loans and equity. There is little security either in the business or in its assets, so it is difficult to obtain significant amounts of bank finance.

(3) *The development stage* is the expansion of a business with a proven product during which further markets are identified and developed. This stage will normally be funded by a mixture of equity and loans. Many 'venture capitalists' are in fact 'development capitalists' and will only invest at this stage and then only under the conditions indicated earlier.

At each stage the risk of failure is diminished, and therefore the value of the company increases. In consequence, a smaller proportion of the more highly valued equity needs to be sold to finance each succeeding stage.

A final observation on sources of funds is the low level of third-party equity participation, and in particular the almost total absence of investments under the Business Expansion Scheme (BES). BES support was only mentioned as a source of funds in 2 per cent of cases, a disappointingly low level, given that these were precisely the types of company which the scheme was devised to support. It would appear that taxpayers seeking to exploit the tax break available under the BES have taken the low risk route and concentrated on asset-backed investments and the BES funds, rather than higher risk small technology companies.

The lack of any significant equity involvement may also be a reflection, in part, of the reluctance of founders to share their business with outsiders. It was apparent in discussion with some founders that they were unwilling to assume the risks associated with rapid growth. They were reluctant to expand by taking on extra management or by diluting their control through expanding equity participation and were content to restrict the scope of their operations to a level compatible with a comfortable lifestyle. This attitude is likely to coincide primarily with the one-third of companies which were not particularly ambitious and were still expecting to employ less than ten people in five years time.

10.4.3 Factors affecting ability to raise finance

The possible impact of such factors as management background and technical content of the product were also examined to see whether this had any effect on a firm's ability to raise external funds.

10.4.3.1 Management background

The firms with management teams containing individuals who already had entrepreneurial, management or financial backgrounds did not find it significantly easier to obtain finance at start-up, nor were the patterns of the type of finance raised significantly different. In contrast, the age of the key founder does seem to have had an effect on the problem of raising finance. The results suggest, perhaps not surprisingly, that younger and older entrepreneurs had significantly more problems (see Table 10.11).

Table 10.11: Funding problem related to founder's age

	Companies with problems of obtaining finance by age of key founder						
Age	< 25	26–30	31–35	36–40	41–45	46–50	51 +
%	50	29	33	22	25	26	41

10.4.3.2 Product

The technical content of the product or service is relevant to the ability to raise funds. Some 42 per cent of those with leading-edge technology had difficulty raising finance compared with only 22 per cent of other high tech firms. This may be because there was more technological risk associated with such companies, or because they had not yet identified suitable commercial applications for the new technology.

10.4.3.3 Profitability

Current profitability also had a bearing on the ease with which respondents obtained finance at start-up. This suggests that either potential funders were successful in identifying a good prospect or that firms achieved profitability through their ability to obtain finance. However, for many new technology-based firms, losses are likely in the early years in view of the necessary expenditure on research and project development. Moreover, the gestation period for these businesses can be considerable: many get under way as part-time occupations (21 per cent off-park and 31 per cent on-park). It is likely to be many years before such firms achieve profitability and this is incompatible with many providers of finance who require a short-term pay-back. Several founders were disappointed, in particular by venture capitalists, who required a yield from day one.

10.4.3.4 Motivation

The attitudes and motivation of the firm founders and managers is another key factor in the ability to raise funds. Those firms with dynamic and positive leadership which are seeking strong growth are much more likely to be successful. Not only do they inspire more confidence but are likely to achieve the rates of growth and profitability attractive to outside equity investors. This contrasts with those founders who are less aggressive and are unwilling to assume the risks associated with rapid growth. They may well have development opportunities open to them but prefer a more relaxed life-style and therefore do not appeal to investors seeking high growth and high returns.

10.4.4 Management constraints

Chapter 11 examines in detail the performance of the surveyed firms and shows that high technology firms have recorded impressive growth. Among the firms surveyed, employment increased between 1985 and 1986 by 80 per cent among the firms on Science Parks and by 28 per cent among off-park firms. This compares with a decline of 1 per cent among small firms in the comparable Occupational Study Group (OSG) study (Johnson and Storey, 1987) covering small firms in all sectors. Not only have these small high technology firms recorded impressive growth, they have equally ambitious growth expectations for the future. Almost three-quarters of firms want to diversify and expect to more than quadruple employment in five years' time. In turn, almost a third have ambitions for obtaining a public listing, at least on the Unlisted Securities Market.

To fulfil these development ambitions the firms will be faced with the normal management and organisational problems associated with rapid growth. The nature of these problems is indicated in Table 10.8, in which lack of management time was identified as the overriding major operational constraint. In addition, lack of management skills, although not such a constraint, is still a significant problem. In effect, these two constraints interact even where managerial skills are available, time pressure on managers prevents their effective utilisation.

The statistical analysis of the firms surveyed is also supported by qualitative evidence. Each interviewer was asked to summarise his own impressions of each company, and typical of the comments made were the following:

'Reason for success or failure will not be linked to technology but more to management expertise.'

'They have management experience but extra skills will be required for long term growth.'

'They require help in planning for the future.'

'A fundamental lack of financial understanding; money regarded as a problem not a resource.'

The problem of management development associated with entrepreneurial growth is a well-known phenomenon. A small group works long, hard and informally to establish the enterprise. This single-minded dedication takes the business so far but its growth needs start to exceed the grasp of a few individuals. At this stage, however, there is often a reluctance to let go of the reins and broaden the management talent base. Many entrepreneurs find this transition a difficult one to make, but if they fail to make it, then long-term growth prospects will be severely curtailed.

As well as needing to adopt a different style of management,

209

there is a need for a different kind of organisation: to make the transformation from a spontaneous, free-spirited enterprise to a more formally planned, organised and disciplined entity. As the company becomes more structured, however, so the danger arises for technology-based firms that the informal and creative environment which is often considered essential for innovative development will be destroyed; and that increased straight-jacketing with procedures and systems will alienate staff and negate creative flair. In large organisations there is no doubt a danger that bureaucracy, remoteness and slowness of response can crush innovative flair and incentive. The recognition of this has led to such developments as sponsored spin-outs and strategic partnering whereby large companies seek to secure the benefits of a small company able to meet new challenges and opportunities as they arise.

These dangers are unlikely to arise in any serious way in the immediate future with the small technology firms surveyed. However, if the ambition of securing a listing, to which many of the firms aspire, is to be realised, it will be necessary to impose at least a minimum of management and organisational discipline. This will require adopting:

— market and business planning;
— systematic development of products and services;
— acquisition of resources (physical, financial, human);
— development of operational systems; and
— development of management systems.

It is the process of moving from entrepreneurship to professional management. It will occur at different stages with different companies, but will need to be addressed by all those firms seeking sustainable growth.

10.5 CONCLUSIONS

Many of the development issues relating to high technology firms are common to all small growing businesses, but these are intensified along certain dimensions for the high tech firm. In particular:

— the need to move quickly to establish distribution channels to reach the markets and thereby maximise the returns available

in a fast changing market-place;
— the need for a constant flow of new products to offer in the market-place — one- or two-product companies are high risk;
— the need to avoid an overemphasis on technology and ensure that the products developed serve a market need; that there is a clear understanding of who will buy and why;
— the need to build a management team and the recognition that marketing and business skills are essential for long-term growth;
— the need to evolve towards more structured organisational and operational arrangements and to institute business planning.

In respect of funding, it is clear from the survey that most firms did not obtain their finance at start-up from institutional sources. Even once established, they tended to be funded by personal savings and retained profits rather than through institutional investors, although there is a clear increase in financing by banks and venture capitalists. The low level of financing by third-party investors is, to an extent, a function of the young age of most businesses, and would be expected to increase with time and growth. However, unless there is the potential for growth, and the entrepreneurial drive to achieve that growth, self-financing will remain the only financing option available to many new technology-based firms.

The technology firms surveyed demonstrated considerable potential. They are growing faster than other types of firms and have achieved success in their markets. A solid base of business has been established and if they can continue to develop their marketing abilities and establish a broadly based management team, the ambitious growth which many of the firms are seeking should be achievable.

11

The Performance of High Technology Firms

11.1 INTRODUCTION

The high technology sector is thought to offer a major source of new wealth and employment opportunities. However, there has been very little formal evidence presented to show the extent to which British small firms in the high-tech sectors perform better than otherwise similar small firms generally. There has also been little appraisal of the extent to which the performance of the small high-tech firm varies according to age, location, whether or not it is located on a Science Park, and according to its level of technological sophistication.

This chapter presents original data on these issues derived both from the current survey and the study of British small firms referred to in Chapters 5 and 6 (Johnson and Storey, 1987). It will be recalled that both are 'face-to-face' interview surveys and hence only the performance of existing, surviving firms can be analysed.

In the analysis, 'performance' will be examined under three headings: employment creation, value of sales turnover, and profitability. A further measure of performance which is relevant for smaller firms is their likelihood of ceasing to trade, but in an interview survey of this type it is not possible to incorporate this important element. All that can be said is that there appears to be some — albeit somewhat circumstantial — evidence that the failure rates of small high-tech firms are somewhat below those for small firms in general. Segal Quince (1985), for example, are able to identify very few high-tech firms which ceased to trade in Cambridge. Whilst this evidence is far from conclusive it is very unlikely that small high-tech firms have failure rates higher than the 'norm', and they could have rates which are below it.

The remainder of this chapter will examine performance in terms of the criteria of employment, sales and profitability. It begins with a comparison between the current sample of small high-tech firms and the small firms in the All-Sector OSG study (Johnson and Storey, 1987). It then examines only the current survey of high-tech firms and subdivides the sample in several ways. Firstly, it distinguishes between firms on and off Science Parks in an effort to identify any element of added value which the park provides for the firms. Secondly, it distinguishes between firms located in the north and those in the south. Thirdly, it distinguishes between those firms in the survey which are genuinely 'leading-edge', as discussed in Chapter 7, and those which are merely 'high-tech'. The final section examines only those firms located on a Science Park, where a distinction is made between those firms established by academics and those which locate on the park, but where the founder has no previous employment links with the HEI.

As was shown in Chapter 5, Science Parks contain not only independent, entrepreneurially managed firms but also firms which may be part of a group and where the ultimate ownership is outside the park. In order to make valid comparisons both between this study and others, and to make comparisons between firms within the survey, only single-plant independent firms are included. This is because this group is much more likely to be affected by the environment which the park provides, rather than, for example, a subsidiary unit, the performance of which will be affected by decisions taken at head office.

When comparing the performance of small firms, it is of paramount importance to recognise the importance of age. Thus, for example, it is easy to observe illusory differences in growth amongst a group of small firms over time if one group is younger than the other, since, in proportionate terms, younger firms grow faster than older firms. For this reason, all data on comparative performance is expressed in terms of firms in a given age-group.

11.2 THE PERFORMANCE OF SINGLE-PLANT INDEPENDENT FIRMS IN THE HIGH-TECH AND CONVENTIONAL SECTORS

In Table 11.1 a comparison is presented between employment levels in single-plant independent firms of different ages. The All-Sector OSG survey results are compared with the current survey. The table shows that small firms in the All Sector group do not increase

Table 11.1: Employment in small firms

		Firm age in years			
		0–2.9	3–5.9	6–9.9	10+
All sectors survey	$\overline{X}$	5.68	6.15	8.91	7.42
	X^{median}	3.0	4.0	4.0	4.0
	n	38	65	35	125
			*	*	*
High-tech survey	$\overline{X}$	6.71	11.04	20.57	26.44
	X^{median}	5.0	8.0	11.0	16.0
	n	42	84	35	23

* Denotes statistically significant differences between the two groups of figures at the 5 per cent level.

employment with age, i.e. the average UK small firm does not grow larger as it grows older, once it is more than three to six years old. Arithmetic mean employment, however, does rise from 5.68 workers in firms less than three years old to 8.91 workers in firms between six and ten years old, but this is simply because of the growth in relatively few firms. For surviving firms which are more than ten years old, mean employment falls to 7.42. These results are consistent with expectations from other analytical and survey work (Storey, 1985a), which shows that the median surviving manufacturing firms reached a peak employment within three to four years of start up.

For high-tech firms, however, the pattern is significantly different. Both mean and median employment increase with age, showing that not only are high-tech firms larger in terms of employment when they are young, but that they continue to grow. Thus, high-tech firms which are less than three years old have a median employment of five workers, compared with three workers in firms in the All Sector survey. For firms which are more than ten years old, this differential has widened appreciably from a median of four workers in the All Sector survey to sixteen in the current survey.

Table 11.2 presents data on sales turnover and finds a broadly similar pattern. Median sales turnover in the All Sector firms rose from £63,500 in those less than three years old to £100,000 in those between six and ten years old. For the high-tech firms, median sales turnover for firms less than three years old was £72,500, but for firms more than ten years old, this had risen to £850,000.

Profitability measures of performance do *not*, however, follow the same pattern. All firms in both surveys were asked to indicate

Table 11.2: Sales turnover in small firms (£000)

		\multicolumn{4}{c}{Firm age in years}			
		0–2.9	3–5.9	6–9.9	10 +
All sectors survey	$\bar{X}$	124.6	168.3	167.7	233.9
	X^{median}	63.5	76.0	100.0	78.8
	n	16	38	22	56
			*	*	*
High-tech survey	$\bar{X}$	133.4	324.5	876.4	1,098.0
	X^{median}	72.5	121.5	340.0	850.0
	n	34	92	37	27

* Denotes significance at 5 per cent level.

Table 11.3: Pre-tax profitability as a percentage of turnover

		\multicolumn{4}{c}{Firm age in years}			
		0–2.9	3–5.9	6–9.9	10 +
All sector survey	% with profit > 10%	39.1	41.7	38.5	38.9
	% making losses	26.0	16.7	23.0	11.1
	n	23	48	26	90
High-tech survey	% making profits > 10%	24.0	34.2	30.0	40.9
	% making losses	40.0	29.1	23.3	18.1
	n	25	79	30	22

the broad level of profitability which their business achieved, where profitability was defined as pre-tax and expressed as a percentage of turnover. Table 11.3 shows for each survey the proportion of the sample which claimed to be making a profit rate in the previous year which was in excess of 10 per cent and the proportion which claimed to make a loss in that year. Two points are immediately apparent: first, that in both groups the youngest firms are the most likely to have made losses; and secondly, that apart from firms which are more than ten years old, a lower proportion of the high-tech firms, of all ages, claimed to be making high profits than the firms in the more conventional sectors. The fact that the All Sector survey was undertaken in 1985 and the current survey in 1986, and so the profitability data in the All Sector survey refer to a year closer to the trough of 1980–1 recession, may explain these differences, at least in part. Even so, it is curious that the data on profitability performance of high-tech firms is very different from that on the other measures of performance. It is also important to note that high rates of profitability in the All Sector survey do not vary with age, so that 39 per cent of young firms are making high rates of profit, which is exactly the same proportion as in the oldest age-groups. For the high-tech firms, however, profitability fairly consistently increases with age so that the best-established firms appear to be making the highest rates of profit. The low proportion of high-tech firms making profits in their early years of life are also, of course, attributable to the fact that many actually start without any formal product to sell.

11.3 PERFORMANCE OF HIGH-TECH FIRMS: ON AND OFF SCIENCE PARKS

If an estimate of the benefits of a Science Park location is to be made, it is clearly important to compare the performance of high-tech firms on and off a park. If, for example, it were shown that the firms located on a park grew significantly faster than those located elsewhere, this would be important supportive evidence — provided the two groups of firms were appropriately matched — of the added value of a park location.

To this end, Tables 11.4, 11.5 and 11.6 examine the performance of firms by distinguishing between those located on a Science Park and those located elsewhere. In broad terms, they show that whilst performance in terms of employment size, sales turnover and profitability depends upon the age of the firm, there are only four statistically significant differences between firms located on and off a Science Park. The first two are in Table 11.4, and these show that off-park firms between the ages of three and ten years are significantly larger in terms of employment than firms of a similar age located on the parks. On the other hand, Table 11.5 shows that ten year old firms on the Science Park had significantly higher sales turnover than those not on a park. Table 11.6 shows the profitability of six to ten year old firms on a Science Park is significantly higher than similar firms located off-park.

There is therefore some conflicting evidence of differential performance of firms on a Science Park. Clearly, this should not come as a surprise since the off-park firms were specifically chosen to be 'comparable' with those on the park in terms of sector and technological sophistication. It is also clear that, in terms of firm performance, whether or not a firm is in the high technology sector is of greater importance than whether or not it is located on a Science Park.

216

Table 11.4: Employment in single-plant independent high-tech firms: on- and off-park

| | | Firm age in years | | | |
		0–2.9	3–5.9	6–9.9	10+
Science Park	$\overline{X}$	5.44	9.78	14.5	31.3
	X^{median}	5.00	7.00	9.5	19.0
	n	36	54	18	7
Off-park	$\overline{X}$	14.3	13.3 *	27.0 *	24.3
	X^{median}	6.0	11.0	13.0	14.0
	n	6	30	17	16

* Significant at 5 per cent level.

Table 11.5: Sales turnover in single-plant independent high-tech firms: on- and off-park (£000)

| | | Firm age in years | | | |
		0–2.9	3–5.9	6–9.9	10+
Science Park	$\overline{X}$	132.5	240.6	572.8	2,515 *
	X^{median}	100.0	120.0	400.0	1,525
	n	25	55	17	6
Off-park	$\overline{X}$	136.0	449.3	1,134.4	693.1
	X^{median}	70.0	170.0	330.0	600.0
	n	9	37	20	21

* Significant at 5 per cent level.

Table 11.6: Profitability in single-plant independent high-tech firms: on- and off-park

| | | Firm age in years | | | |
		0–2.9	3–5.9	6–9.9	10+
Science Park	% with profit > 10%	31.6	26.7	41.2 *	50.0
	% making losses	42.1	35.5	17.6	0.0
	n	19	45	17	4
Off-park	% making profits > 10%	0	44.1	15.4	38.9
	% making losses	33.3	20.5	30.8	21.3
	n	6	34	13	18

* Significant at 5 per cent level.

These conflicts between performance indicators between the on and off park firms, therefore, lead to a questioning of whether there are any performance differences between groups of firms within the sample.

11.4 NORTH–SOUTH DIFFERENCES

A key concern in the growth of high technology small firms has been the concentration of this activity in the existing prosperous south of England. To determine whether this is reflected in the performance of firms in this survey their location was broadly categorised as to whether they were in the north or south of Britain, where south was defined as south of a line from the Wash to Bristol.

Tables 11.7 and 11.8 provide evidence of a North–South Divide. High-tech firms in the north in the age groups 3–5.9 years and 6–9.9 years have significantly fewer employees and lower sales turnover than those located in the South. Indeed, for *every* age group in terms of employment and sales turnover, the southern firms are, on average (arithmetic mean), larger than their northern counterparts. The groups identified above indicate where these differences are statistically significant, at least at the 5 per cent level.

In terms of profitability, shown in Table 11.9, there are no significant differences between northern and southern firms. If anything, there appears to be a higher proportion of northern firms recording high rates of profit. However, it must be recognised that, as before, this may reflect the difficulties of obtaining a satisfactory common definition of profit in this context.

11.5 TECHNOLOGICAL SOPHISTICATION

Whilst all firms in this survey are classified as being in the high technology sectors, not all have identical levels of technological sophistication. In Chapter 7, a distinction was made between firms using 'leading-edge' technology based upon the latest research, or which were producing entirely new products, and the remainder of firms in the survey. It might be assumed that the former group would perform more successfully than the latter. To test this hypothesis, the sample of single-plant independent firms was subdivided between 'leading edge' and 'high tech'. The former included only those which claimed to be using leading-edge technology and/or

Table 11.7: Employment in single-plant independent high-tech firms: North and South

| | | Firm age in years | | | |
		0–2.9	3–5.9	6–9.9	10+
North	$\bar{X}$	5.45	9.47	11.59	27.33
	X^{median}	5.00	7.00	7.00	19.00
	n	29	58	17	15
South	$\bar{X}$	9.54	14.54	29.1*	24.8
	X^{median}	6.00	10.5	12.5	12.5
	n	13	26	18	8

* Significant at 5 per cent level.

Table 11.8: Sales turnover in single-plant independent high-tech firms: North and South (£000)

| | | Firm age in years | | | |
		0–2.9	3–5.9	6–9.9	10+
North	$\bar{X}$	115.5	241.3	721.1	1,082.5
	X^{median}	60.0	120.0	199.0	850.0
	n	22	64	21	19
South	$\bar{X}$	166.3	514.7*	1,082.3	1,134.8
	X^{median}	129.0	225.0	715.0	799.0
	n	12	28	16	8

* Significant at 5 per cent level.

Table 11.9: Profitability in single-plant independent high-tech firms: North and South

| | | Firm age in years | | | |
		0–2.9	3–5.9	6–9.9	10+
North	% with profit > 10%	22.2	35.2	35.7	47.1
	% making losses	33.4	32.5	7.1	11.8
	n	18	54	14	17
South	% making profits > 10%	28.6	32.0	25.0	20.0
	% making losses	57.1	24.0	37.6	40.0
	n	7	25	16	5

Table 11.10: Employment in single-plant independent high-tech firms: leading-edge and high-tech

| | | \multicolumn{4}{c}{Firm age in years} | | | |
		0–2.9	3–5.9	6–9.9	10+
Leading-edge	$\overline{X}$	5.14	12.5	37.6 *	36.0
	X^{median}	4.5	9.0	20.0	12.5
	n	14	28	11	4
High-tech	$\overline{X}$	7.48	10.65	12.50	25.00
	X^{median}	5.00	7.00	9.0	17.50
	n	27	51	20	18

* Significant at 5 per cent level.

Table 11.11: Sales turnover in single-plant independent high-tech firms: leading-edge and high-tech (£000)

| | | \multicolumn{4}{c}{Firm age in years} | | | |
		0–2.9	3–5.9	6–9.9	10+
Leading-edge	$\overline{X}$	77.5	312.1	1,092.6	1,585.0
	X^{median}	60.0	150.0	476.0	1,125.0
	n	11	27	11	4
High-tech	$\overline{X}$	149.3	332.7	806.9	1,013.3
	X^{median}	109.0	115.0	177.0	630.0
	n	22	62	23	23

Table 11.12: Profitability in single-plant independent high-tech firms: leading-edge and high-tech

| | | \multicolumn{4}{c}{Firm age in years} | | | |
		0–2.9	3–5.9	6–9.9	10+
Leading-edge	% with profit > 10%	25.0	39.1	22.2	—
	% making losses	50.0	21.7	22.2	—
	n	8	23	9	0
High-tech	% making profits > 10%	25.0	32.7	27.8	40.9
	% making losses	31.4	32.7	22.2	18.1
	n	16	55	18	22

introducing entirely new products. Apart from a small intermediate group, all other firms were classified as high-tech.

Using these distinctions, Tables 11.10, 11.11, and 11.12 show the performance comparisons in terms of employment, sales turnover and profitability respectively. In all three tables the only group where there appears to be any statistically significant support for the notion that leading-edge firms out-perform others in high technology is in Table 11.10, for 6–9.9 year old firms. In this group, leading-edge firms appeared to have higher levels of employment, although interestingly, the younger leading-edge firms appeared to have (non-significantly) lower employment.

11.6 ACADEMIC-OWNED BUSINESSES

There are two major elements in estimating the added economic value of a Science Park. The first is that it provides a location which, utilising the facilities of the HEI and the high quality accommodation, enables a high-tech firm to grow faster than it would at an alternative location. The second is that it gives the academic a clear opportunity to start a business to commercialise his research. If all the firms in the survey were identical in all other respects, then the fact that Table 11.4 showed that Science Park firms of a given age achieve lower rates of employment might be a source of concern. Science Parks, however, comprise both business which might well have located elsewhere *and* those which are established by academics.

It seems reasonable to assume that without the Science Park, most of the academic-owned businesses would not have been established in the first place. This is illustrated by the fact that of the Science Park businesses, more than one-fifth of firms are founded by existing or ex-academics, compared with only 2 per cent of off-park firms. The vast majority of the academic-owned firms are therefore making a gross contribution to national welfare since without the existence of the park, they would never have been established.

For current purposes, however, the importance of academic-owned business on a Science Park has significant consequences since it is likely, for several reasons, that such firms will perform less well than those owned by 'professional' business men. This is because many may be owned by academics who remain in full-time employment in the university or polytechnic. They may therefore be less committed, from the point of view of generating income, to the growth of the firms than someone who depends exclusively upon the firm for income. Secondly, academics, by their choice of occupation, are more likely to be committed to the ideas and the scientific research underlying the business, than to achieving high growth and

221

Table 11.13: Employment in independent high-tech firms founded by academics

		Firm age in years			
		0–2.9	3–5.9	6–9.9	10+
			*		
Ex-academic	$\bar{X}$	5.6	7.9	7.3	6.5
staff	X^{median}	5.0	4.0	8.0	6.5
	n	14	19	4	2
Others	$\bar{X}$	7.3	12.0	22.3	28.3
	X^{median}	5.0	9.0	12.0	18.0
	n	28	65	31	21

* Significant at 5 per cent level.

Table 11.14: Employment in independent firms: excluding academic-owned firms on Science Parks

		Firm age in years			
		0–2.9	3–5.9	6–9.9	10+
Science Park	$\bar{X}$	5.4	10.8	16.5	14.2
	X^{median}	5.0	8.0	11.0	27.0
	n	22	35	14	5
Off-park	$\bar{X}$	14.3	13.3	27.0	24.3
	X^{median}	6.0	11.0	13.0	14.0
	n	6	30	17	16

the income associated with this. Finally, it seems likely that the academic will not have the experience of the professional businessman, and is more likely to make mistakes which could hinder the growth of the business. For these reasons, it may be argued that academics make less growth-orientated businessmen and it is therefore not surprising that Science Park firms, as a group, in terms of employment creation, appear to perform somewhat less successfully than the off-park firms.

We now test the extent to which the under-performance of Science Parks is due to disproportionate presence of academic businesses on the Parks. Table 11.13 shows employment data, by age of firm of *all* independent businesses in the survey established by academics and by non-academics. It will be recalled that almost all the businesses established by academics are on Science Parks. Table 11.13 shows that there is some support for the view that businesses established by academics are less likely to grow than others. For firms less than three years old, academic businesses have fewer employees, but the difference is significant only at the 10 per cent level. For those firms between three and six years old, there is a difference which is significant at the 5 per cent level. For all business age-groups the academic-owned businesses perform less well, in terms of employment creation, than the 'professional' businesses.

Table 11.14 therefore excludes all businesses which are owned by academics, from both the on- and off-park groups. This shows that once the academic businesses are excluded, there is no significant difference between the performance, in terms of employment, of firms on and off Science Parks. The apparently inferior performance of the former group is attributable to the stronger presence of academic-owned businesses on Science Parks.

11.7 CONCLUSIONS

This chapter has demonstrated that the small independent firm in the high technology sectors exhibits significantly faster employment and sales turnover growth than a firm of comparable age in the more conventional sectors. It demonstrates the importance of this group to economic development. Employment creation of high-tech firms located in the north is, however, significantly inferior to those located in the south. From the viewpoint of estimating the impact of Science Parks upon the performance of firms, the results are less clear-cut. Broadly speaking, it appears that a distinction can be made between businesses owned by academics and ex-academics, and those owned by 'professional' businessmen. There is clear evidence that the former group appear to exhibit slower employment growth than the latter — although they may be equally profitable. Since almost all the academic-owned businesses are on Science Parks, this serves to 'depress' the overall employment performance of high-tech firms on the parks when these are compared with off-park firms of a similar age.

When only 'professionally' owned firms, on and off Science Parks, are compared, it appears that there is no significant difference between the two groups. It does not, however, provide any evidence that amongst this group the Science Park firms perform better than the off-park firms of a similar age.

In estimating the contribution of a Science Park, it therefore appears that the benefits are two-fold. One is to provide the opportunity for an academic to commercialise his scientific research, and

223

that a number of academics have taken that opportunity. Secondly, it provides an opportunity for 'professional' high-tech businesses to perform as well, but apparently no better, than at other locations.

Appendix: Cameos of Six Tenant Firms

MANAGEMENT AND CONTROL TECHNOLOGY (MCT)
ASSOCIATES LTD

Anyone looking from a distance at the progress of MCT Associates since its formation in 1979 might be forgiven for assuming that here is a classic case of the 'soft to hard' phenomenon — a company starting as a consultancy, learning from this and perceiving a market niche, later standardising its service, and then moving into products and manufacture.

That is how it may look, but MCT's founder, Alan Lewis, was planning this business for 15 years before start-up and, unlike the above description, he had a well thought-through strategy in which it was always intended to move into products. Start-up as a consultancy was necessary to help finance the development period for MCT's high value-added products.

Alan Lewis had been with GEC Elliott before going to Birmingham University, first to obtain a business qualification, and then working as a Senior Research Fellow. With two colleagues from Birmingham and his brother, who also had a background in instrumentation and control engineering, he established MCT at Hinkley, Leicestershire, in 1979. The firm started as a design and development consultancy and was an authorised consultant under the DTI-sponsored Computer Aided Engineering (CAE/CADCAM) scheme, and for the Microprocessor Applications (MAP) scheme.

However, the goal that MCT was working towards was the development of a range of computer-aided systems for monitoring, checking and calibrating gauges in scientific and other precision instruments. Gauge calibration and management systems are now available off the shelf or to meet special requirements, and can either be retro-fitted to existing metrology equipment or supplied as turnkey systems. Such high value-added systems required considerable investment in development time. Initially, 80 per cent of staff time was spent in development, and even today such work continues to occupy over 60 per cent of staff activity. As with so many small firms, capital for start-up came from personal savings, with second-round funding in 1983 coming from bank loans and an overdraft, and an additional mortgage on the Managing Director's house.

The situation changed somewhat when in May 1984, MCT

became the third firm to move on to Aston Science Park. Looking for a site in the West Midlands MCT chose Aston principally because of the financial backing the Park could offer, and secondly because the Science Park site would make MCT more visible and help the firm's market image. Birmingham Technology Ltd (BTL), who manage Aston Science Park, have a venture capital fund backed by Birmingham City Council and Lloyds Bank. Thus, they were able to offer MCT an equity capital injection, together with loans. Interestingly, BTL took into account the many years of unpaid development time which had been put into the business and agreed to a substantial 'sweat equity' with the existing shareholders.

Nevertheless, MCT was not over-capitalised, and the desire to keep borrowing down, together with the cash flow problems associated with low-volume, high-cost products, meant that growth was slower than hoped for. The effort put into development has paid off, however, and the two marketable products MCT had ready when it moved on to the park have become a whole range of modular software products which can 'bolt together' to meet customers' needs quickly. MCT also has close relationships with some of the world's leading metrology OEMs, who incorporate MCT products in their own instruments.

From its small but purposeful beginnings, MCT has developed into what the Managing Director believes is the leading company in the world in its market niche. And true to past form, he has a clear plan for continuing development over the next five years.

BRADFORD UNIVERSITY SOFTWARE LTD

Ten years ago, Judy Butland worked in the Electrical Engineering Department of Bradford University, providing programming advice to students. These students could write programmes but were often stumped when they wanted to convert their data into graphical form for presentation in their theses. With no off-the-shelf software being available, Judy Butland set about producing some FORTRAN software to do the job on the University mainframe computer. This developed into a library of software tools, which, not surprisingly, the students found very useful. Other universities showed an interest, and many copies of the software, by now known as Simple Plot, were given away.

Meanwhile, Judy's husband, Dr David Butland, moved from the University's Computer Centre User Services Department to BURL, Bradford University Research Ltd, which was a unit set up to assist in the commercialisation of University research. It became clear to the Butlands that there was a demand for Simple Plot from industrial companies. Eventually, Bradford University Software Ltd was set up as an independent company in a city centre office in 1982, marketing and developing Simple Plot. Judy and David Butland were joined as directors by Lawrence West, the University's Director of External Relations.

Original finance for the business came from the directors themselves, but later sources included equity participation by the National Enterprise Board and the University, and the Department of Trade and Industry provided software development grants. However, the directors' contribution remains an important source of funding. In May 1983, the company moved on to the newly opened Listerhills High Technology Development on Bradford's Science Park. Employment has risen gradually and BUSL currently has eleven staff. The original Simple Plot has been further developed, and other versions, including one called ESP (Even Simpler Plot) added to the range. Everyone in the firm works full-time, developing and supporting Simple Plot and its related products. The market for the software packages is now largely the R & D departments of industrial corporations, as well as universities, and the firm has few direct competitors. Most of its customers are located in the south of England, but a small export market is opening up through agents in Japan, West Germany, Holland and the US.

Here, then, is a software company clearly originating in a technological university, developing its product in the university and

227

then bringing it to the market. Its strategy is one of continuous development based on their present products, and the firm has built up such good relations amongst the staff and management that there is a reluctance to grow much larger, for fear of losing that special relationship.

CAMBRIDGE LIFE SCIENCES

Cambridge Life Sciences is a rare creature in the UK — an independent company in the biotechnology field. Its 20,000-square foot, two-storey building, with shallow sloping roof and continuous windows around the first floor, is surrounded by grassy banks and overlooks a lake on the Cambridge Science Park.

Cambridge Life Sciences was founded in 1981 by William McCrae and Michael Gronow. The joint Managing Directors saw an opportunity to commercialise the fruits of research taking place in UK government-sponsored research laboratories and universities. They identified human and animal diagnostics as an area in which a small medical biotechnology firm could start up: alternative areas such as therapeutics require the resources of a large company and were not a practical start-up field. Cambridge Life Sciences benefited from the directors' broad research and commercial experience; William McCrae's background as a consultant helping to set up Celltech; and Michael Gronow's experience in setting up PA's biotechnology arm after many years of involvement in life sciences research.

The directors saw a clear opportunity for the new company to build on the world-class research taking place in government laboratories and universities, and to manage R & D effectively. There were few biotechnology firms in the UK and British discoveries, such as monoclonal antibodies, were being exploited overseas. Cambridge Life Sciences negotiated exclusive agreements to commercialise research output from Ministry of Agriculture research institutions, and has research agreements with twelve universities. The company sees itself as being in the business of the management of research, and this research base, which would cost millions of pounds to replicate in-house, gives the firm a strong competitive advantage.

In spite of the strength of its research base, Cambridge Life Sciences initially had great difficulty in raising finance. Every avenue was tried, but UK financial sources were found to be unsupportive of new, high technology businesses. Eventually, equity participation by 3i's investors, together with £1m raised from private investors in one of the first BES issues, launched the firm on a sound footing in 1982.

The company's first product resulted from research carried out at the Public Health Laboratories at Porton Down and Addenbrookes Hospital in Cambridge, into diagnosis of overdose poisoning by

229

Paracetamol. Eighteen months of R & D at Cambridge Life Sciences preceded the market launch in 1982. Once the firm had a marketable product, the investment problems receded. In 1984 five major financial institutions invested £1.5m and in 1986 the company raised £7m in the City by means of a share placement. There is now a strong realisation that the research base provided by Cambridge Life Sciences' formal access to government-funded research gives the company a major strength in the international market-place.

Company strategy has moved from being initially 'technology-driven' towards a 'market-driven' approach. This means they identify market opportunities and then organise the R & D accordingly. This in turn has meant that some technologically sweet projects had to be abandoned because they were not sufficiently market-orientated. This does not mean, however, that the firm has moved away from state-of-the-art developments. Recent projects include DNA probes for the detection of infectious diseases, diagnostics for detecting whether animals are on heat, and for drug overdoses. Such innovations so drastically cut down the time for a diagnosis (for example, kidney screening in one minute) that they enable GPs to do tests in their surgery that formerly required hospital laboratory analyses.

LASER-SCAN LABORATORIES LTD

There are perhaps two main archetypal models for high technology start-up companies. The first type starts up anonymously in back-street garages, and the second type is born in the rarified atmosphere of the laboratories of the world's leading universities. Laser-Scan represents the second type, and is in many ways an archetypal model for a Science Park firm. With its origins in the Cavendish physics laboratories at Cambridge, Laser-Scan is based on the successful commercialisation of leading-edge university research. It was, in 1973, the first company to move on to Cambridge Science Park. From the three original founders, the company has grown to employ around 130 staff and in 1986 moved into new, larger, purpose-built premises on the Park.

The origins of Laser-Scan lie in experiments in high energy physics in the mid-1960s in the Cavendish Laboratories. The founders were researchers who developed a scanning device using the new laser technology. The original purpose of the instrument was to assist in the analysis of photographs of collisions between sub-atomic particles in bubble chamber experiments. There proved to be a market for these devices from other researchers, and several machines were sold to other universities. Laser-Scan was formed as an independent company in 1969. When the business activity of the three founders became too great for the Cavendish host, the firm moved on to the newly opened Science Park.

Clearly, high energy physics is a limited market, and the founders sought other fields where their instrument's ability to process and analyse large quantities of visual data could lead to new applications. Links with the geography department, aided by a well-timed international conference, led to Laser-Scan focusing on cartography. However, considerable development was required to take the technology out of the physics lab and into other environments. The need for funding to develop the cartography application was provided by the Ministry of Defence (MOD). Technical assistance also came from the CAD Centre in Cambridge. Following the first cartographic application, Laser-Scan's computer-controlled laser deflection technology has been developed into a variety of systems such as image digitisers, plotters, editors and displays, including the largest liquid crystal display screens in the world. Later application areas include the security printing market, including banknotes, and large screen displays for aircraft location, for which the MOD provided R & D support.

Laser-Scan systems incorporate many innovative features, the company holding many patents, and gaining a Queen's Award for Technological Achievement in 1982. They have virtually no direct competitors in the world.

Such systems are necessarily expensive and are sold only to large organisations such as the MOD, the Ordinance Survey, water authorities and foreign government bodies. The infrequent sales of very large systems can lead to cash-flow problems and so other income sources have been developed. Laser-Scan offers cartographic bureau services to enable smaller users to have access to the technology. The firm has strong in-house hardware and software development expertise and undertakes software development for other organisations. Sixty per cent of the 130 staff are professionally or academically qualified, and technicians are very highly skilled.

Laser-Scan became a public company in 1982, with its holding company quoted on the New York stock market. The early crucial links with Cambridge University have decreased over the years but the present Chairman, Peter Woodsford, previously worked in the Cavendish Laboratories, as did the original founders.

SOURCE COMPUTER SYSTEMS LTD

'Source' is located on Aston Science Park, where they are a small but fast-growing firm producing shop-floor data collection equipment designed to assist production management. Their product thus incorporates both hardware and software. Most interestingly, Source owes its origins to a Teaching Company Scheme which brought the founder members together, and provided the support for their initial development work.

The three founders met through a Teaching Company Scheme set up by Birmingham Polytechnic and Brandauer Ltd, manufacturers of precision electronics components. Brandauer provided the original problem to be solved — the development of a computer terminal to monitor their production equipment, and feed information back to a central computer. Brandauer rented them space for around two years at very low cost, and provided a phone, with the Teaching Company Scheme backing them up. This environment enabled the development of their first system to be completed in comparatively sheltered circumstances, and meant that at the end of this period, they had a product to market, not just a set of ideas. Working on Brandauer's real-world problem was felt to have been a particularly useful exercise. In return, Brandauer benefited from having an in-house development team with backgrounds in production engineering, computer-aided design, and production efficiency.

Source came out of the Teaching Company Scheme with a reasonably well-developed first product, and much experience of user needs, customer liaison, and the many problems encountered along the way. It also had some ideas for other applications and markets.

Source was set up as a partnership in 1983, supported by the personal savings of the founders, and became a private limited company in 1984. Its first single product was launched in 1984, but clearly the firm needed access to capital in order to develop its product range. This was provided by Birmingham Technology Ltd (BTL), who manage Aston Science Park. BTL did for Source what it has been able to do for so many of its tenant firms — it put together a financial package of equity participation and loans from its venture capital fund, which provided a crucial influx of growth capital. In addition, BTL put one of its experienced business managers on the Source board, from whom the Source directors 'learned more about business in six months than ever before', as Source Managing Director Neville Howarth put it.

Source obtained further funding through the Small Firms Loan Guarantee scheme, an illustration of how subsequent funding becomes easier once initial financial backing has been secured. The firm then set about enhancing its intelligent data collection terminals. These take information from shop floor operators, either via a simple keyboard or a bar code reader. The information is 'time and date stamped' and stored in the terminal ready for transmission directly to the host computer. Following development, its new range of products was launched in February 1986. It has grown to employ 18 staff, and is currently working flat out to keep up with orders.

KGB MICROS LTD

KGB Micros is a business micro-computer dealer based in Windsor and on the South Bank Technopark in London. The owners and directors have built up the business strongly since 1981, and particularly in the last three years. Annual turnover is running at £5m and an annual growth rate of 50 per cent is being achieved. The company currently has a staff of 45.

KGB provides business systems for all types of companies and computer-aided design systems to engineers, architects, planners and designers. Recent growth has been built on the latter and the company is a leading distributor of Autocad Software. Like many of the companies surveyed, KGB does not manufacture but buys-in all its products. The market is highly competitive and KGB has succeeded by providing high-quality added value services based on technical expertise and strong technical back-up. It thus reflects the attributes which many of the surveyed companies claimed provided their greatest competitive strength — namely quality, flexibility and speed of response.

KGB also provides a good example of a technology-based company which did not follow the soft-hard route of product evolution, but rather the reverse. On the back of successful product sales it has developed into training and systems consultancy. This provides higher margin services to complement the lower margins available on product sales.

KGB has achieved sales to a broad range of private sector customers, but has been less successful in selling to the public sector. Despite being listed as an approved supplier, it is very seldom given the opportunity to tender. This is very surprising, given KGB's leadership in the provision of CAD systems and calls into question the attitude of government departments to small company suppliers, especially as only 8 per cent of sales of all independent companies surveyed were to central government.

The funding sources used by KGB at different stages of its growth reflect the typical pattern for small firms. Initial funding was primarily through the owners' capital with minimal support from a clearing bank. As the business took off, it had to rely upon internally generated funds to finance growth and for a period was heavily exposed to the risks of over-trading. It was only when several years of successful trading could be demonstrated that significant bank finance became available. This is the Catch 22 situation faced by many successful young firms: the need to demonstrate a successful track record to obtain external funds, but not being able to obtain the funds in order to achieve this.

Throughout this period KGB was unsuccessful in obtaining finance from venture capital sources, despite discussions with two different funds. The accusation often levelled at venture funds, that they demand an 'arm and a leg', was fully borne out by KGB's experience. Not only did the company find the attitudes and approach of the funds totally unsympathetic, but the degree and nature of the operational involvement sought was such that the management felt it would lose control of the company.

As KGB grew, it suffered from the problem endemic to all small companies — lack of management time. This resulted in basic clerical and book-keeping work falling behind schedule. The company only knew how much it was (or was not) making 3–6 months after the event, and the inability to produce up-to-date accounting figures prejudiced the company's attempt to obtain credit from the bank. KGB would like to see accounting and clerical bureau facilities provided by the Science Parks to help with these types of problems.

KGB is, however, enthusiastic about its Science Park location. In particular, the ability to expand premises in a flexible manner has been of great value and contrasts with the problems faced at its Windsor office. It has also received excellent co-operation and support from the park management.

The company now recognises the need to diversify its product range, both to reduce dependence on a relatively narrow base and to provide the impetus for continued growth. To assist in this process, it has commissioned outside research and consultancy advice to identify development opportunities in its existing and related market areas. At the same time, strong growth is forcing the company to augment its functional skills in marketing and to introduce more formal management information systems.

Part III

Evaluation and Policy Implications

12

The Added Value of Science Parks and the Implications for Policy

12.1 INTRODUCTION

Part I of this study briefly reviewed the evidence relating to the role of science and technology in economic development. It was noted that in recent years, there had been a growth in both the relative importance of small firms and universities as vehicles for transferring and diffusing new technology. A key element combining both these trends has been the growth and development of Science Parks, and Part II therefore reported the results of a survey of firms in the high technology sector located both on and off British Science Parks.

This chapter uses the information collected in Part II as an input to a preliminary, and necessarily sketchy, discussion of the economic value which Science Parks contribute to the economy of both their immediate areas and, where relevant, to the national economy. It then highlights the implications of these conclusions for the major groups with an interest in Science Parks — government, universities, the property investors and the managers of Science Parks.

12.2 ESTIMATING THE ECONOMIC VALUE OF NTBFs AND SCIENCE PARKS

It is very difficult to appraise the effectiveness of Science Parks because the objectives of the different partners in the Parks may differ considerably. Thus, a university may be interested in achieving a satisfactory level of income from the park by promoting business activities closely linked to its own research interests. It may also be interested in ensuring that its academic staff have an

239

opportunity to exercise the entrepreneurial option or to ensure a two-way flow of information between its departments and commercial organisations. On the other hand, local authorities may view the park as perhaps the 'flagship' of their economic development policies, the ultimate objective being the creation of employment opportunities for voters in the locality.

Private sector organisations such as banks, pension funds and property organisations are likely to have a more strictly commercial set of objectives towards investments in the park or its constituent firms, although they too may view involvement as being at least partly socially responsible. It is not our intention here to evaluate the extent to which each of these organisations has achieved these differing objectives. Instead, we shall take a wider view, by examining the net contribution which parks make to the local and national economy. In undertaking this analysis, it has to be recognised that Science Parks, other than Cambridge and Heriot-Watt, are relatively new. For this reason it is only possible to speculate broadly upon the contribution of the second phase of parks. It also has to be recognised that some, perhaps very important, roles of Science Parks, particularly in the transfer of technology, may be underestimated by the narrow criteria chosen, since it can be difficult to identify and isolate the full extent of the ripples of technological change.

Recognising these provisos, we examine the economic impact of parks according to six criteria where the survey has provided some helpful evidence:

(1) Gross job creation
(2) Deadweight
(3) Displacement
(4) Technology diffusion effects
(5) Demonstration effects
(6) Multiplier effects

12.2.1 Gross job creation

The results obtained in Chapter 11 show that NTBFs have a rate of job creation which is substantially higher than that for small firms generally. They also probably have a lower rate of firm failure than is the norm for small firms. In this sense, therefore, initiatives to promote NTBFs, of which Science Parks are one, will yield much higher rates of gross job creation than policies to help conventional small firms. If, however, we are to estimate the added value of Science Parks, we have to distinguish between NTBFs located on a Science Park and those located elsewhere. Chapter 11 showed that when a direct comparison was made, and taking account of the different ages of the firms, those on Science Parks had achieved somewhat *lower* levels of employment by a given age than otherwise comparable firms located off parks. This might suggest that parks were actually hindering the development of such firms. Further analysis, however, indicated a more plausible explanation, which was that almost one-fifth of businesses on Science Parks were founded by academics and ex-academics, and it was those businesses which under-performed, in terms of employment growth, compared with the other businesses. When the academic businesses were removed, firms on Science Parks performed almost identically, in terms of job creation, to off-park firms.

This illustrates an important distinction: it shows that, in terms of employment creation, there is no evidence that NTBFs established by non-academics (which we shall now call 'professionals') benefit from locating on a Science Park, in the sense that this enables them to grow faster than might otherwise have been the case. A direct case cannot be made for this group unless it can be shown that it was only the availability of premises on the Science Park which enabled the businesses to start. In short, if the 'professional' business would have started in the absence of a Science Park, there is no clear evidence that locating off a park hinders their development. For this particular group, it is therefore difficult to identify a direct employment-related benefit from Science Park locations.

There is, however, some 'softer' evidence that 'professional' businesses benefit from a Science Park location. The general levels of satisfaction expressed by those which do locate on Science Parks was considerably higher than for off-park firms. Furthermore, on-park firms were much more likely to be considering expanding on the park than those located elsewhere. It therefore seems likely that there are benefits to 'professional' firms from a Science Park location, but these have not yet been reflected in a superior performance in terms of employment creation.

241

12.2.2 Deadweight

In estimating the contribution of an economic initiative, it is important to recognise that something would have happened in the absence of the initiative. In the case of the employment created by firms currently located on Science Parks, it is clear that some such firms would have been established without the park and perhaps could have grown to their current size (or larger) at an alternative location.

To estimate the true effect of a policy initiative, it is necessary to take the total number of jobs created and eliminate those which would have occurred if the policy had not been in operation. In practice, of course, it is difficult to estimate what would have happened to a given firm without the Science Park. Nevertheless, as was argued above, there is little evidence that 'professional' off-park firms are hindered in their employment growth. It also seems likely that many of the 'professional' businesses would have found an alternative location at which to start and, once there, may not have found their growth seriously inhibited, at least in the short term.

For the 'academic' businesses, however, it seems much less likely that many would have started in the absence of a park. Hence, there would be a much lower deadweight element in the jobs created by these businesses: for example, amongst the off-park firms, only 2 per cent of founders were ex-academics, compared with 19 per cent on the park. Clearly, some academics would have started their businesses even if the park had not existed, but it seems likely that the presence of the park has provided a major stimulus to academics to starting their business. Hence, even though these businesses grow significantly more slowly in terms of employment than the 'professional' businesses, it seems likely that once the deadweight effect is removed, these types of firms may make a larger contribution to net job creation than the 'professional' business.

In the wider context, of course, the question has to be raised as to whether transforming a perhaps first-rate academic into a second-rate business man is desirable in terms of the national interest. Nevertheless, it certainly appears from the survey that a major contribution is made by the academic entrepreneur.

12.2.3 Displacement

Whilst jobs may be created by an economic initiative such as a Science Park, if this merely leads to a loss of jobs elsewhere in the economy, with no benefit to the consumer, then the overall impact of the initiative is negligible. In the case of a business which sells the whole of its output in the immediate locality, such as a window cleaner or vehicle repairer, a new entrant to that industry may simply displace another vehicle repairer or window cleaner without any benefit to the consumer in the form of lower prices or greater choice.

It is clear, however, that the Science Park businesses have a minimal local displacement effect. It was shown that NTBFs sell only 19 per cent of their output within a ten-mile radius compared with 78 per cent for small firms generally. Furthermore, 12 per cent of NTBFs, output is exported compared with 1 per cent for small firms. The displacement effect of policies to promote NTBFs and Science Parks is therefore much more likely to be felt by overseas competitors than is the case more generally for policies to promote small firms. In this context, it is not easy to distinguish between NTBFs on and off Science Parks, since the performance of the two groups is broadly similar, but it is clear that all such firms are likely to have a positive impact upon the competitiveness of the British economy.

12.2.4 Technology diffusion effects

Another key role of NTBFs is to accelerate diffusion of technology and so enhance the competitive position of users. Generally, the sale of 'new technology' to commercial and industrial customers impacts on the quality of their products or improves production processes, enabling them to become more competitive; and this generates new sales both at home and overseas (or greater profits), with consequent effects on investment and employment. The survey results show that 61 per cent of all firms had introduced at least one new product in the last two years.

In addition to the direct diffusion effect of technology, account must also be taken of the negative cost to the UK of its firms exploiting technology less rapidly than those from overseas. Failure to exploit new research ideas fully can quickly result in uptake in another country, with resultant loss in market share in the high technology product itself and knock-on effects arising from the more rapid diffusion in other countries by 'user' firms, who thus obtain a competitive advantage. Thus, there is a high premium on a country's ability in the area of technological innovation and entrepreneurship, and it is the links between research and commerce which are of crucial importance. In providing these links, a Science Park should assume a central role.

The survey makes it clear that the proportion of firms on Science Parks with links with HEIs is comparatively high: for example, 60 per cent mentioned that they have informal links with academics and it is also clear that a higher proportion of Science Park tenants now use university facilities than had expected to at the time that they decided to locate on the park. Even so, there is no unambiguous evidence that location has increased the *formal* relationships between the HEIs and firms. However, there is some evidence that *informal* relationships and use of facilities have increased and that these have become more important than firms first anticipated.

12.2.5 Demonstration effect

At a more qualitative level the Science Park, in facilitating the development of NTBFs, may have a considerable, long-term effect on changing the attitudes of young scientists towards business. The contributions of Sinclair, Acorn and Amstrad in alerting such individuals to these opportunities could, in the long term, be a major factor leading to an increase in the formation rate of new firms. It must be emphasised, however, that the survey method used is an inappropriate tool for determining whether any such attitude changes have occurred, or might occur in the future.

12.2.6 Multiplier effects

There are several respects in which the activities of Science Park firms could be considered to exert substantially greater multiplier effects than small firms in general. Firstly, the survey shows that they employ a much higher (52 per cent) proportion of the work-force as professional management, scientists and technologists compared with the small-firm sector as a whole (14 per cent). These are likely to be well-paid individuals whose spending in the local community will generate additional demand. Secondly, the NTBFs create a demand for high value-added services in the local economy such as advertising, marketing, banking and financial services. Thirdly, there is much evidence in the survey that NTBFs, on and off Science Parks, have a considerable 'downstream' effect. Thus, for example, it was shown that 60 per cent of Science Park firms sub-contract some production to other firms, and that overall, 15 per cent of the total output of NTBFs in the survey is subcontracted. Whilst no directly comparable figures are available from elsewhere, it is clear that this exceeds substantially the norm for small firms in general.

To summarise, therefore, it is clear that the economic impact of policies to promote NTBFs is likely to have considerably greater effect than policies to promote small firms generally. It appears that the major net effect in terms of observed employment creation is upon those academics for whom the Science Park acts as a stimulus for commercialising their research. For 'professional' business, the effect of a Science Park location is less clear in terms of performance, although satisfaction with the location and a willingness to expand on-site suggest that there may be performance benefits in the medium- to longer-term. There can therefore be little doubt that there have been benefits from the development of Science Parks, but it is vital that these are fully appreciated by all the parties involved, and that important new steps are taken to exploit their full potential. In the next section, we highlight these directions for the key participants.

12.3 IMPLICATIONS FOR THE FUTURE

12.3.1 The implications for government

Any review of the role of Science Parks and high technology firms has to begin by considering attitudes and policies towards technology itself. As noted in Part I, there appear to be significant differences in approach between the United States (and increasingly, Japan) on the one hand, and many European countries on the other, concerning the role of technology in society and the priorities for government policy. In the United States, there is a greater apprecia-tion of the fact that technology and economic progress are fundamentally linked. It is also increasingly recognised that a central issue is how to translate technology into new business opportunities. Emphasis is increasingly placed on technological innovation and entrepreneurship within large firms, as well as by agencies support-ing the formation and growth of NTBFs. In contrast, European emphasis has been directed more towards research and development through, for example, pre-competitive collaborative research involving universities and larger companies.

Although there has been a growth of high technology firms in places such as Cambridge, and venture capital has also grown rapidly in Britain in recent years, innovation and entrepreneurship still remain undervalued in terms of their contribution to improving the competitive position of the UK economy. Matters are beginning to change, however. Increasingly, attention is being focused on 'exploitable' areas of science and the development of research centres of excellence, but still with large companies in mind. The urgent task of identifying new ways of translating research into enterprise has still to be developed.

For Britain, and other European counties which less readily accept US attitudes towards technology and economic growth, changes in policy require some justification. Measures to facilitate greater technological innovation and entrepreneurship impinge on the overall science budget, and/or require justification in terms of net economic gain. As our analysis of Science Parks has shown, evaluation in terms of short-term additional employment can lead to an overemphasis upon short-term quantifiable benefits, perhaps at the expense of longer-term gains.

There are two key conclusions that have emerged from this survey, both of which have crucial implications for government policy. The first is that NTBFs stand out as a special group of small firms in terms of performance and their contribution to employment and the economy. The second is that Science Parks are uniquely placed as a local delivery mechanism for a range of technological innovation and entrepreneurship policies directed at NTBFs.

Despite the performance and contribution of NTBFs to the economy, the survey identified several constraints on the ability of NTBFs in general to fulfil their economic potential. These included management capacity, finance and weakness in sales and marketing. The extent to which Science Parks can help firms overcome these constraints depends partly on the quality of the on-site management resources, and partly on access to appropriate sources of equity and loan funds. Already, considerable public funds have been committed to physical developments, but if the wider economic benefits are to be realised, greater attention now needs to be given to the role and resourcing of the on-site management facility in Science Parks. To stimulate the formation and growth of NTBFs effectively, management resources need to be supplemented in four ways:

(1) facilitating start-ups via access to small tranches of seedcorn and venture funds;

(2) promoting access to top quality, pro-active advice for rapidly growing firms;
(3) providing practical assistance to firms on topics such as exports, development, joint ventures and the formation of subsidiary companies, etc. and
(4) providing an interface between university research and industry which will actively facilitate knowledge and technology transfer.

Science Parks are also one element of government regional and inner city policies, designed to encourage new employment opportunities in deprived areas. Because of the low failure rate and high employment growth of high-tech firms, Science Parks fulfil an important objective of regional policy. They may in the longer term contribute to reducing the regional imbalance in employment opportunities in the less-favoured UK regions. However, their success is dependent on maintaining the supply of adequate property facilities in line with demand, combined with the provision of related services for on-park firms. Furthermore, the generally lower rates of employment growth of northern high-tech firms is a cause for concern in terms of whether, without policy changes, NTBFs can generate jobs in the localities where they are most needed.

Science Parks should become a focus for the delivery of government technology transfer policies implemented both by the British Technology Group and through more direct measures such as SMART, a pilot scheme based on the successful SBIR programme operating in the United States. Such programmes are directly relevant for Science Parks if the latter are to play a lead role in actively stimulating the formation of new high technology firms. In their turn, Science Parks, with their expertise in technology transfer, should be used more extensively in administering these programmes.

Science Parks also nowadays assist governments in attracting firms from other countries to locate in the UK. With an increasing proportion of overseas investment in the high technology sector, the high quality environments of some Science Parks, together with the technological back-up of the universities, offer suitable locations for such firms. This potential of Science Parks has been recognised by Locate in Scotland and Winvest, the overseas promotion agencies in Scotland and Wales respectively. These 'flagship' developments have meant that inward investment is changing character somewhat, away from a routinised plant and towards having a greater scientific and managerial component. There remains further scope for a more

247

co-ordinated approach towards marketing UK Science Parks to potential inward investors.

The growth of Science Parks raises problems for the delivery of government economic policy, however. Firstly, several departments in central government have an interest in Science Parks, and even within the same department, several divisions may have separate interests. This is further complicated because Science Parks are essentially local economic initiatives and therefore in some cases are established to fulfill objectives set by local authorities. Despite their relevance to different policy initiatives, Science Parks have yet to be recognised as a key policy instrument; and consequently, the resourcing of Science Parks has come from several sources — central and local government, and regional development agencies, all of whose policies, objectives and assessment criteria differ. The effect is that some parks lack appropriate resources fully to meet both the property and non-property objectives in a balanced way.

Although there can be no doubt that the development of the second wave of Science Parks in the 1980s coincided with, and was probable partly caused by, reductions in central government funding for universities, further funding reductions will be counter-productive. Indeed, it is important that, as part of a policy to recognise the importance of science in economic development, government both begins a process of selective increases in the scientific budget and also begins to emphasise the important role which universities play in the economy. Now that Science Parks and other 'commercial' elements are present within the universities, it would be unfortunate if these promising developments were stifled by a shortage of resources.

There are two final areas in which our survey has shown that the government could make a significant contribution to the growth of NTBFs and of Science Parks. Firstly, it has been shown that the use of external equity capital at start-up, even in this group, is not common. It is also clear that entrepreneurs believe that a 'shortage' exists, and that current initiatives such as the BES are not achieving their objectives of closing this gap. A solution worth considering is that efforts are made to redirect BES funds away from their current targets and towards the NTBF sector, perhaps by placing further restrictions on eligible investments. Finally, the area of public procurement also needs to be reviewed, since several firms felt that government discriminated against them even when they had over-come the hurdle of becoming included on public tender lists. It has to be emphasised that the objective here is to remove discrimination against smaller firms, rather than positively to discriminate in their favour.

12.3.2 The implications for universities

If government is to provide universities with adequate resources, then the latter have to recognise that they are not 'ivory towers', isolated from the realities of the outside world. Whilst the broader educational objectives of universities must be protected — and in particular, basic research must continue to be adequately funded — government reasonably requires reassurance that universities are facilitating the transfer of knowledge and technology into the wider economy. Science Parks are a high profile element demonstrating this commitment to technology transfer. The park should be adequately managed and not simply a property-based initiative on a university campus. Instead, the examples of well-established and thriving 'managed' parks such as those at Warwick and Aston should be emulated.

Within universities, it is not simply the science and engineering faculty which may be entrepreneurial. Indeed, the pressures upon resources in the arts and social science faculties make it currently inevitable that those groups will need to increase their involvement in 'outside' commercial activities. There is no reason in principle why the Library cannot provide specialised advice on information retrieval, the Language Department assist in providing specialist translation service, or the historians become involved in tourism-related activities. If this means that these types of businesses locate on the Science Park, then this might lead to a change in name to reflect these developments — such as an Enterprise or Business Park. It cannot be too strongly emphasised that there is no reason why the commercialisation of research is the exclusive province of the science and engineering faculty. Such commercialisation need not be regarded as a *substitution* for academic activities, but rather as providing *additional* opportunities for the staff involved.

Whilst these developments are to be encouraged, it is also important to emphasise that the returns to the university are not of a short-term nature. The developments at both Cambridge and Heriot-Watt have taken more than ten years to come to fruition, so it is unlikely that in these more difficult times, a time-scale of less than ten years can be envisaged.

Our analysis also has other implications for universities. It is clear, for example, that in very few instances was there much contact between the university Business School and the Science Park, even though the firms themselves were clearly aware of their own deficiencies in a variety of management skills. In some cases these skills could have been supplemented by access to managerial specialists on the campus. A strengthening of Business School–Science Park links appears to be justified.

It needs to be recognised, however, that no single university will provide the full range of scientific, technical or management skills required by park firms. There may be park-based firms which have the vast majority of their formal links with other universities, and perhaps even abroad. In no way should such a firm be regarded as of secondary importance to a Science Park and it would be unwise to exclude firms on these grounds. It seems clear that those parks which have been most successful are those which have been the most pragmatic in their entry policies, and that, once established on the Park, firms can increase and strengthen their links with the university to the mutual benefit of both parties.

A similar philosophy needs to be pursued over whether or not to allow manufacturing on the park. Some, but by no means a majority, of firms develop by becoming 'harder' through becoming more manufacturing-based. There has been a tendency to prohibit manufacturing on the park on the grounds that this may discourage 'research-based' firms from locating there. Clearly this is a risk, but it appears to be of less importance than the risk of losing a business which needs to develop a manufacturing capability on site. The most successful parks have been willing to accept some manufacturing as the price for maintaining economic buoyancy.

Another practical consideration is that universities have to look carefully at their attitudes to employment contracts of both teaching and research staff. Although it may pose additional administrative difficulties, universities should be examining innovative ways in which academics can begin businesses, perhaps on a part-time basis, without jeopardising either their pension entitlements or their ability to re-enter the profession after some years away.

Finally, it must be recognised that pressures on universities to become more commercially oriented must not end up destroying their strengths. University teaching and research do require some independence from overly short-term economic pressures and a balance has to be struck between the need to speed up the process of technology transfer and the ability to undertake fundamental research of the highest quality. It would be very unfortunate if

British universities were forced too far towards meeting short-term objectives at a time when competing countries such as Japan are investing much more heavily in long-term basic research.

12.3.3 The implications for property

A major problem for both Science Park managers and tenant firms is the availability of premises to meet the requirements of existing tenants and the provision of facilities for firms wishing to locate on the park. For many parks, the primary constraint will increasingly be a lack of land. For other parks, the critical problem is to secure sufficient finance to maintain a regular flow of developments to cater for demand. Whilst some Science Parks have access to public funds via local authorities, regional development agencies and Urban Development Grants from the Department of Environment, the future growth of Science Parks will increasingly depend on the activities of the private property investment institutions. The survey suggests that Science Parks could be an attractive proposition to such bodies. Firms located on parks show above-average rates of growth. The risk to the institutions is further reduced by the role of the Science Park manager, who is well placed to manage the estate and the tenant portfolio. There is also evidence that with intensive on-site management and an ongoing marketing policy, significant growth rates are being achieved. At Bradford, for example, compound rental growth rates of 5 per cent are being achieved since the park was opened in 1983 (English Estates, 1987). Science Parks would therefore appear to present the investment institutions with a new, and exclusive, type of property investment in unique locations with little fear of competition, and with satisfactory rental yields and growth prospects.

12.3.4 Implications for Science Park managers

The survey results suggest that considerable scope exists for Science Parks to benefit from a more pro-active and effective management support programme for park tenants. In some cases it may be necessary to increase substantially the level of resources that is set aside for the ongoing management of the park.

Priority needs to be given by park managers to four areas:

(1) identification of advisors and consultants able to provide high

251

quality advice to park firms;

(2) the development of a Science Park Venture Fund providing seedcorn and small amounts of equity capital, or at least the strengthening of links with existing venture capital organisations willing to forge a relationship with Science Park firms;

(3) practical assistance and contacts to assist park firms to develop internationally; and

(4) the provision of an interface between the university and the park firms to facilitate knowledge and technology transfer.

Science Parks are a particularly suitable location for new businesses. Opportunities exist for park managers to develop training and business placing programmes to assist potential technological entrepreneurs. It is these new business ventures which otherwise might not start up, which can have a significant economic impact in terms of net additional jobs.

Opportunities also exist for Science Park managers to develop 'added value' networks with similar organisations overseas. These networks assist tenant firms in establishing new market outlets internationally by facilitating, for example, training and agency arrangements. Individual links, fostered by an EEC initiative, have been forged between several Science Parks in the UK, including Aston and Newtech, with European partners to promote the links and collaborative research and development programmes between tenant companies. At South Bank Technopark, reciprocal arrangements have been established with the University of New Mexico with the objective of assisting high-tech companies on the Science Park and further afield to diversify their product portfolio by taking up proven products, developed in American universities under licensing agreements. These arrangements need to be strengthened if firms are to be assisted to develop in overseas markets.

12.4 CONCLUSION

There can be little doubt that Science Parks have made a promising and useful contribution to economic development in the UK. Nevertheless, because of the relative newness of almost all parks, our approval has to be qualified. Perhaps the most useful result of our work is to demonstrate the promise which the concept provides and to highlight the importance of new technology-based firms. It is to be hoped that governments will adequately resource these developments in future and that universities, for their part, will become more entrepreneurial and involve themselves fully in providing 'managed' parks, where networks within and without the university are fully developed.

Bibliography

ACARD (Advisory Council for Applied Research and Development) (1983) *Improving the research links between higher education and industry*, HMSO, London
―――― (1986) *Exploitable areas of science*,HMSO, London
Altshuler, A., Anderson, M., Jones, D.T., Roos, D. and Womak, J. (1984) *The future of the automobile*, MIT Press, Cambridge, Mass.
Armington, C. and Odle, M. (1982) 'Small business — How many jobs?', *Brookings Review*, Winter, pp. 14–17
Armington, Harris and Odle (1983) 'Formation and growth in high technology businesses: a regional assessment', Brookings Microdata Project, Washington, DC
Arrow, K.J. (1962) 'Economic welfare and the allocation of resources to invention' in National Bureau of Economic Research, *The rate and direction of incentive activity: economic and social failures*, Princeton University Press, Princeton
Batelle Research Institute (1973) *Interaction of science and technology in the innovative process: some case studies*, Batelle Research Institute, processed
Bernal, J.D. (1939) *The social function of science*, Routledge and Kegan Paul, London
Bolton, J.E. (1971) *Small firms: report of The Commission of Inquiry on small firms*, Cmnd 4811, HMSO, London
Bowles, J.R. (1985) 'Research and Development in the United Kingdom', *Economic Trends*, August, no. 382, pp. 82–93
Bragard, C., Donckles, R. and Michel, G. (1985) *A study of Belgian entrepreneurs*, KMO, Ufsal, Brussels
Braun, E. and MacDonald, S. (1978) *Revolution in miniature: the history and impact of semi conductor electronics*, Cambridge University Press, Cambridge
Breheny, M.J. and McQuaid, R. (1987) 'H.T.U.K. The development of the United Kingdom's major centre of high technology industry' in M.J. Breheny and R. McQuaid (eds), *The development of high technology industries*, Croom Helm, London
Bullock, M. (1983) *Academic enterprise, industrial innovation and the development of high technology financing in the United States*, Brand Bros and Co., London
Burns, P. and Dewhurst, J. (eds) (1986) *Small businesses in Europe*, Macmillan, London
Cambridge City Council (1986) *Employment development strategy: high tech and conventional manufacturing industry*, Cambridge, UK
Channon, P. (1987) 'Opening address' in H. Sunman (ed.), *Science Parks and the growth of technology-based enterprises*, UK Science Park Association and Peat Marwick McLintock
Clapham, J.H. (1963) *An economic history of modern Britain*, Cambridge University Press, Cambridge

Clarke, R. (1985) *Industrial economics*, Blackwell, Oxford
Cooper, A.C. (1970) 'The Palo Alto Experience', *Industrial Research*, May, pp. 58–60
—— (1973) 'Technical entrepreneurship: what do we know?', *R & D Management*, vol. 3, February
Coopers and Lybrand (1980) *Provision of small industrial premises*, Department of Industry, Small Firms Division, London
CURDS (1987) *Research and technological development in the less favoured regions of the community*, Centre for Urban and Regional Development Studies (CURDS), University of Newcastle
Curran, J. (1986) *Bolton fifteen years on: a review and analysis of small business research in Britain, 1971–86*, Small Business Research Trust, London
Currie, J. (1985) *Science Parks in Britain — their role for the late 1980s*, CSP Economic Publications, Cardiff
Dalton, I. (1985) 'The objectives and development of the Heriot-Watt University Research Park' in J.M. Gibb (ed.), *Science Parks and Innovation Centres: their economic and social impact*, Elsevier, Amsterdam
—— (1987) in H. Sunman (ed.), *Science Parks and the growth of technology-based enterprises*, UK Science Park Association and Peat Marwick McLintock
Davies, S.W. (1979) *The diffusion of process innovations*, Cambridge University Press, Cambridge
Debenham, Tewson and Chinnocks (1983) *High-tech: myths and realities: a review of developments for knowledge-based industries*, London
Demsetz, H. (1969) 'Information and efficiency: another viewpoint', *Journal of Law and Economics*, vol. 12, pp. 1–22
Denison, E.F. (1967) *Why growth rates differ*, Brookings Institution, Washington, DC
—— (1974) *Accounting for United States economic growth 1929–1969*, Brookings Institution, Washington, DC
Dorfman, N. (1983) 'Route 128: the development of a regional high technology economy', *Research Policy*, vol. 12, pp. 299–316
Economist Intelligence Unit (EIU) (1985) *Universities and industry*, Special Report no. 213, EIU, London
Ellin, D. and Gillespie, A. (1983) 'The geography of high technology in the UK', mimeograph, CURDS, University of Newcastle
English Estates (1985) *A survey of firms in start-up units*, Gateshead
—— (1987) 'A review of developments for high technology industry', unpublished
Eul, F.M. (1985) 'Science Parks and Innovation Centres — property, the unconsidered element' in J.M. Gibb (ed.), *Science Parks and Innovation Centres: their economic and social impact*, Elsevier, Amsterdam
Fishlow, A. (1986) 'Productivity and technological change in the railroad sector 1840–1910' in *Output, employment and productivity in the US after 1800*, Studies in Income and Output, no. 30, National Bureau of Economic Research, New York and Amsterdam
Flood, M. (1986) *Invention: water turbines and solar cells*, Design and Innovation, Block 1, Open University, Milton Keynes

255

Foxall, G.R. (1984) *Corporate innovation: marketing and strategy*, Croom Helm, London

Freeman, C. (1982) *The economics of industrial innovation*, 2nd Ed., Frances Pinter, London

—— (1986) The case for technological determinism, paper presented at ESRC Cambridge Conference 11–12 April 1986

Galbraith, J.K. (1967) *The new industrial state*, Penguin, Harmondsworth

Gibbs, D.C. *et al.* (1985) *The location of Research and Development in Great Britain*, Final report to the Department of Trade and Industry/EEC, University of Newcastle upon Tyne

Gilfillan, S. (1935) *Inventing the ship*, Follett, Chicago

Gould, A. and Keeble, D. (1984) 'New firms and rural industrialisation in East Anglia', *Regional Studies*, vol. 18, no. 2, pp. 189–201

Gudgin, G., Fothergill, S. and Brunskill, I. (1979) 'New manufacturing firms in regional employment growth', *Centre for Environmental Studies, Research Series*, no. 39, London

Hall, P., Breheny, M., McQuaid, R. and Hart, D. (1987) *Western sunrise: the genesis and growth of Britain's major high tech corridor*, Allen and Unwin, London

Henneberry, J.M. (1984) 'Property for high technology industry', *Land Development Studies*, vol. 1, pp. 145–68

Hessen, B. (1968) 'The social and economic roots of Newtons *Principia*' in G. Basalla (ed.) *The rise of modern science: external or internal factors?*, Heath, London

Hobsbawm, E.J. (1969) *Industry and empire*, Penguin, London

Illinois Institute of Technology (1968) *Technology in retrospect and critical events in science*, National Science Foundation, Washington, DC

Jewkes, J., Sawers, D. and Stillerman, R. (1969) *The sources of invention*, MacMillan, London

Johnson, S. and Storey, D.J. (1987) *Employment and occupational change in the small firms sector*, mimeograph

Kaldor, M., Sharp, M. and Walker, W. (1986) 'Industrial competitiveness and Britain's defence', *Lloyds Bank Review*, October, pp. 31–49

Keeble, D. and Kelly, T. (1986) 'New firms and high technology industry in the United Kingdom: the case of computer electronics' in D. Keeble and E. Wever (eds), *New firms and regional development in Europe*, Croom Helm, London

Keil, G. (1986) *New instruments in the promotion of NTBF founders in the Federal Republic of Germany*, BMFT, Bonn

Kelly, T. (1987) *The UK computer industry*, Croom Helm, London

Kulicke, M. (1987) 'The formation, relevance and public promotion of new technology based firms', *Technovation*, Amsterdam

Little, A.D. (1979) *New technology based firms in the UK and Federal Republic of Germany*, Wilton House Publications, London

Lowe, J. (1985) 'Science Parks in the UK', *Lloyds Bank Review*, April, no. 156, pp. 31–42

MacDonald, S. (1987) 'British Science Parks: reflections on the politics of high technology', *R & D Management*, vol. 17, no. 1, pp. 25–37

Markusen, A., Hall, P. and Glasmeier, A. (1986) 'High Tech America: The What, how, where and why of the Sunrise industries*, George Allen and

Unwin, Boston, Mass.

Mole, V. and Elliott, D. (1987) *Enterprising innovation: an alternative approach*, Frances Pinter, London

Monck, C.S.P. (ed.) (1986) *Science Park Directory*, UK Science Park Association

—— (1986) 'The growth of Science Parks — a progress report' in C.S.P. Monck (ed.), *Science Parks — their contribution to economic growth*, UK Science Park Association

—— (1987) 'Science Park tenants and their growth potential and policy implications' in H. Sunman (ed.), *Science Parks and the growth of technology-based enterprises*, UK Science Park Association

Mowery, D.C. and Rosenberg, N. (1979) 'The influence of market demand upon innovation: a critical review of some recent empirical studies', *Research Policy*, vol. 8, pp. 103–53

Nolan, M.P., Oppenheim, C. and Withers, K.A. (1980) 'Patenting profitability and marketing characteristics of the pharmaceutical industry', *World Patent Information*, vol. 2, pp. 169–76

Norris, W.K. and Vaizey, J.E. (1972) *The economics of research and technology*, George Allen and Unwin, London

Oakey, R.P. (1984) *High technology small firms: innovation and regional development in Britain*, Frances Pinter, London

OECD (1982) *Innovation in small and medium firms*, Paris

—— (1986) *Science and technology indicators no. 2: R & D innovation and competitiveness*, Paris

Office of Director of Defence Research and Engineering (1969) *Project Hindsight: final report*, Washington, DC

Office of Technology Assessment (OTA) (1984) 'Technology, innovation and regional economic development — encouraging high technology development', O.T.A., Washington D.C.

Pavitt, K. (1982) 'R & D patenting and innovative activities', *Research Policy*, vol. 11, no. 1, p. 33–51

—— (1987) 'The objectives of technology policy', *Science and Public Policy*, vol. 14, no. 4, pp. 182–8

—— Robson, M. and Townsend, J. (1987) 'The size distribution of innovating firms in the UK: 1945–1983', *Journal of Industrial Economics*, vol. 35, pp. 297–306

Pickles, A.R. and O'Farrell, P.N. (1987) 'An analysis of entrepreneurial behaviour from male work histories', *Regional Studies*, vol. 21, no. 5, pp. 425–44

Pizzano, W. (1985) 'Essential elements for Scientific Parks and programmes: three Appalachian models', *Seminar on Science Parks and technology complexes*, OECD, Paris

Roberts, E.B. and Wainer, H.A. (1968) 'New enterprises on Route 128', *Science Journal*, December, pp. 78–83

Rose, H. and Rose, S. (1969) *Science and society*, Penguin, Harmondsworth

Rothwell, R. (1979) 'The relationship between technical change and economic performance in mechanical engineering: some evidence' in M.J. Baker (ed.), *Industrial innovation: technology, policy, diffusion*, Macmillan, London, pp. 36–59

—————— (1980) 'Policies in industry' in K. Pavitt (ed.), *Technical innovation and British economic performance*, MacMillan, London

—————— (1983) 'Information and successful innovation' in R. Rothwell and W. Zegveld (eds), *Reindustrialisation and technology*, Longmans London

—————— (1985) 'Innovation and the smaller firm', paper prepared for First International Technical Innovation and Entrepreneurship, Salt Lake City

—————— (1986) 'The role of small firms in technological innovation', in J. Curran, J. Stanworth and D. Watkins (eds), *The survival of the small firm*, vol. 2, Gower, Aldershot

Roy, R. (1983) *Design: processes and products*, Block 2, Open University, Milton Keynes

Sayer, A. and Morgan, K. (1985) 'The electronics industry and regional development in Britain', in A. Amin and J.B. Goddard (eds), *Technological change, industrial restructuring and regional development*, Allen and Unwin, London

Segal Quince (1985) *The Cambridge phenomenon: the growth of high technology industry in a university town*, Brand Brothers

Segal, Quince Wicksteed (1988) *Universities enterprise and local economic development: an exploration of links*, HMSO, London

Schmookler, J. (1966) *Innovation and economic growth*, Harvard University Press, Cambridge, Mass.

Schumpeter, J. (1928) 'The instability of capitalism', *Economic Journal*, vol. 38, pp. 361–86

—————— (1939) *Business cycles*, McGraw High, New York

—————— (1942) *Capitalism, socialism and democracy*, Harper and Row, New York

Scott, M. (1986) 'Small business and occupational choice: some perceptual issues amongst northern undergraduates', *Northern Economic Review*, no. 14, pp. 24–32

Southern, P.H.S (1986) 'The experience of English Estates in the development of United Kingdom Science Parks', seminar on Science Parks and technology complexes, OECD, Paris

Storey, D.J. (1982) *Entrepreneurship and the new firm*, Croom Helm, London

Storey, D.J. (1985a) *Small firms and regional economic development: Britain, Ireland and the United States*, Cambridge University Press, Cambridge

—————— (1985b) 'The problems facing new firms', *Journal of Management Studies*, vol. 22, no. 3, pp. 325–45

—————— and Johnson, S.J. (1987) *Job generation and labour market change*, MacMillan, London

Storey, D.J., Keasey, K., Watson, R. and Wynarczyk, P. (1987) *The performance of small firms*, Croom Helm, London

Taylor, C. and Silberston, A. (1973) *The economic impact of the patent system*, Cambridge University Press, Cambridge

Thwaites, A.T. (1982) 'Some evidence of regional variations in the introduction and diffusion of industrial products and proceses within British Manufacturing', *Regional Studies*, vol. 16, pp. 371–82

Usher, A. (1929) *A history of mechanical inventions*. 2nd edition, Harvard University Press, Cambridge, Mass.

Von Hippel, E. (1976) 'The dominant role of users in the scientific instrument innovation process', *Research Policy*, vol. 5, no. 3, pp. 212–39

Walker, D. (1986) *Design and innovation: an introduction*, Open University, Milton Keynes

Walker, W. (1980) 'Business industrial performance 1856–1950: a failure to adjust' in K. Pavitt (ed.), *Technological innovation and British economic performance*, MacMillan, London, pp. 19–37

Whittington, R.C. (1984) 'Regional bias in new firm formation in the UK', *Regional Studies*, vol. 18, no. 2, pp. 253–6

Williams, B.R. (1985a) 'The direct and indirect role of higher education in industrial innovation — what should we expect?', Technical Change Centre, London

———— (1985b) 'The role of universities and research institutions in the development of high technology based new firms', paper given at UK–German Symposium on High Technology Based New Firms, Cambridge, 9–10 April

Young, K. and Mason, C. (1983) (eds) *Urban economic development: new roles and relationships*, MacMillan, London

Yoxen, E. (1983) *The gene business: who should control biotechnology?*, Pan Books, London

Index